D0440193

降击神通
AVATAR
THE LAST AIRBENDER

Nickelodeon Avatar: The Last Airbender
Official Strategy Guide

NICKELODEON AVATAR: THE LAST AIRBENDER

Xbox® videogame system, Nintendo GameCube™, & PlayStation®2 computer entertainment system Versions

GameCube, PS2, & Xbox Versions

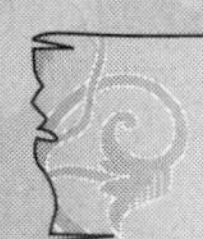

Getting Started

After pressing START at the title screen, you are prompted to start a NEW game or LOAD an existing game. From the Game Menu, you can PLAY the game, change OPTIONS, view EXTRAS, or return to the TITLE SCREEN.

Options

GAME OPTIONS include turning on/off tutorials (on-screen messages), subtitles, vibration, damage indicators, and the automatic assignment of moves. SOUND OPTIONS let you increase/decrease the volume of the Music, Sound Effects, and Speech.

Extras

This option allows you to enter a Code, view Level Art, Storyboard, and Character Galleries (which you can unlock by playing the game) and view Trailers and Credits.

Pause Menu

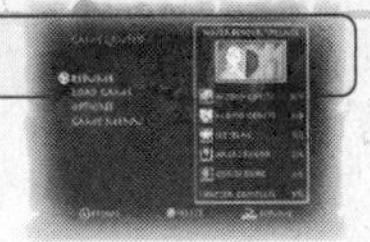

During the game, press START to bring up the Pause menu. From this menu, you can review statistics showing the number of objects found and the percentage of the chapter completed. Resume the game, Load a saved game, change Options, or quit back to the Game Menu.

In Game Menu

During the game, press the SELECT (PS2), BACK (Xbox), or Z (Game Cube) button to bring up the In Game Menu. Here, you can view your Inventory, Journal, Moves, and a Map of the chapter/world.

Main Screen

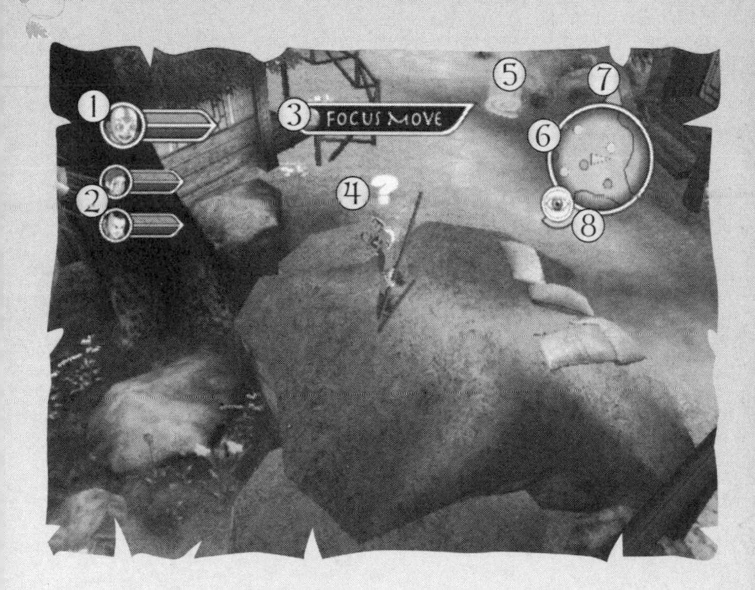

1 Active Character Health/Chi Meters

The top meters correspond to the character you are controlling. Green represents health and Purple represents Chi; both regenerate over time and can be increased with medicine.

2 Supporting Character Health/Chi Meters

Although the other members of your party can hold their own against enemies, these meters let you know how much health and Chi they have remaining.

3 Action Prompt

This small graphic prompts you to take actions such as Opening chests, Using Focus, or Talking to non-playable characters.

4 Character

This represents the character that you're controlling. A "?" appears if your character is near a hidden item.

5 Save Point

Look for glowing blue spirals on the ground—they represent SAVE POINTS where you can save your progress.

6 Radar

Along with an outline of the environment, the radar shows your location (orange arrow) and the location of objectives (green dots), enemies (red dots), friendly characters (yellow dots), and characters you need to speak with (blue dots).

7 Objective Arrow

Green arrows on the edge of the radar screen point in the direction of your objectives. Depending upon how many quests are active at the same time, you may see multiple arrows. They glow when you are close to completing an objective.

8 Stealth Meter

The orange meter lets you know how long you can remain invisible (eye closed) or how much longer until you will be able to use stealth again (eye open) when you are visible.

Controls Summary

Action	PS2	Xbox	GameCube
Movement	Left Analog Stick	Left thumbstick	Control Stick
Camera Zoom	Right Analog Stick	Right Thumbstick	C-stick
Select Aang	D-Pad Up	Directional Pad Up	+ Control Pad Up
Select Haru	D-Pad Down	Directional Pad Down	+ Control Pad Down
Select Katara	D-Pad Left	Directional Pad Left	+ Control Pad Left
Select Sokka	D-Pad Right	Directional Pad Right	+ Control Pad Right
Interact	△	Y	Y
Block attacks	□	X	B
Stealth	○	B	X
Attack	✕	A	A
Target Lock	L1	Left Trigger	L
Use Health from inventory	L2	White Button	N/A
Enter/Exit Momo Mode	R1 + ○	Left Trigger + B	L + X
Advanced Moves	R1 + ○, △, □, ✕	Right Trigger + Y, B, X, A	R + Y, X, B, A
Use Chi from inventory	R2	Black Button	N/A
Pause	START	START	START
In-Game menu	SELECT	BACK	Z
Bring up Map	R3	Click Right Thumbstick	N/A

Equipment

Each character can be equipped with six items. Three are Armor items (headbands, robes, boots, sandals, etc.) and three are Trinkets (necklaces, amulets, pendants, charms, rings, bands, etc.). Each item has a different effect upon your characters' status—Life, Chi, Agility, Regeneration, etc. Negative effects are represented by red bars; Positive effects by green bars.

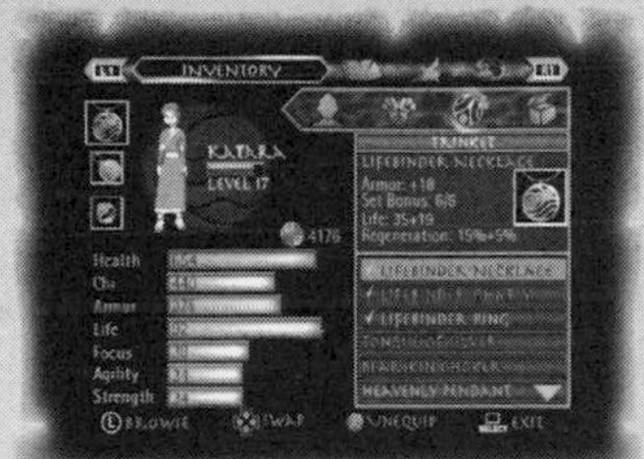

As you obtain items in your quest, sell unneeded Armor and Trinkets to Merchants. Items in White are weak; Green items are stronger but commonplace; Purple items are rare and valuable; Blue items are part of a Quest and cannot be sold or dropped; Orange items are part of a Set and are rewarded for completing Quests and can also be found in hidden chests.

Equip a character with all six Set items for a special bonus. Give ***Lifebinder*** items to Katara, ***Four Winds*** items to Aang, ***Soul Iron*** items to Sokka, and ***Core*** items to Haru.

Four Nations Game

Four Nations is a game of luck and skill. The object of the game is to be the first player to use all your tiles or to prevent your opponent from making a move.

Each tile consists of two colored icons: fire (red), water (blue), earth (green), or wind (yellow). There are three types of tiles: Doubles Tiles, Linking Tiles, and Avatar Tiles. Doubles Tiles contain two of the same icon and are placed horizontally, allowing you to make another move. Avatar Tiles are wild and can be used to match any of the four icons if you don't otherwise have a tile that matches.

As the game begins, each player is randomly given five tiles from the chosen set. When it is your turn, you must place one of your tiles onto the game board. The first player to start must match the starting icon on the board. For example, if the starting icon is fire (red), you can only play a tile that has a red fire icon on it. The tile is placed adjacent to the starting tile, oriented vertically. The opponent must now match a tile with the icon at the opposite end of the tile just played. Players alternate turns until one player is out of tiles or until one player cannot move (for example, none of his tiles have a blue icon to match the blue icon on the board).

You are able to view the tiles in your opponent's hand. Note how many of each color your opponent has and compare that with your own hand. If your opponent has no blue icons, for example, you'll want to play a tile with a blue icon, forcing him to forfeit since he cannot make a match.

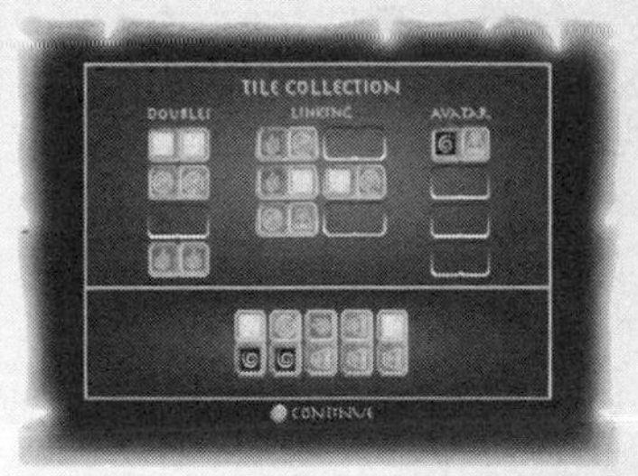

Before playing a tile, consider how your opponent will react. If you need to match a yellow icon, for example, and you have one Linking Tile that is yellow/red and one Linking Tile that is yellow/green, check your opponent's hand for red and green icons. Let's say, for example, that he has a red/blue and a green/yellow Linking Tile. You, however, have no more blue icons, but you do have a yellow one. Play the yellow/green Linking Tile instead of the yellow/red Linking Tile; otherwise he'll counter with a red/blue tile that you cannot match.

Chapter 1: Waterbender Village

Katara has traveled to the North Pole with Aang to assist him with his training. It seems, however, that Aang would rather be penguin sledding than taking his role as the Avatar seriously.

CHAPTER CHECKLIST

Hidden Chests	4
Momo Objects	8
Set Items	1

AREAS

1	WATERBENDER TEMPLE
2	WATERBENDER VILLAGE
3	FISHERMAN'S FLOAT
4	ICEBERG COVE

QUESTS

1	MISSING WATERBENDER
2	CRYSTAL COLLECTION
3	HARD CATCH
4	HELP AROUND TOWN-COLD VILLAGER
5	ZUKO ATTACKS
X	RESCUE KATARA

Area One: Waterbender Temple

As the game begins, Appa is waiting outside the Temple where Aang is undergoing his training. You control Aang, who would much rather go penguin sledding. Maybe you can have some fun with your friend, Katara.

Press the Attack button to perform a strike with your staff. You can break the jars outside the temple by striking them. Some jars contain copper pieces and other helpful items.

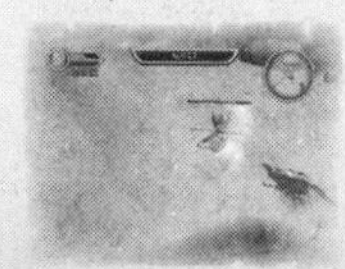

You'll also need to use your staff to attack and defend yourself against enemies. There are several wolves in this area, represented by red dots on the radar. Hold the Block button to defend yourself; press the Attack button to knock the wolves out.

Follow the path leading away from the temple and towards the village. As you do so, the controller rumbles and a question mark appears above Aang's head. Carefully walk around the area until you see the text prompting you to press the Interact button to use Focus.

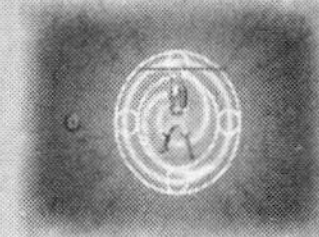

In Focus mode, capture the action button icons as they move from the edges of the screen towards Aang. Press the corresponding button just as the icon enters the small circle. If you press the button too late, the icon reaches Aang and you'll fail this task. Don't worry, you can try again!

Hidden Chest: 1 of 4

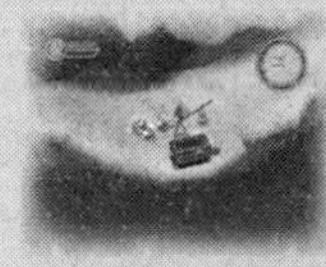

Focus helps Aang and his companions reveal hidden chests. The statistics screen tells you how many chests are hidden in the current level. If you find or purchase a treasure map, an icon will be placed on the world map showing you the precise location of the hidden chest. Grab the goodies from the chest and continue down the path.

You can talk to the people you encounter by standing in front of them and pressing the Interact button. Some of them just want to chat, but others may reveal important information. The fisherman here tells you that Katara is at the village looking for you.

Always keep an eye on the radar for the presence of enemies. The red dots indicate that a trio of wolves can be found up ahead. Block their attacks and fight back with your staff.

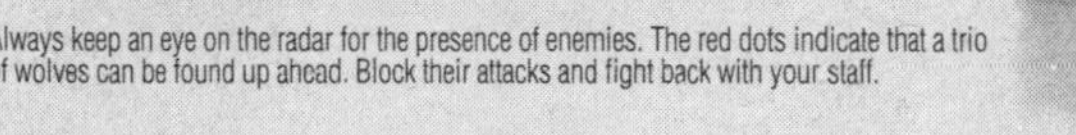

SAVE POINT

The glowing symbol on the ground represents a SAVE POINT. Whenever you encounter one of these, it is a good idea to take a moment to save your progress.

Area Two: Waterbender Village

Just past a second Fisherman, you'll spot the entrance to the Waterbender Village. Sure enough, Katara is here near the statue—and she isn't ready to go penguin sledding! She tells you that Master Wei is looking for you.

DIRECTIONS

Characters will frequently tell you to head in a certain direction, such as left or right. They will also point you in directions such as South, West, North, or East. You do not have a compass, but the world maps should help you find your way. Just remember that North is up, West is left, East is right, and South is down.

Chapter 1

Head to the left (West) of the statue and make your way up the stairs. If you stop to talk to the villager, she'll tell you that someone named Hiryu has gone missing. Continue to the upper level, breaking any jars you may see. Master Wei is waiting here.

CONVERSATION SYMBOLS

A small blue symbol appears over the head of a character who wants to talk with you. When the symbol is green, you have completed a task for that character and should talk to him/her once again.

Master Wei gives you the first of your five Quests. He informs you that a Waterbender named Hiryu has gone missing. Your job is to figure out what happened to him.

Quest 1: Missing Waterbender (Main Objective)

Search for clues about Hiryu, the missing Waterbender

You can undertake several Quests at once, and can complete them in a different order than suggested by this strategy guide. You won't be able to continue to the next Chapter before completing Quests labeled "Main Objective," however. Press the Open/Close Menu button to check the Journal for a list of active Quests.

QUEST LOCATOR

A green arrow appears at the edge of your radar, pointing in the general direction of the active Quest. If there are several active Quests, you will see more than one arrow. The arrows glow Green when you're about to complete a Quest.

Before searching for clues about Hiryu, you may wish to wander around the village and get to know the layout. Break as many jars as you can to collect money and items. You will encounter a chest in the village which cannot be opened even using Focus. Just remember to come back to it later on.

A villager named Da-Xia is standing near the fountain in the center of the village, on the lower level. He has a blue symbol over his head, so he must want to talk with you. Speak to him and he'll tell you that he needs you to locate eight ice crystals.

Quest 2: Crystal Collection

8 Crystals for Momo to find

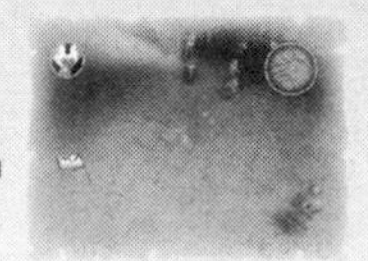

In every level, one of your Quests involves collecting a number of items. You cannot find these items on your own—instead, you will have to rely upon Momo. Hold L1 (PS2), Left Trigger (Xbox) or (GameCube) and press the Stealth button to enter "Momo Mode." Aang will remain in place while you take control of Momo for as long as necessary. To return to Aang, hold the L1, Left Trigger, or and press the Stealth button once again.

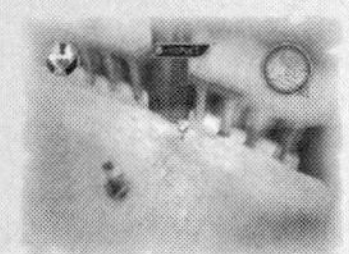

The Eight Crystals can be collected in any order. Five are located within the confines of the village; Three are on the path between the village and the Temple. While playing as Momo, a question mark appears above its head and the controller vibrates when you near the location of one of the crystals.

Momo Objects 1-3 of 8

One crystal is located near the old woman, Ming, who lives on the West side of town. Another can be found near the chest that Aang is unable to open on his own. A third can be found near the town's Vendor (represented by a yellow dot on the radar).

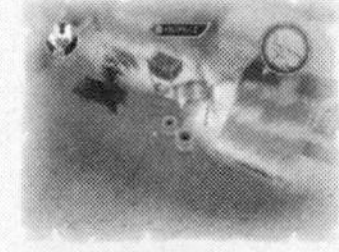

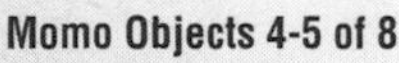

Momo Objects 4-5 of 8

On the Northeast side of town, a spiral staircase leads to a chest. Beneath the staircase you'll find a crystal. A walkway on the East side of town comes to a dead-end at another chest. In the middle of the walkway, near the top of an observation tower, you'll find the last crystal in the village.

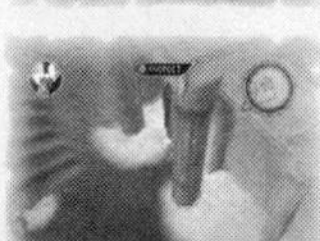

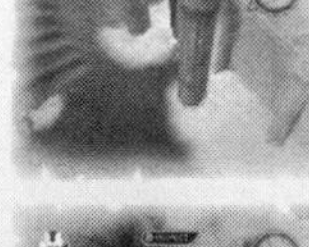

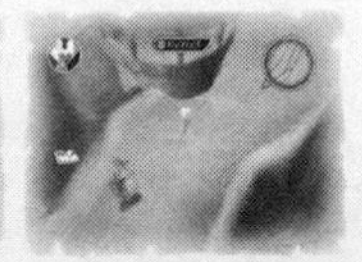

Momo Objects 6-8 of 8

Venture outside the village to obtain the final three crystals. Don't worry about the wolves; they'll ignore Momo as long as you don't attack them first. (Momo can't be injured by enemies) One crystal is near the SAVE POINT just outside of the village. Two more are along the North side of the path leading to the Temple. When you've retrieved all eight of them, take control of Aang and return to Da-Xia to accept a reward.

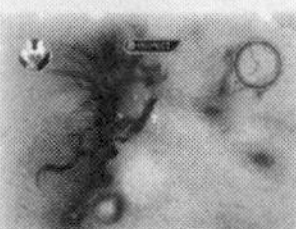

QUEST 2: COMPLETED

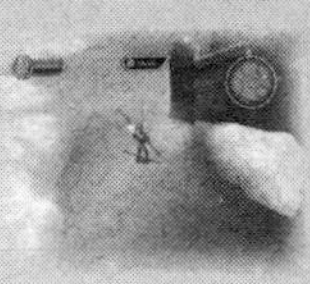

Follow the green arrow on the edge of the radar to search for clues about Hiryu. Talk with other villagers and you may learn that Hiryu was last seen to the West of the village. Before venturing out of the village, take advantage of the SAVE POINT. If you are dishonored, you can restart from this point.

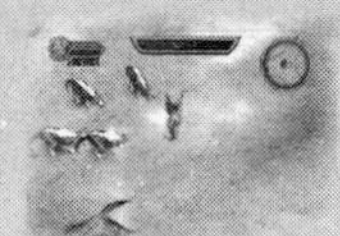

You'll encounter multiple wolf packs outside the village, so be prepared to defend yourself. Although the path leads both North and South, you want to head South towards the fishermen.

LEVEL UP

Aang is swift enough to avoid combating the wolves, but fighting them is the best way to earn experience points (and often to find items). Once you have gained a certain amount of experience, the game lets you know that you have leveled-up your character, thus earning a more powerful attack move.

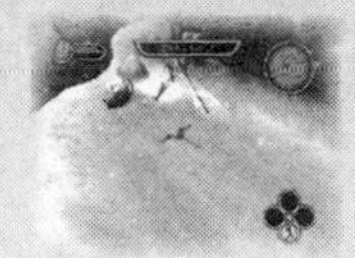

Use the rocks to cross the small stream and follow the path to the West/southwest. You'll encounter the Dark Wolf—a stronger enemy than the ordinary Wolf. Press the Block button when he attacks, and hold the Target button to move around him as you fight back.

Not too many people are brave enough to venture out here. On the ice bridge you'll spot a Fisherman named Tarym. Talk to him for more clues regarding Hiryu's whereabouts.

Hidden Chest: 2 of 4

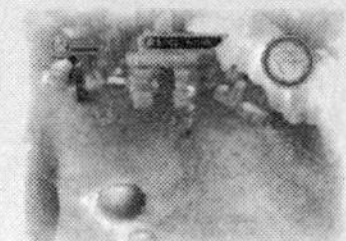

On the other side of the ice bridge you'll spot a Chest. The vibration clues you in that another chest is hidden nearby. Find the proper location and press the Interact button to use your Focus power and reveal the Hidden Chest. Don't forget to take the goodies with you!

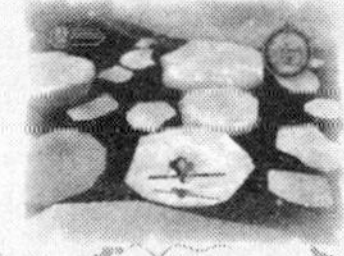

Lo Ku tells you to check the Northern caves for the missing Waterbender, but you aren't finished exploring just yet. Look for an ice flow to the South that you can use to walk across to a larger piece of ice. Look for a Chest on the right side.

Area Three: FISHERMAN'S FLOAT

QUEST 3: HARD CATCH

Help the Fisherman Cast His Nets Out to Sea

Another Fisherman is here. Yun-Li is having trouble tossing his net. He promises to give you some Oil if you can help him out. Sounds like a good deal! Approach the net and press the Interact button when prompted to do so. Using your Focus, you can toss the net out into the sea. That wasn't so hard, was it? Talk to Yun-Li afterwards to receive the Oil. If you don't need it, someone else will.

QUEST 3: COMPLETED

Make your way all the way back to the village, battling any wolves that get in your way. At this point, you may want to stop off at the Merchant's place to sell your unwanted items (and buy better armor and trinkets).

Save your progress at the SAVE POINT near the stairs leading up to the Merchant (represented by a yellow dot on the radar). The Merchant is selling a Treasure Map (50 copper) and a Blue Woven Gi (150 copper) among others.

Hidden Chest: 3 of 4

Explore the area to the East of the Merchant. Vibration, and a question mark, indicates the presence of a hidden chest. Find the spot where you are prompted to press the Interact button and use Focus to open the chest.

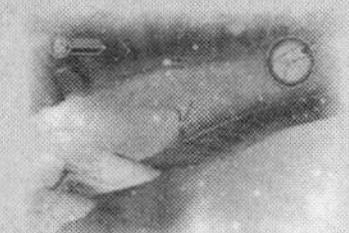

Leave the village to the West, but this time head to the North. Once again, you'll encounter multiple wolf packs. If your health is running low, use one of the potions from your inventory. You can also stop and take a break ***in a safe area*** and let your health regenerate.

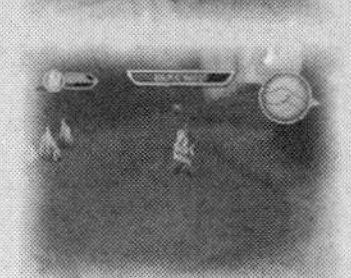

The path eventually leads into a cave. Break the large ice crystals on the ground—some of them contain items. Wind your way through the cave, fighting off the wolves in your path.

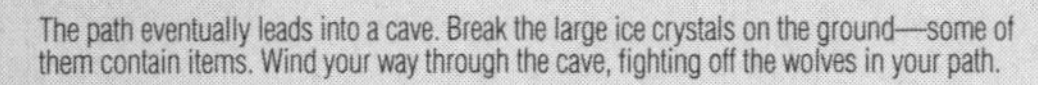

Area Four: Iceberg Cove

As you battle the wolves around a large hole in the ground, you'll spy a couple of discarded objects. Dispatch the wolves first, and then grab the Machine Part and the Waterbender Pouch.

Quest 1: Missing Waterbender - Update

Show Master Wei the Waterbender Pouch you found. It could be an important clue.

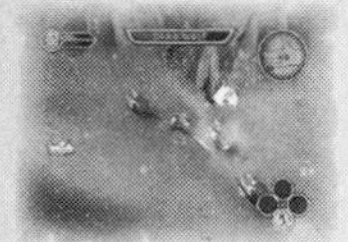

The bad news is that you must battle even more wolves on your way back to the village. The good news is that by now you should have leveled-up, allowing Aang to perform advanced moves such as the Dragon Attack.

If you want to visit the Merchant once again to unload collected items, go ahead. You can also save your progress at the SAVE POINT outside the village near the Merchant. While there, purchase a Wick; it will save you time later.

Follow the green arrow on the edge of the radar to return to Master Wei. Speak to him and show him the items that you found in the Iceberg Cove. He thanks you for the information, and rewards you with the Four Winds Charm. Don't forget to equip it!

Quest 1: Completed

Quest 4: Help Around Town

Speak to villagers around town, and see if you can help out

Master Wei recommends that you talk to the villagers to see if there are any tasks that you can perform. Speak with a few of them, and you'll learn that there is an old woman (Ming) in need of Oil. She lives on the West side of town, across a small bridge on the upper level.

Quest 4: Cold Villager - Update

Return to Ming with her wick

Speak with Ming and give her the Oil which you earned from the Fisherman for casting his net. Ming tells you that she also needs a Wick. If you purchased it earlier, give it to her now. Otherwise, find the Merchant and buy one with the money she gives you.

Quest 4: Completed

QUEST 5: ZUKO ATTACKS (Main Objective)

Zuko has launched an attack on the city. Help the nearby Waterbender fend off the Firebender.

No sooner have you assisted the old woman than the entire village comes under siege from the Firebenders. Use your staff to fight off any Fire Soldiers in your way. The attack has destroyed many of the village's bridges, requiring you to find alternate routes.

QUEST 5: ZUKO ATTACKS - UPDATE

Master Deszu has asked you to help Sokka. He's in trouble on the front wall.

As you approach Master Deszu, he asks you to help Sokka. Your friend is on the walkway at the far East of the village. Battle your way over to him as quickly as you can, following the green arrow on the side of the radar.

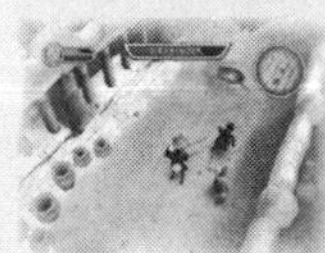

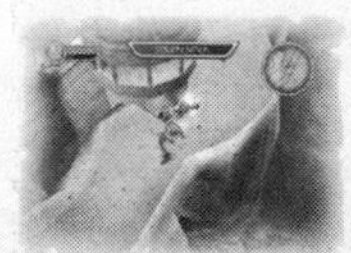

Fight off the Firebender that is attacking Sokka. A cinema scene shows Zuko directing the battle. His soldiers attempt to kill Master Wei, but Katara stops them. Zuko then decides to grab Katara before retreating.

QUEST 5: COMPLETED

Having assisted Sokka, he now joins your party. To take control of him, press Right on the Control/Directional Pad. To switch back to Aang, press Up. Open the chest at the far East end of the pathway before continuing.

Quest: Rescue Katara

You managed to push back Zuko's attack on the city, but Katara was captured. Talk to Master Wei, who is calling for you.

◇ Hidden Chest: 4 of 4 ◇

Before meeting up with Master Wei, you'll need to find the final Hidden Chest. Remember that Chest Aang couldn't open earlier? Make your way over to it and take control of Sokka. Press the Interact button when prompted to use Sokka's Focus to reveal the Hidden Chest.

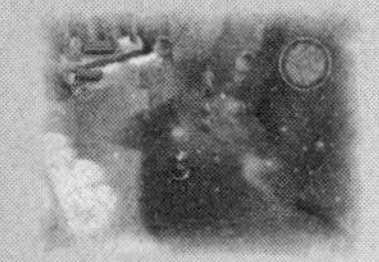

Master Wei is waiting for you near the entrance to the village. Speak with him to learn more about the Waterbender's disappearance and to get advice for rescuing Katara.

Quest: Rescue Katara - Update

Find Appa so you can follow Zuko's ship

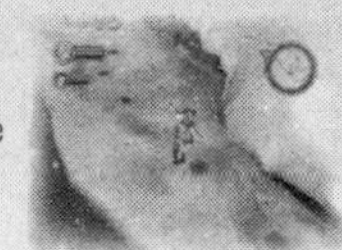

Leave the village one final time, with Sokka at your side, heading along the path toward the Temple. Just before you reach Appa at the Temple, the game asks if you are ready to fight the level Boss. If you have not completed all your quests, you need to finish them first. You will also be prompted to save your progress.

Quest: Rescue Katara - Update

Destroy the massive machine blocking your path to Appa

The Firebenders have left a machine known as the Colossal Inferno. Hanging from an ice bridge, it shoots fireballs at Aang and Sokka and also spreads a swath of fire.

You cannot block either the fireballs or the fire itself, so don't even try it or you'll take damage. Instead, run back and forth, left and right, to avoid the fireballs. When the Colossal Inferno spreads fire, keep your distance to avoid getting burned.

After the fire spray, the Colossal Inferno needs to take a breather to cool down. That's your cue! Approach the machine and target the exposed orange center. Use your advanced moves to cause greater damage. You can strike it several times before it becomes active once again.

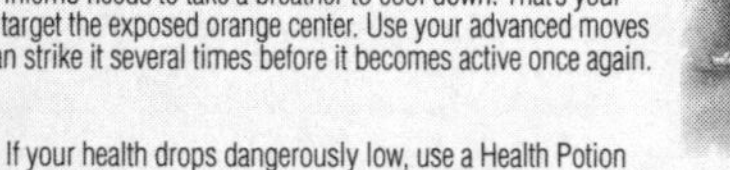

If your health drops dangerously low, use a Health Potion from your inventory. You can also switch back and forth between Aang and Sokka if necessary, controlling the character who has the greatest amount of health. If one of the characters expires, don't worry—keep on fighting!

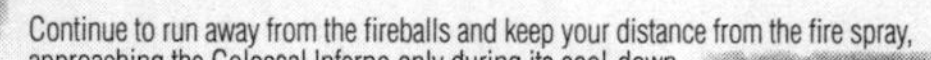

Continue to run away from the fireballs and keep your distance from the fire spray, approaching the Colossal Inferno only during its cool-down time. After striking it a few times, run away before it comes back to life. The bar above its head indicates its status. You'll have to repeat the process several times before depleting the life bar.

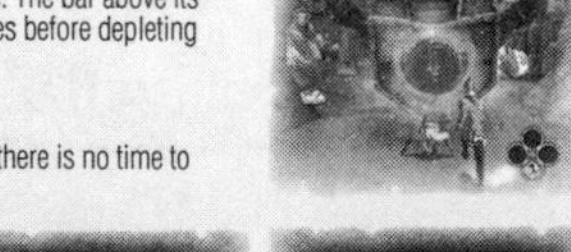

After a fierce battle, you've finally destroyed the Colossal Inferno. But there is no time to celebrate! Zuko still has Katara, and you must get her back.

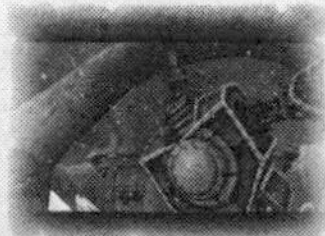

Chapter 2: Amongst the Enemy

Aang and Sokka have followed Zuko in an attempt to rescue their friend, Katara. Their journey has taken them straight into the heart of enemy territory.

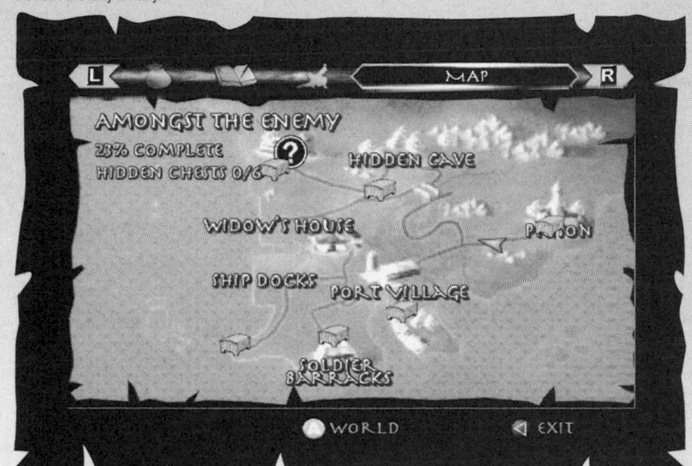

CHAPTER CHECKLIST

Hidden Chests	6
Momo Objects	8
Set Items	3

AREAS

1	PORT VILLAGE
2	SOLDIER BARRACKS
3	HIDDEN CAVE
4	SHIP DOCKS
5	WIDOW'S HOUSE
6	OUTPOST
7	PRISON

QUESTS

1	RESCUE KATARA
2	HERBAL REMEDIES
3	TOMATO COLLECTION
4	DISAPPEARING FOOD
5	FRIENDS AND ENEMIES
6	GOOD CAPTAIN, BAD CAPTAIN
7	HELP THE WIDOW
8	HOUSE ARREST
X	FREE THE MAKER

Quest 1: Rescue Katara (Main Objective)

Zuko's ship has been captured by the Fire Nation. Talk to the village Elder and ask if she knows anything about Katara.

Appa will wait on the beach South of the village, so as not to attract attention. Aang and Sokka must travel the remainder of the journey on foot. The red dots on your radar indicate the presence of enemy soldiers up ahead. You can either fight them, or avoid them by using stealth.

STEALTH

Once Stealth is activated, a stealth meter appears at the bottom left corner of the radar. When the timer runs out, the eye will open, and you will become visible once again. Make sure that you reach a hiding place before that happens! You won't be able to use this power if you've already been spotted by the enemy.

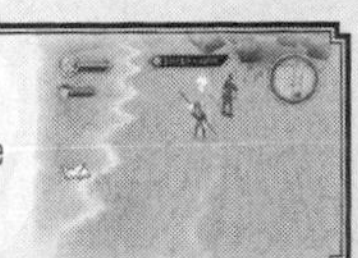

You'll walk slower than usual while using stealth, so don't delay as you move past the soldiers on the beach. There's a hidden chest nearby, but neither Aang nor Sokka are able to open it using Focus. Keep moving toward the village.

Area One: Port Village

There is a SAVE POINT right outside the Port Village. Although you haven't completed any quests yet, you still might want to save your progress. Talk to the old woman Elder at the village entrance and she'll give you some helpful advice.

Quest 1: Rescue Katara - Update

Search the Barracks for small uniforms that can be used as disguises

The Elder is also a merchant—she sells Honey and purchases your surplus items. Unlike the merchant in the last chapter, this one is an Herbalist who is able to craft items such as Health Medicine, Chi Medicine, Anti-Heat Salve, and Perfume.

CRAFTING ITEMS

Each hand-crafted item is made from common items you'll find on your journey. Follow the recipe! The Merchant lets you know if you're missing any of the necessary ingredients.

To the left of the village entrance, represented by a yellow dot on the radar, is an Artisan. He buys and sells items and can also hand-craft special armor items for you. Ask him to craft something, and check the list for the ingredients you'll need. Unfortunately, you haven't found enough silk and leather. After speaking with him, explore the rest of the village.

There are numerous jars, barrels, and crates scattered throughout the village which can be broken with your staff. On the West side of the village, you'll spot a girl with a blue symbol over her head. She wants to talk to you, so approach her and engage her in a conversation.

Quest 2: Herbal Remedies

Find Jin Wei Some Herbal Soap to Soothe Her Grandfather's Aching Bones

The girl's name is Jin Wei, and when you talk to her she will tell you all about her Grandfather's condition. Keep an eye out for some Herbal Soap, and remember to bring it back to her once you've found it.

Look for another villager represented by a yellow dot—he's in a courtyard to the North. Speak to him to play the Four Nations Game and win prizes. *[For game information, see the GETTING STARTED section]*.

Quest 3: Tomato Collection

8 tomatoes remaining for Momo to collect

At the North end of the village, a blue dot on the radar represents the location of a Merchant. He's got a special quest for you—locating tomatoes! You must use Momo to locate the items.

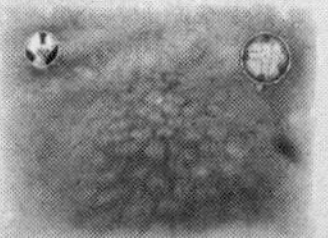

Although you can look for the tomatoes while undergoing other quests, you can also locate them all at once. If you decide upon the latter, keep Aang and Sokka in the village and venture out as Momo. Seven of the tomatoes are found in bushes along the paths between the village and the outlying areas. The eighth tomato is on the North side of the Outpost.

MOMO THE SCOUT

Until you've found a disguise, you will be attacked by any Fire Soldier who sees you. You can use stealth to avoid them, but it is difficult when you don't know where you are going in advance. Switch to Momo mode and use him to check out the area, watching for enemy locations and looking for places to hide.

Although you can use stealth to investigate the areas to the North and East of the village, it will be much easier if you obtain a disguise first. The old woman told you to look for uniforms at the barracks, which are located to the Southwest of the village.

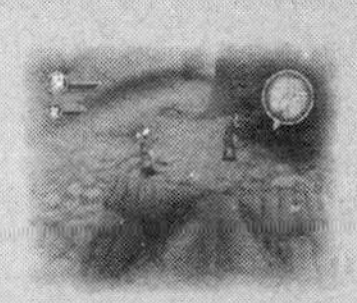

After using Momo to scout ahead, press the Circle button to activate stealth and sneak by the groups of soldiers one at a time. Look for hiding places near rocks and trees. Even if you are stuck out in the open, as long as you are in between the groups of soldiers when your stealth wears off, you won't be seen and attacked.

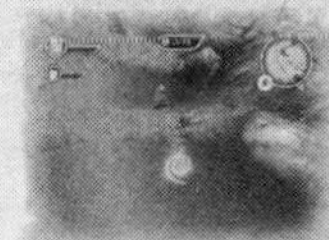

If you accidentally become visible near a soldier, or are spotted before you can use stealth, you'll have no choice but to fight them. Use your special advanced moves, block their attacks, and circle around them as you fight back. Never allow yourself to become surrounded by multiple enemies. If necessary, run away to a more defensible position.

Just because you fought one group of soldiers does not mean you'll have to fight them all. If none of the nearby soldiers saw the battle, you can still use stealth to sneak past them. Follow the path to the West and then as it curves South. Just outside the barracks you'll find a SAVE POINT. Take advantage of it to save your progress.

Area Two: Soldier Barracks

Hidden Chest: 1 of 6

Just inside the barracks area, you can take cover behind a wall on the right. A chest is visible behind this wall. Aang cannot open it, but Sokka can. Take control of him and press the interact button when prompted to use Focus. Grab the goodies and get ready to make a final run to the barrack building.

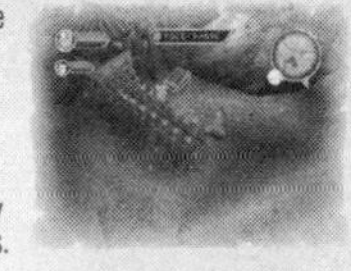

Using stealth, head towards the building. Look for temporary cover near rocks or barrels in between the groups of soldiers. If you are spotted, ignore the soldiers and run towards the building as fast as you can.

When you reach the building, don't bother with the front door, but look for a door on the South (bottom) side. Open it and enter. You'll watch as two pint-sized Fire Soldiers are chewed out by their superior officer. Looks like you've found your disguises!

Follow the green arrows surrounding the radar to locate the pint-sized soldiers. Use stealth to sneak past the soldiers whenever possible—at least until you've located the SAVE POINT upstairs.

Having saved your progress, you can now dispense with the sneaking around. Battle the soldiers inside the rooms to obtain experience points and treasures.

Upstairs, to the far left, you'll find the Herbal Soap that Jin-Wei's Grandfather was looking for. To the right, you'll spot the pint-sized soldiers who were disciplined earlier. Fight them, and any other soldiers who might happen to be in the room. When the battle is over, take the uniforms they leave behind.

Quest 1: Rescue Katara - Update

Return to the Elder. She might have some information about Katara.

Now that you are wearing uniforms as a disguise, you won't have to worry about being spotted by all the soldiers outside the barracks. Explore the area, breaking all the crates and jars you encounter. When you've filled your pockets with items, head back towards the village.

Back at the village, locate Jin Wei and give her the Herbal Soap that you found in the barracks. She thanks you on behalf of her Grandfather, and tells you to find him. He is located in the center area of the village. Speak with him and he'll give you the Soul Iron Band as a reward.

Quest 2: Completed

Quest 1: Rescue Katara - Update

Help the Elder with the missing supplies while she collects information about Katara

Return to the Elder after you've found the disguises. She asks for your help while she searches for information about Katara. The villagers' supplies have been disappearing, leaving them in danger of starvation. Volunteer to look for the supplies—the Elder suggests you find traces of what the thief may have left behind.

Quest 4: Disappearing Food

Search the surrounding area for the villagers' missing supplies.

The green arrow on the edge of the radar points to the East. Make your way through the village to the East side. As you leave the village, you'll spot a broken crate of food. It's a clue! Footprints lead to the Northeast, so follow them!

At the next intersection, the footprints near the dropped food lead North. The disguises may have fooled the enemy soldiers, but they don't have any affect on the Hog Monkeys blocking your path. You can use stealth to avoid them, but you won't earn experience points or acquire items. Instead, use your staff to defeat them.

Momo Objects 1 of 8

Just past the first group of monkeys, before the path turns to the left (west), you'll spot a large leafy green bush. Switch to Momo mode and inspect the plant. Sure enough, Momo finds a tomato here.

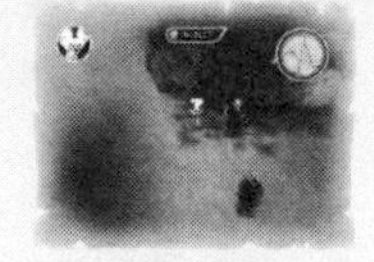

Quest 5: Friends and Enemies

Stop the angry villagers pelting the Fire Nation Commoner with fruit.

A cinema scene shows villagers tormenting one of the Fire Nation Commoners. Even though you are at war with the Fire Nation, you can't stand by and watch this happen. Break the fruit crate with your staff and the villagers will scatter. The Commoner is grateful for your help, and promises not to reveal your identities.

Quest 5: Completed

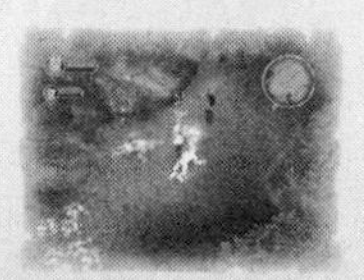

Can you trust the Commoner? In any case, he quickly runs off. Focus on the task at hand - following the trail of the thieves. More Hog Monkeys block the path as you head to the South. Teach these beasts to stay out of your way!

Momo Objects 2 of 8

Just before the path starts to curve back to the West, you'll spot another large leafy green bush near a tree. Switch to Momo mode and inspect it to find another tomato.

If you need to take a break and regenerate your health, do so now. You're about to face two more groups of Hog Monkeys on the path ahead. Wipe them out and follow the path as it leads to a wooden bridge.

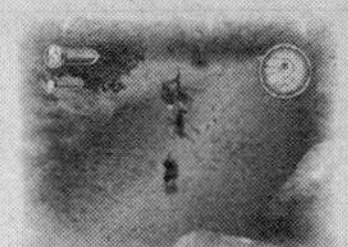

There is yet another broken food crate here, with footprints leading to the North over the footbridge. Ignore the enemy soldiers as you cross the bridge and turn to the right. At the corner ahead is another broken crate—and more of those darned monkeys!

Momo Objects 3 of 8

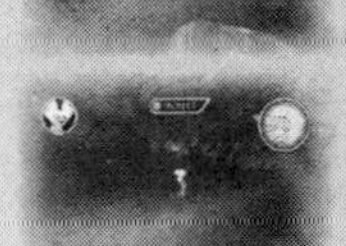

The leafy green bush in the corner should clue you in time to take control of Momo! Inspect the bush and you'll find one more tomato. Switch back to Aang and continue on your way.

Momo Objects 4 of 8

The path leads up a hill. On the South side of the path, you'll find a crate of goodies. On the opposite side of the path from the crate is another leafy green bush beneath a tree. You guessed it! Momo finds another tomato here.

Look for a SAVE POINT as the path ends at a clearing of enemy soldiers. After saving your progress, cross the stream over the small rocks and look for a broken food crate to the North.

Before investigating the cave near the broken food crate, explore the entire clearing. There is another stream crossing to the South. The controller vibration and question mark above your head clues you in to the presence of a hidden chest. Walk to the left side of the clearing until you are prompted to use Focus.

Hidden Chest: 2 of 6

There are enemy soldiers nearby, so you must be sure to stand far enough away from them before using Focus. If you hit them with your staff - even accidentally - they attack you. Use Focus to reveal the hidden chest. Opening it attracts the soldiers' attention, but you have no choice. If they attack, remain near the chest and fight back. The nearby soldiers won't notice as long as you keep the battle contained to this area.

Head back to the North and stand at the entrance to the cave near the broken food crate. The opening is blocked by vines, but the prompt lets you know that you can use Focus. Take control of Sokka, not Aang, as only he will be able to clear the entrance. After using Focus, venture inside.

Area Three: Hidden Cave

Quest 4: Disappearing Food - Update

Defeat the greedy soldiers who stole the village supplies

Inside the cave you'll find a large crate containing some of the villagers' missing supplies. It looks as if the Fire Soldiers have been stealing them. Teach these soldiers a lesson!

Follow the path inside the cave as it leads over a bridge.
Break the nearby barrels and battle any additional soldiers who get in your way. Up ahead you'll spot the remainder of the villagers' missing supplies. Unfortunately, there is a large gathering of soldiers who don't intend to let you escape with this information. Use your advanced moves and quickly refill your Health and/or Chi as needed.

Quest 4: Disappearing Food - Update

Tell the Elder the supplies can be safely collected from the hidden cave.

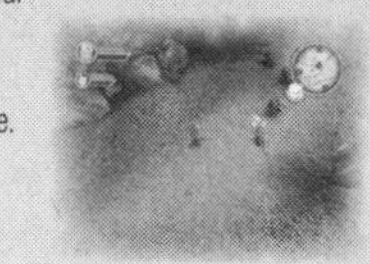

Having defeated all the enemy soldiers inside the cave, the villagers will now be able to come and retrieve their stolen supplies. Don't forget to open the small chest before turning around and exiting the cave the way you came in.

The enemy soldiers outside the cave still are unaware of your disguise—or whether you know their secret. You can walk by them without starting a fight. Cross the stream and save your progress at the SAVE POINT you spotted earlier.

You'll still have to fight any monkeys who get in the way, but they aren't a serious challenge. You can use stealth to walk past them if you aren't in the mood for fighting. Cross the wooden bridge and follow the green arrow on the outside of the radar, battling or sneaking past the rest of the monkeys.

When you reach the intersection, take a left turn towards the village. Find the Elder at the far West side of the village and talk to her. She thanks you for solving the mystery of the disappearing food, and suggests that you visit the docks to find information about Katara.

Quest 4. Completed

Quest 1: Rescue Katara - Update

Speak to the Dock Merchant. He may know if Katara was among the prisoners the Elder heard about.

Check your main world map. The Dock can be reached by taking a North at the intersection on the path between the village and the barracks. Save your progress at the SAVE POINT near the village entrance before leaving.

Talk to some of the villagers and they'll tell you about a widow who lives to the West. Leave the village to the West and, when you reach the intersection, take the path North to the dock area. Be careful not to strike an enemy soldier when breaking open barrels with your staff.

Area Four: Ship Docks

Take the first left turn and walk past the tents to reach the dock area. The Dock Merchant is here, with a blue symbol over his head. Ask him about the morning's events. He'll tell you that they captured Zuko's ship and dragged him away—along with a Water Tribe girl!

Hidden Chest: 3 of 6

Explore the dock area to collect items from barrels and crates. Check the piers for additional barrels. To the South, at the farthest end of the dock area, you'll find a hidden chest. Take control of Sokka and open the chest using Focus. If you want to save your progress, use the SAVE POINT at the North end of the dock area.

Quest 1: Rescue Katara - Update

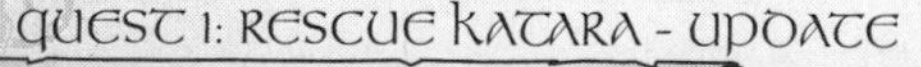

Save Katara from the Fire Nation prison to the East.

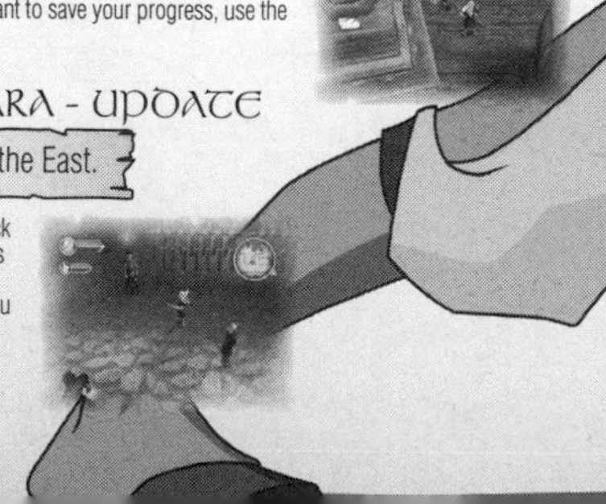

Leave the dock area and walk through the tents. If you check your radar, you'll spot a blue (friendly) dot to the North. It is the Fire Nation Commoner you rescued earlier. When you tell him about the theft of supplies, he recommends that you talk to his Captain.

Quest 6: Good Captain, Bad Captain

Speak to the Good Captain about the thieving soldiers. Beware of the Bad Captain!

The Good Captain is standing nearby. Look for the green dot on your radar and approach him. Talk to him about the theft. He thanks you for speaking up, and promises to put an end to it. He also gives you a Carved Charm.

Quest 6: Completed

Momo Objects 5 of 8

There are three areas on the map which you haven't yet visited. The Prison, to the East, is your final destination, so don't enter it until you've completed the other quests. For now, explore the area to the North of the docks. As the path curves to the West, you'll find another leafy green bush. Switch to Momo mode and grab the tomato before moving on.

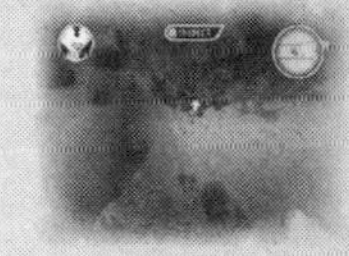

Momo Objects 6 of 8

At the intersection, make a left turn and follow the path to the West. Just past another smashed food crate, you'll encounter a group of monkeys. Take them out and, as Momo, search the leafy green bush nearby for yet another tomato. Look for a chest on the path.

Area Five: Widow's House

The path ends at the Widow's House. She is standing here with a blue symbol above her head, indicating that she has something to tell you. Speak to her and she'll tell you about her plight.

Quest 7: Help the Widow

Defeat the corrupt Tax Collector to stop him from hoarding the villager's taxes

After you give the widow some of your own money, the Tax Collector arrives and takes it from her. You aren't going to let him get away with this! Immediately follow the Tax Collector represented by a green dot on the radar. You've got to take him down while he is still out of sight of the other soldiers, or else they will join in attacking you.

Quest 7: Help the Widow - Update

Find the chest the Tax Collector's Key opens and retrieve all the village taxes

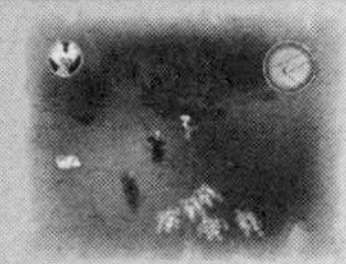

Momo Objects 7 of 8

The vanquished Tax Collector drops the Tax Collector's Key. Leave the Widow's House behind and make your way along the path to the East. Just past the intersection, you'll spot another leafy green bush. Inspect the area as Momo to acquire the seventh tomato. One more to go! Switch back to Aang and continue along the path to the East.

The path branches off to the East and Northeast. If you continue straight ahead, you'll reach the wooden bridge on the way to the Hidden Cave area. Instead, take the top route and follow the path as it curves around the corner and back to the West.

Area Six: Outpost

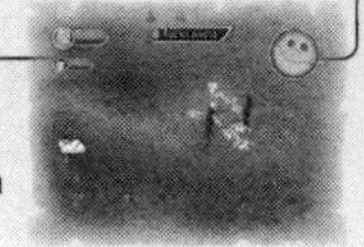

Hidden Chest: 4 of 6

The path ends at a Fire Nation Outpost. Inside the compound, to the right, you'll spot a chest sitting out in the open. On the South side of the compound, your senses tell you to look for a hidden chest. As Aang, use Focus in the appropriate area to reveal the chest.

Momo Objects 8 of 8

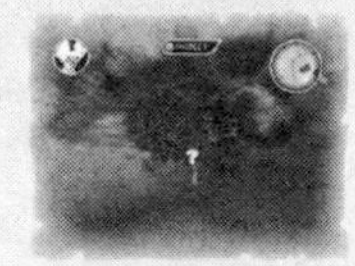

Before entering the Outpost building, look for a leafy green bush to the left of it. Switch to Momo mode and grab the last tomato found here; that's all of them! You'll also want to break the nearby barrels and crates to collect items.

Open the door and enter the Outpost. Since you are still in disguise, the soldiers won't pay you any heed. Make your way to the right of the building and look for a hallway that comes to a dead end. The large chest sitting there is locked, but you have the Tax Collector's Key needed to open it.

As you open the chest, a cinema scene shows additional soldiers entering the building. When control is returned to you, quickly use stealth to sneak past the soldiers and avoid a fight. If you are spotted before leaving the building, make a run for the exit. Once you are outside, you can use stealth once again as you leave the Outpost.

Quest 7: Help the Widow - Update

Return the Widow's share of the retrieved taxes

Fortunately for you, the soldiers on the path are unaware of what you've done. Return to the Widow's House and speak to the old woman to give her back her share of the money. Before leaving, look for a handful of crates and jars in the area that can be broken for items.

Quest 7: Completed

While you are at the village, take the time to find the Merchant who asked you to locate eight tomatoes. Speak to him and receive a Heavenly Pendant in exchange for the tomatoes.

Quest 3: Completed

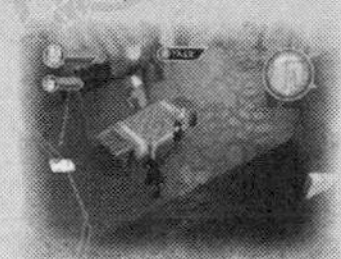

Having completed your other quests, you can now focus on rescuing Katara. Make your way through the village, exiting to the East. When you come to the intersection, keep moving straight ahead (to the right). The path eventually ends at the prison. Just as you arrive, there is a big commotion—it appears that Zuko has managed to escape!

Quest 1: Rescue Katara - Update

Use the confusion of Zuko's escape to enter the Prison.

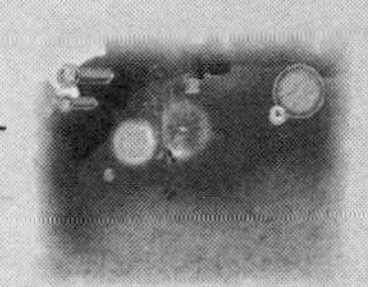

Hidden Chest: 5 of 6

Break the crates and jars outside of the prison. On the right side of the main gate you'll find a hidden chest. Only Sokka can use his Focus to open this one. After grabbing all the items you need, save your progress at the SAVE POINT to the left side of the main gate.

Quest 1: Rescue Katara - Update

Rescue Katara from her prison cell.

As you enter the prison, you'll discard your disguises. From here on out, you must battle all the soldiers (or use stealth to sneak past them) as you make your way to Katara's cell.

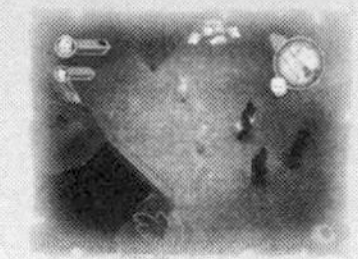

Sneak past the group of guards on the next platform. Don't bother trying to break the crates, as it will attract their attention. Whether you head up or to the left, you'll reach a set of cells. A Fire Nation Soldier asks for help, but without the key you won't be able to open the cells.

Quest 8: House Arrest

Free the Fire Nation Soldier.

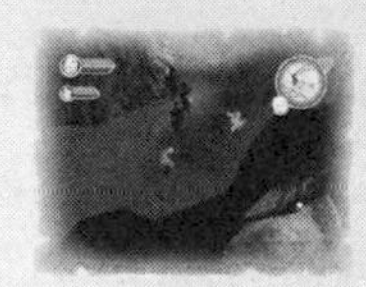

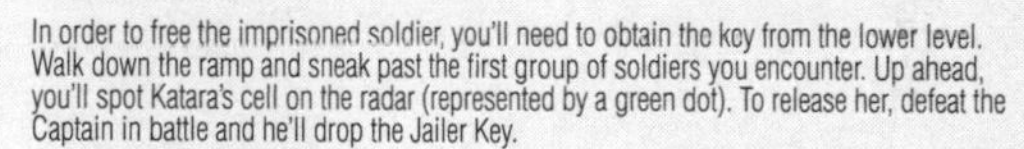

In order to free the imprisoned soldier, you'll need to obtain the key from the lower level. Walk down the ramp and sneak past the first group of soldiers you encounter. Up ahead, you'll spot Katara's cell on the radar (represented by a green dot). To release her, defeat the Captain in battle and he'll drop the Jailer Key.

Use the Jailer Key to open Katara's cell. She tells you that the Fire Nation has imprisoned someone named Lian, also known as "The Maker." They are forcing her to make machines for the war. Katara insists that you help free "The Maker" who is being held against her will.

Quest 1: Completed

Quest: Free the Maker

Find and defeat the Prison Jailer. He is holding Lian, the Maker, captive.

Katara now joins your party. To take control of her, press left on the D-pad. Before going anywhere, save your progress at the nearby SAVE POINT.

Now that you have the Jailer's Key in your possession, you can open all of the prison cells. Make your way back up to the upper level of the prison, freeing a prisoner you spot along the way.

You'll have to sneak past or battle the soldiers before you can reach the ramp leading to the upper level. At the top, you'll spot an imprisoned Fire Soldier in the first cell. Set him free to complete the quest.

Quest 8: Completed

Remember that Hidden Chest along the beach where you first began this Chapter? Neither Aang nor Sokka could open it, but Katara can. Yes, it is a long way back there, but you do want to find everything don't you? Leave the Prison the way you came in and make your way towards the village. Don't forget that the enemy soldiers will now attack you, as you are no longer in disguise.

◇Hidden Chest: 6 of 6◇

Pass through the village and head to the main entrance at the South. On the beach, look for the group of rocks on the left side at the water's edge. Take control of Katara and find the appropriate spot to activate her Focus.

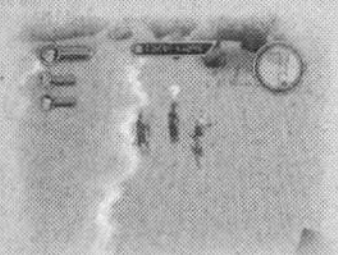

If you wanted the Elder or the Artisan to craft anything for you, now is the time to ask them. You might also want to sell excess items and purchase armor or potions before returning to the Prison. You won't be coming back to the village.

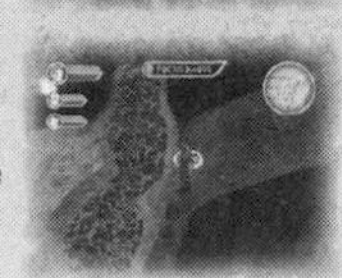

With every item accounted for, and all quests complete (save one), return to the Prison. Make your way down to the lower level until your path is blocked by lava. Neither Aang nor Sokka can help out here. Take control of Katara and use her Focus to create a path over the lava. As you enter the bottom cell, you are prompted to save your progress before the Boss battle.

Quest: Free the Maker - Update

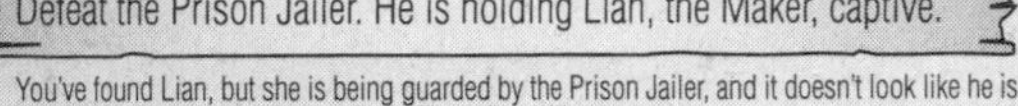

Defeat the Prison Jailer. He is holding Lian, the Maker, captive.

You've found Lian, but she is being guarded by the Prison Jailer, and it doesn't look like he is willing to set her free without a fight. That's fine with you…

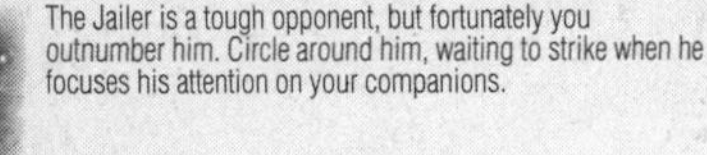

The Jailer is a tough opponent, but fortunately you outnumber him. Circle around him, waiting to strike when he focuses his attention on your companions.

At first, it won't appear that your attacks are causing the Jailer any damage. Keep up the attacks, hitting and running away before he can strike back. He's strong, but eventually he'll start to tire. When he drops to one knee to catch his breath, it's your signal to press the attack.

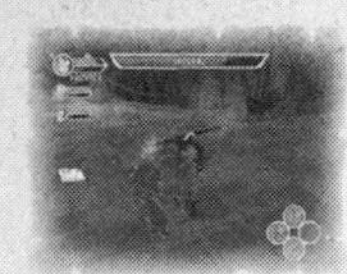

Switch back and forth between the three characters to catch the Jailer off balance. If he is pursuing you as Aang, for example, you can quickly take control of Katara and hit him from behind.

When the Jailer shoots fire at you, keep your distance and run around the cell away from him. At one point, he will curl up and roll towards you in an attempt to flatten you. Maintain your distance, striking from behind and the sides when his attention is elsewhere.

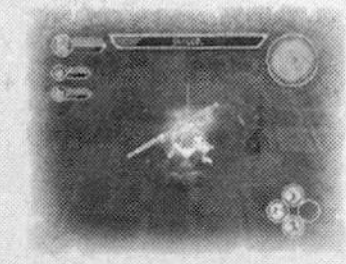

Continue the hit and run attack until the Jailer takes a knee, then close in and deliver advanced attacks. Repeat this process until his health bar is completely depleted.

At last, the Jailer falls down for good in defeat. Lian, however, has run away during the battle. A map left behind in her cell suggests that the Earth Bender training area is the next target—and thus your next destination!

Chapter 3: Forest

From the map left behind in the Maker's cell, our heroes have determined that the Fire Nation's next target is the Earthbender Training Camp. Aang leads them to it, although it is no longer familiar to him. Much has changed in the 100 years since he last visited!

CHAPTER CHECKLIST

Hidden Chests	6
Momo Objects	6
Sct Items	5

AREAS

1	FOREST VILLAGE
2	TRAINING CAMP
3	POACHER HIDEOUT
4	DEEP FOREST GLADE
5	ENCHANTED GROVE

QUESTS

1	THE EARTHBENDERS
2	TRAPPED
3	FEED APPA
4	IN SEARCH OF ORE
5	CHILD'S PLAY
6	THE POACHERS
7	INVESTIGATION
8	HEALING HANDS
9	BROTHERS AT ARMS
X	FIND THE SAGE

Area One: Forest Village

Quest 1: The Earthbenders (Main Objective)

Find the training camp to the Northeast, and assist in the battle Choi spoke of.

As you arrive at the village, you are approached by an injured villager named Choi. He tells you that the Earthbender training camp is already under attack and asks for your help. Other villagers will tell you that the camp can be found through the forest to the Northeast.

Although you'll want to come to the aid of the Earthbenders as soon as you can, you do have time to walk around the village and become familiar with the surroundings. A handful of blue dots on the radar indicate the location of people - or animals - that want to speak with you.

QUEST 2: TRAPPED

6 Moon Peaches remaining for Momo to find

Your faithful companion Appa is here and he's very hungry! Aang, Sokka, and Katara won't be able to help. You'll need to switch to Momo mode to find the Moon Peaches needed to satisfy Appa's hunger. Fortunately, they grow on blue-colored trees which are easy to find.

The Order of Things

You must complete this quest before speaking with Tyro to open the boss's lair. *Trapped* becomes unavailable once you begin the *Find the Sage* quest. However, 100% completion is not possible unless *Trapped* is completed early in the chapter.

Complete the training camp area by rushing through and destroying the machines. Proceed to the Enchanted Grove once the area's been cleansed. There are rocks blocking the path and they've enclosed the goal of the quest. Use Haru's focus move to push the rocks out of the way and free the poachers.

QUEST 3: FEED APPA

QUEST 4: IN SEARCH OF ORE

Find some black ore for the village Artisan so he can make his best armor

The Village Artisan, J'in (you can call him Whacky), also wants to speak with you. He buys and sells items and can craft items such as the Primal Headband, Robe of Kyoshi, Lightwind Charm, Vest of Power, and Transient Emperor. J'in needs Black Ore to create his best armor, however, and he asks your help in obtaining some. The mine where the Black Ore can be found is located to the Southwest.

QUEST 5: CHILD'S PLAY

Return the lost toys to Liang in the Southern part of the village

You'll also spot a woman named Liang with a blue symbol over her head. Speak to her and she'll tell you that she tossed her daughter's toys into the forest as punishment. Now she wants them back, so she asks you to help find them.

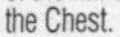

Hidden Chest: 1 of 6

While exploring the village, your senses (vibration and a question mark above your head) should tell you that there is a Hidden Chest near the wishing well. Make your way to the top of the hill above the well and, as Aang, use Focus to reveal the Chest.

Not far from the wishing well is a SAVE POINT. Although you haven't yet completed any quests, you may want to save your progress—especially if you've recently traded with any of the Merchants.

There is a Four Nations player on the West side of the village (near Appa). It costs 10 Copper to play the game, but you can win Unagi Boots, a Linking Tile, or a Renewal Headdress if you beat him. *[Strategies for the Four Nations game are found in the GETTING STARTED section of this guide].* The village merchant sells a Treasure Map, a Blue Shell Headband, Binding Sandals, Perfume, Herbs and Silk (among others). If you want the Artisan to craft anything for you, this is the place to purchase ingredients.

The village Elder is also an Herbalist who can craft Health medicine, Chi medicine, Regen medicine, Yin-Yang Paste, Anti-Heat Salve, Hard Leather Strips and Perfume.

You now have four active quests, and can complete them in any order. Your main objective, however, is to find the Earthbenders. Exit the village via the path to the Northeast.

If you thought you had seen the last of wolves back at the Waterbender Village, think again—Grey wolves inhabit these parts! Use stealth to sneak past them if possible, pausing in safe zones in between packs, or battle them head on to gain experience and earn items.

Momo Objects 1 of 6

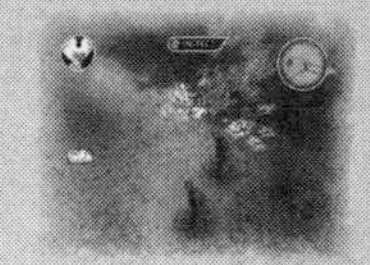

At the intersection, the path curves South or heads straight across to the East. Notice the blue tree on the East side? Switch to Momo and collect a Blue Moon Peach for Appa. Now switch back to Aang and continue to the East. When you find a SAVE POINT, use it to save your progress.

MUSHROOMS

Along the paths of the forest world, you'll spot large mushrooms. As with barrels, crates, and jars, you can break open these mushrooms. Some of them contain copper or valuable items.

Area Two: TRAINING CAMP

QUEST 1: THE EARTHBENDERS - UPDATE

Help the Earthbenders defeat the machines

You arrive at the Earthbenders' training camp to find that it is indeed under attack. The Fire Nation is using machines known as Stompers to do their dirty work. There are seventeen of them scattered throughout the camp.

Stompers spin around, causing damage to anyone in close range, before coming to a stop. Keep your distance while they are still spinning and hold the block button. When they stop moving, get in close and hit them hard. You can use Aang's Whirlwind attack to throw the machines off balance. Check the radar for the location of all seventeen Stompers. The same strategy works for defeating all of them. Your teammates, and several Earthbenders, will join in the battle.

QUEST 1: COMPLETED

After destroying all of the machines, speak with Master Tyro. He tells you that the machines captured Yuan, their youngest and most talented Earthbender. You agree to help. Another Earthbender named Haru joins your party. To control him, press down on the Directional Pad.

QUEST 7: INVESTIGATION (Main Objective)

Inform the Village Elder that the training camp is safe

QUEST 8: HEALING HANDS

Heal the Earthbenders who were injured in battle.

Master Tyro wants you to return to the village and let the Elder know that the camp is safe. Before you go, however, you have another task to perform. Several Earthbenders were wounded in the battle with the Spinners. Take control of Katara and look for them.

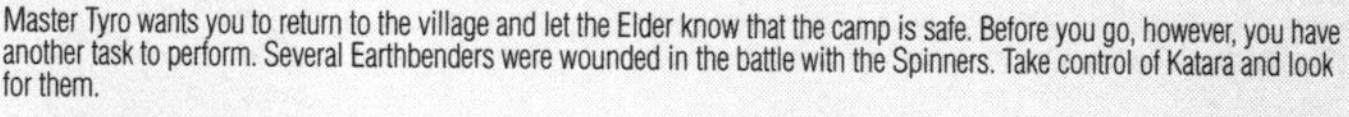

The injured Earthbenders are easy to spot—they are the ones grabbing their sides. There are four of them located in the training camp. As Katara, use Focus on them to heal their injuries. The final Earthbender that you heal gives you a Core Charm.

Head back the way you came, and once at the village look for a green dot on your radar. Talk to the Elder as Master Tyro requested. As you discuss the attack, an explosion rocks the area. It came from the mine to the Southwest of the village.

QUEST 7: INVESTIGATION - UPDATE

Assist the Elder while Tyro searches for information on the Machines. Investigate the mines in the Southwest, then return to the Elder.

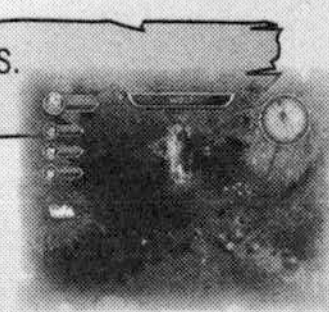

Check your map and you'll realize that you haven't explored the area to the Northwest of the village yet. The mines can wait for now. You'll find a Child's Doll along the path leading out of the village to the Northwest. Grab it and remember to give it back to Liang later on. For now, continue forward battling the wolves which block the path.

Momo Objects 2 of 6

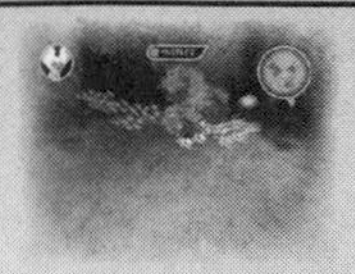

A blue tree is growing at the intersection ahead. Switch to Momo and inspect the tree. You'll find one of the Moon Peaches that Appa is hungry for. The path leads right (east) or left (west). For now, follow it to the right.

Hidden Chest: 2 of 6

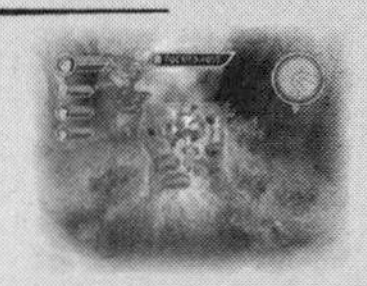

As you cross the rocks over the stream, your senses tell you that a Hidden Chest is nearby. Only Katara is able to reveal it using Focus.

Quest 6: The Poachers

Heal the cub

On other side of the stream, you'll come across an injured bear cub. Katara's healing powers will come in handy. Take control of her and use Focus to heal the cub.

Quest 6: The Poachers - Update

Search for the cub's mother. Tracks lead to the East

The bear tracks in the mud on the path ahead let you know that you are on the right track. Follow the path and stop to save your progress when you see the SAVE POINT.

Area Three: Poacher's Hideout

Just around the corner you'll find a new area—the Poacher's Hideout. A cinema scene shows you that the cub's mother is being held in a cage to the Northeast. There are a lot of poachers here, however, so it won't be easy to reach her. Instead of fighting your way through them, perhaps you can disorient them first.

Near the entrance to the Poacher's Hideout is a large bell. Aang can use Focus to ring the bell, causing the poacher's to scatter in a panic. Make your way up the East side of the encampment, taking out any remaining poachers on your way to the bear's cage.

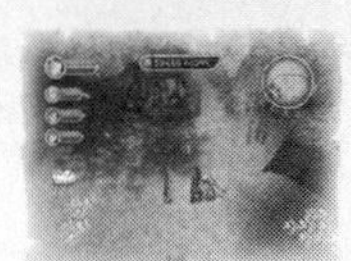

Sokka can open the bear cage using Focus. Now you've got one very large bear following you! Fortunately, she appears grateful and isn't a threat.

Quest 6: The Poachers - Update

Guide the mother bear back to her cub

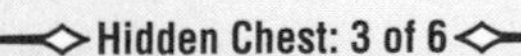

Hidden Chest: 3 of 6

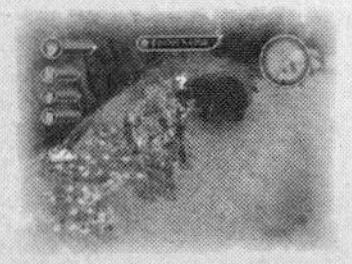

Lead the bear out of the Poacher's Hideout by taking the path to the West. Near the stream overlook, your senses tell you that a Hidden Chest is nearby. The only party member who can use Focus to reveal it is Haru.

The bear will continue to follow you, so defeat any remaining poachers and exit the encampment. The bear cub is here where you left it, just past the SAVE POINT. Walk over to the cub to complete the quest.

QUEST 6: COMPLETED

Return across the stream towards the village. When you reach the intersection, this time continue straight across to the West. Up ahead, in a clearing near the water, you'll encounter three Fire Nation soldiers. One is mounted on the back of a creature, making him much more difficult to defeat. Circle around the creature and attack it from the sides or from the rear.

Hidden Chest: 4 of 6

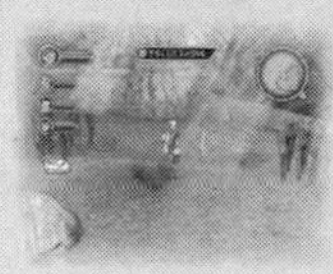

After defeating the trio of Fire soldiers, look for a Chest nearby. You'll also sense a Hidden Chest at the water's edge. Move in closer and use Katara's Focus to reveal the location of the Hidden Chest. After grabbing the goodies, return to the village.

Now it is time to head towards the mine to investigate the explosion. Perhaps you'll also be able to find the Black Ore that the Artisan is looking for. Find the path leading Southwest from the village and take it.

You won't get too far down the path when you'll spot a Child's Ball. This is the second of the two lost toys you promised to find for the mother in the village. You can keep it for later, but it is just as easy to turn back around and give the Ball to Liang right now.

QUEST 5: COMPLETED

Back on the path leading Southwest from the village, you'll run into a group of Fire Nation soldiers. Take them out before they can call for reinforcements!

Momo Objects 3 of 6

The blue-colored tree nearby reminds you that you still need to collect Blue Moon Peaches for Appa. Switch to Momo mode and inspect the tree to obtain another piece of fruit.

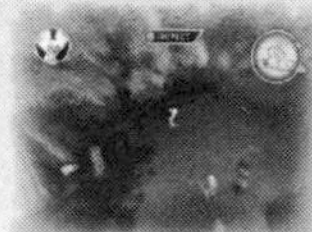

Momo Objects 4-5 of 6

Remain in Momo mode for the time being and continue down the path as it curves to the South. Across the wooden bridge you'll encounter another group of Fire Nation soldiers. Fortunately, they'll ignore Momo. Look for two blue trees nearby—one to the West, and one to the East of the intersection. Inspect them to obtain two more Blue Moon Peaches before switching out of Momo mode.

Now that Momo has scouted ahead, you know what you are up against. Be sure to equip your most powerful armor as you follow the path to the South. You can try to sneak past the Fire Nation Soldiers on the other side of the wooden bridge, but it won't be easy to find a hiding place amidst all those enemies.

You're going to have to become visible anyway if you want to obtain the Hidden Chest nearby. Target the Fire Soldier mounted on the creature first, as he is the biggest threat. Try to attack him only from the sides and the rear. There's no shame in running away from the battle temporarily to refill your Health and Chi. Circle around the rock formation as you destroy the remaining soldiers.

Hidden Chest: 5 of 6

Once the coast is clear, enter the ruined building to the South. Your senses indicate the presence of a hidden chest. Use Sokka's Focus to open it. Grab the goodies and head to the West, battling Soldiers and Wolves along the way.

Area Four: Deep Forest Glade

The path ends at an open area known as the Deep Forest Glade. Use the SAVE POINT before continuing. Two brothers - Jen and Jun Kai - are here. The blue symbols over their heads can only mean one thing: they want to talk to you!

Quest 9: Brothers at Arms

Search for the brothers' lost Uncle inside the mine.

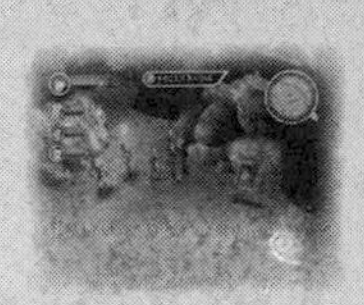

The brothers blame each other for the loss of their Uncle who became trapped inside the mine. This is no time to point fingers—perhaps you can reach him while there is still time. The entrance to the mine is blocked by fallen rocks, but that's no problem for an Earthbender like Haru. Take control of him and use Focus to break the rocks and open an entrance.

THE MINE

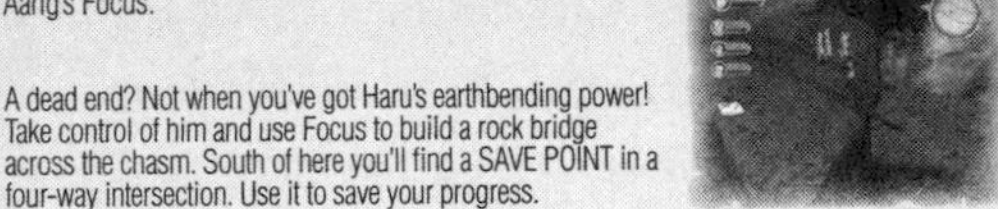

The layout of the mine can seem confusing, but all of the paths eventually connect with each other. There is no one "correct" path to take. Your goal is to find the Uncle, and the Black Ore, and get out as quickly as possible.

Once in the mine, take the path North at the first intersection. You'll encounter multiple Stompers here, but you remember how to beat them. Wait for them to stop spinning before attacking.

Be prepared to switch control between the various members of your party as needed. Each of them has certain abilities that will come in handy. For example, you won't be able to continue to the East until you clear the dust cloud using Aang's Focus.

A dead end? Not when you've got Haru's earthbending power! Take control of him and use Focus to build a rock bridge across the chasm. South of here you'll find a SAVE POINT in a four-way intersection. Use it to save your progress.

Rocks block the passageway to the left (west) of the intersection. Use Haru's Focus to move them out of the way. Behind the now-cleared rocks you'll locate Uncle Kai. He's alive, but injured.

Quest 9: Brothers at Arms - Update

The Uncle is injured and cannot walk until he is healed.

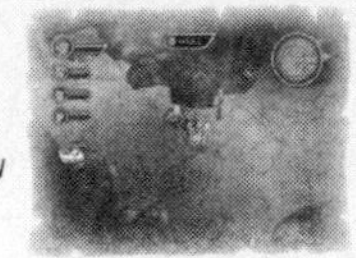

Now it is Katara's turn to be useful! Take control of her and approach the injured Uncle. Use her Focus to heal his injuries. He is grateful for the assistance, and will now be able to follow you out of the mine.

Quest 9: Brothers at Arms - Update

Guide the Uncle safely out of the mine.

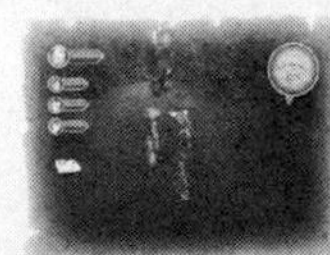

You aren't finished yet. The Artisan asked you to locate some Black Ore for him, remember? East of the four-way intersection you'll find a large piece of it. Grab it and take it back with you. There is also a chest in the passage ahead, although you'll have to battle Stompers if you go any farther.

Quest 4: In Search of Ore - Update

Give the Artisan the Black Ore

Now that you have obtained everything you came for—the Uncle and the Black Ore—it is time to leave the mine. If you take the South or East passage from the four-way intersection, you'll have to use Katara's Focus to bridge the water. The paths eventually link together. There are multiple Stompers, but little else of interest. Unless you are in need of experience points, or want to try to earn items by battling Stompers, don't bother.

Instead, turn around and go back the way you came by heading North away from the four-way intersection. The passage curves towards the West and then heads South. When it reaches an East/west intersection, take a left turn towards the mine's entrance/exit.

Whew! It is good to be back outside! Reunite the Uncle with his nephews to complete the Quest. Tell them about the prisoner you freed from the last Chapter, and Uncle Kai will give you two items as a reward—Dark Iron Ore and Sun Slippers.

QUEST 9: COMPLETED

Hidden Chest: 6 of 6

Before leaving the Deep Forest Glade, look around. Your senses clue you in on the location of another Hidden Chest. It is located near the hut to the West. Use Sokka's Focus to open it.

QUEST 7: INVESTIGATION - UPDATE

Return to the Elder as she may have another task for you

Make your way all the way back to the village, crossing the wooden bridge and keeping an eye out for enemies along the way. Back at the village, before you speak to the Elder, look for the Artisan.

The Artisan is happy to learn that you found the Black Ore he needs. Instead of selling it to him, give it to him as a gift. He'll be so thankful that he will give you a gift in return: the Transient Emperor.

QUEST 4: COMPLETED

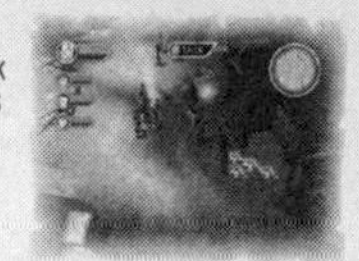

If you didn't already give the two toys to the mother, now is your last chance to do so. Use your radar to locate and speak with the village Elder. As you do so, Tyro appears. He speaks of a legendary forest Sage who is rumored to reside in the Southwest part of the forest.

QUEST: FIND THE SAGE (Main Objective)

Tyro believes a wise spirit, known as the Sage, may have information about the machines. Search for him to the Southeast.

Stop and check your map. There are two ways to reach the Enchanted Grove to the Southeast. You can leave the village to the Southwest, turning East at the intersection on the other side of the wooden bridge, or you can leave the village to the Southeast and then turn South at the intersection.

The Southeast route seems more direct, and hopefully you won't encounter as many Fire Nation soldiers as you did when traveling to the Southwest. Besides, you still need to find one more Peach for Appa!

Momo Objects 6 of 6

Battle the wolves along the path until you find a blue tree. Enter Momo mode and inspect it to acquire the last piece of fruit. Take control of Aang and return to the village, giving the peaches to your faithful flying Bison.

QUEST 3: COMPLETED

With that out of the way, the only thing left for you to do is to find the Sage—if he even exists. Backtrack along the path to the Southeast. At the intersection near the blue tree, head South. There will be a chest on the path ahead.

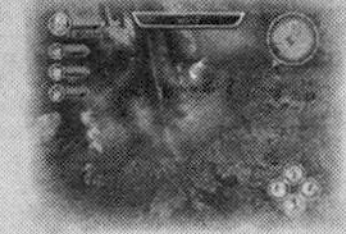

The path curves to the South before heading West. You'll encounter Fire Nation soldiers as well as wolves, but they won't stop you from completing your final quest.

Save your progress at the SAVE POINT just before the next intersection. Another Mounted Captain is here at the intersection. Use stealth to avoid him, or fight him if you must. Although you haven't explored the area between the Glade and the Grove, there isn't anything you need to find there. You'll want to head South.

Area Five: Enchanted Grove

Without much warning, the forest suddenly becomes darker. So dark, in fact, that you'll rely upon the luminescent mushrooms. Multiple Fire Nation soldiers are stationed here. If it's a fight they want, it's a fight they'll get!

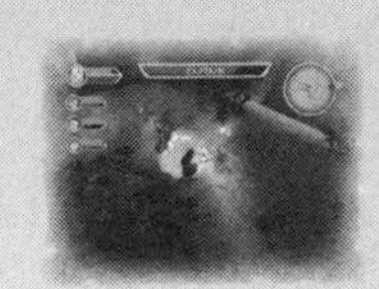

After fighting off the Fire Nation soldiers, continue down the path until it comes to a cave entrance. Inside, you'll be prompted to save your progress before entering the Boss Area. Stop and check your game status—if there are any quests or items left to find, you *don't* want to enter the Boss Area yet.

Quest 10: Find The Sage - Update

Defeat the large, angry bear blocking the path to The Sage.

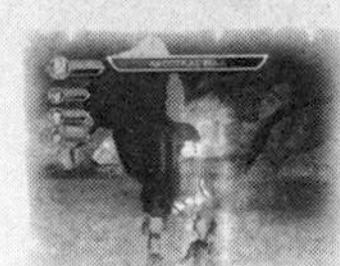

When you are ready, save your progress and be prepared to meet the Boss. It's a giant Ancestral Bear! This angry Ursine will charge your party and swipe at them with its sharp claws. Keep your distance!

There's nowhere to hide, but you can still run away from the Bear's charge. Keep moving in a circle around the edge of the Bear's lair. I don't suppose you can explain how nice you were to that other bear cub, can you?

After several charges, the Bear will stand up on its hind legs and growl. Doing so exposes its weak underbelly. Immediately run towards it and perform a advanced attack before he drops back down to all fours.

You'll have to repeat this four or five times, running from the bear, avoiding swipes of its paw, and waiting for it to stand up before attacking. Watch the health gauge above the Bear's head to see how much damage you are inflicting.

When the Bear's health gauge is depleted, it—transforms into the Sage! Looks like the entire battle was a test! Fortunately for you, you passed.

LEVEL ART GALLERY

By successfully completing this Chapter, you have unlocked the Level Art Gallery from the Extras Menu. Select it to view production artwork for the game's various Chapters. Good job!

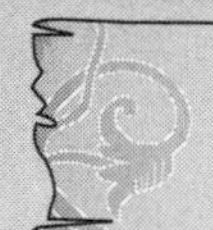

Chapter 4: Omashu

Convinced that the Sage was talking about Omashu, Aang leads his party to the great Earthbender city. Its library must certainly contain the knowledge they need.

CHAPTER CHECKLIST

Hidden Chests	6
Momo Objects	8
Set Items	5

AREAS

1	ROYAL PALACE
2	MAIL CENTER
3	TEA HOUSE
4	ROYAL LIBRARY
5	ROYAL STABLES

QUESTS

1	MACHINE RESEARCH
2	GRANDMASTER
3	PUMPKINS
4	MISSING ARTIFACT
5	CREEPING CRYSTAL
6	THE CONFOUNDED SCHOLAR
7	RETURN TO SENDER
8	PASSWORDS
9	GOOD GOGGLES
10	APPA'S NEW SADDLE
11	MOLLIFYING PASTE
X	ESCAPE OMASHU

Quest 1: Machine Research (Main Objective)

Find the Palace and speak to King Bumi. He may be able to help you find out about the Machines.

You begin this chapter in a tall structure overlooking the town. Appa will remain here as you explore. Speak to the villagers who pass by shortly after your arrival and you'll learn that there is a central marketplace for trading purposes. For fun, kids like to play on the mail carts located to the Northeast of the market.

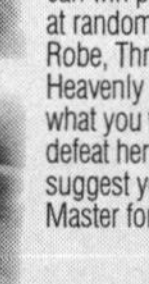

Take the stairs down to the West. On the landing, you'll meet a Four Nations player. It will cost you 20 copper to play against her, but you can win prizes (selected at random) such as a Bear Robe, Threaded Gown, or Heavenly Charm. No matter what you win, when you defeat her three times, she'll suggest you play the Grand Master for a better challenge.

Quest 2: Grandmaster

Defeat the Grandmaster in a game of four nations.

The Grandmaster is found in the seedy part of town, so you won't get to him for a while. In the meantime, take the stairs down to the central marketplace and explore the area. A Merchant in the corner wants to speak with you (note the blue symbol over his head). He sells a Treasure Map and various items, but he is looking for pumpkins.

Quest 3: Pumpkins

8 Pumpkins left for Momo to collect.

Momo Objects 1-4 of 8

Switch to Momo mode immediately upon receiving the request from the Merchant. The first pumpkin is found in the marketplace, not far from the Merchant! Is he lazy, or what? Continue through the marketplace to the East. As the path curves towards the stairs, you'll find one pumpkin on the right and one on the left. Take the stairs up to the landing and search for a fourth pumpkin there. Exit Momo mode with half of the pumpkins accounted for. That was easy!

The Herbalist near a small set of stairs can craft Health medicine, Chi medicine, Regen medicine, Yin-Yang Paste, Anti-Heat Salve, Hard Leather Strip, and Perfume. She also sells Regen, Health, and Chi medicines as well as Honey, Bai Don Kon herb, and Shi Take herb.

Up the small stairs behind the Herbalist is an Artisan. He can craft a Primal Headband, Robe of Kyoshi, and Transient Emperor. He also sells a Swallow Tail Gi and Might of Moho among other items. Buy all the Leather Strips he has to offer—you'll need them later on.

Wind your way East through the marketplace towards the stairs. A woman named Zi is standing at the foot of the stairs. She wants to gain access to the Library in order to search for two parts of an artifact taken from her village. Since you are on your way to the Library yourself, you might as well give her a hand.

Quest 4: Missing Artifact

Search the library for the Moon and Ocean statues and return them to Zi.

Up the stairs is a SAVE POINT. Use it and continue on your way. To the North is a soldier named Tai (represented by a blue dot on the radar). He tells you that there is a jewel thief in the area. You suggest that he uses Gemmanite - a creeping crystal ring - to catch the thief. Tai asks you to keep an eye out for one.

Quest 5: Creeping Crystal

Help the Guards catch a jewelry thief by finding them some Creeping Crystal.

The path leads East and West. For now, make a left turn and walk up the steps to the West. At the intersection, head right to the Northeast. You might be followed by a group of feral cats—they may look harmless, but they are nasty! Fight them off and break any boxes or hay bales in the vicinity to find copper and items.

Check the map. There is a small loop to the left (northwest) of the main path. The vendor here sells a Treasure Map as well as Leather Strips and a Metal Sheet. You'll need five Leather Strips for another Quest, so you might as well purchase them now.

Hidden Chest: 1 of 6

Don't waste your money purchasing a Treasure Map, as you can find the chests on your own. In fact, there is one here in the nearly-deserted market. Your senses will reveal its presence. Use Haru's Focus to locate and open the Hidden Chest.

Momo Objects 5-6 of 8

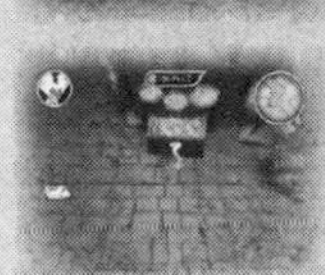

Before leaving the market area, switch to Momo mode and look for two Pumpkins hidden amongst the stalls. Exit Momo mode and return to the main path, heading Northeast.

The blue symbol over the head of a villager here lets you know that you need to speak to her. She is a scholar who, unable to enter the Library, needs you to help her retrieve some information. Why not?

Quest 6: The Confounded Scholar

Discover the real name for Shrinking Crystal and return to the confounded Scholar.

Area One: Royal Palace

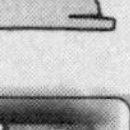

Ascend the multiple sets of stairs. At the top of the stairs, walk between the guards into the Palace. A cinema scene shows Aang's reunion with King Bumi. The King is a little eccentric (to say the least), and doesn't seem to know anything about the Machines. He recommends that Aang check the Library. Unfortunately, as the king's Consul reminds you, the Library is off-limits except to Earthbender masters.

Quest 1: Machine Research - Update

Find a way into the Royal Library without getting caught by the Guards.

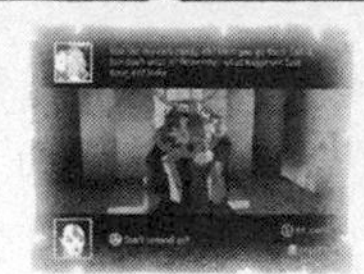

When control is returned to you, don't exit the Palace just yet. King Bumi has a green icon over his head, so speak with him. During the conversation, you can request a Gemmanite Ring which he freely gives to you. This will help the Soldiers catch the jewel thief.

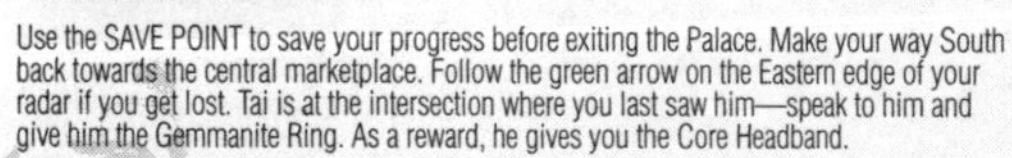

Use the SAVE POINT to save your progress before exiting the Palace. Make your way South back towards the central marketplace. Follow the green arrow on the Eastern edge of your radar if you get lost. Tai is at the intersection where you last saw him—speak to him and give him the Gemmanite Ring. As a reward, he gives you the Core Headband.

Quest 5: Completed

Instead of traveling South back to the marketplace, continue on the past path Tai to the East. Get ready to fend of a group of Feral Cats near a chest as well as any Bandits foolish enough to attack your group.

Hidden Chest: 2 of 6

When the path reaches an intersection, head right to the Southeast. Another group of Bandits is in the corner—not far from where your senses detect a Hidden Chest. Clear the area before using Aang's Focus to reveal the Chest.

Area Two: Mail Center

Return to the intersection and this time continue to the Northwest until you reach the Mail Center. Without warning, Momo jumps into one of the carts and is quickly spirited away. Follow that lemur! Jump into a cart yourself and give chase.

The thrilling cart ride ends suddenly as your cart jumps the track and wipes out a cabbage vendor's stand. The angry vendor calls for the guards—you had better run and hide!

Quest 7: Return to Sender

Hide from the guards!

Quest 8: Good Goggles

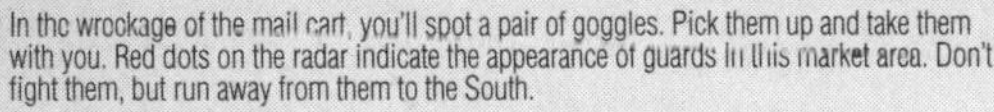

The Goggles look very valuable. Find the owner and return them.

In the wreckage of the mail cart, you'll spot a pair of goggles. Pick them up and take them with you. Red dots on the radar indicate the appearance of guards in this market area. Don't fight them, but run away from them to the South.

Use stealth to sneak past the guards. Break the boxes and hay bales whenever the guards are not around to collect items. The market is a large loop. On the East side, there's a chest in an alcove. Use stealth to get past the guards and exit the market. ***Return to Sender*** can be completed by doing the "cabbage quest" from the cabbage vendor.

Quest 7: Completed

As you head North away from the market with the ruined cabbage stand, you'll reach an intersection. Turn left and make your way past a large lantern—and possibly some Bandits and Rangers. Fight off the robbers and continue to the West. There is a Merchant in the area. Talk to him and purchase Leather Strips if you don't yet have five of them. When you reach the next intersection, talk to the villager for directions to the Library.

The villager at the intersection tells you to take the Earthbender lifts which are located to the North of his location. Walk onto the lifts and press the Action button to activate them. On the top level, you can save your progress at the SAVE POINT.

LIBRARY BACK ENTRANCE

You could head to the Library without the password, using Momo to crawl through the vents and unlock the door from the inside. However, if you do so, you will not get credit for completing a Quest.

Area Three: Tea House

At the top of the lifts, head West and (after fighting off the Feral Cats) walk up the curved path to the Tea House. Inside, you'll spot two guards. One mentions something about a new password, but he won't tell it to his companion until the two of them are alone.

Quest 8: Passwords

Listen in on the Library Guards at the Tea House to learn the password. Make sure you stay hidden!

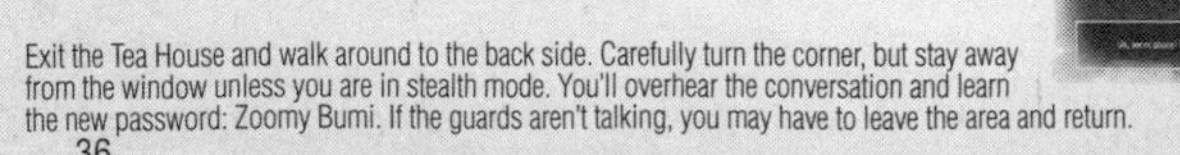

Exit the Tea House and walk around to the back side. Carefully turn the corner, but stay away from the window unless you are in stealth mode. You'll overhear the conversation and learn the new password: Zoomy Bumi. If the guards aren't talking, you may have to leave the area and return.

QUEST 1: MACHINE RESEARCH - UPDATE

Return to the Library Guard and use the password "Zoomy Bumi."

Leave the Tea House, passing by the lifts. There is a chest in the East corner near the lifts, and more Feral Cats to battle up ahead. The path forks to the Northwest or Northeast. Head Northwest for a brief detour.

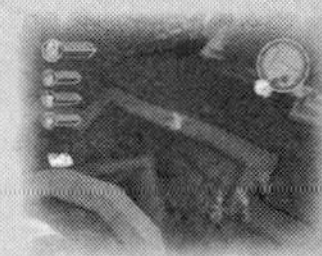

There are multiple groups of Bandits and Rangers in the seedy part of town. You can fight them for the experience points, and a handful of items, but you might also want to use stealth to avoid them altogether.

USING STEALTH

Keep a close eye on your stealth gauge at the edge of the radar. If it is about to run out, find a hiding place quickly. If groups of enemies are off-screen, you can wait in between them while your stealth "recharges."

The green dot on the radar lets you know that you have located the Four Nations Grandmaster. Why is he in this part of town, anyway? It costs 40 copper to play against him, with potential prizes ranging from Badger Boots to a Dragon Ring. More importantly, when defeated he will give you an Avatar Tile.

QUEST 2: COMPLETED

Hidden Chest: 3 of 6

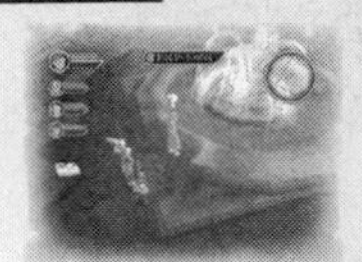

Before leaving the black market, take control of Katara and use her Focus power to reveal a Hidden Chest at the edge of the fountain where the surrounding wall is broken.

Sneak past the remaining Bandits or fight them on your way out. Back at the intersection, head to the Northeast. Haru respects his Earthbender customs and tells you that he cannot go any further. Leave him behind and walk up the spiral path until you reach the Library. Talk to the guards at the door to give them the password.

QUEST 8: COMPLETED

QUEST 1: MACHINE RESEARCH - UPDATE

Search for information about the Machines in the Royal Library.

AREA FOUR: ROYAL LIBRARY

Hidden Chest: 4 of 6

Before entering the Library, take a moment to explore the garden area outside. Your senses tell you that a Hidden Chest is nearby. Use Katara's Focus at the edge of the fountain to reveal then Hidden Chest.

There is a SAVE POINT near the fountain. If you inspect the grating on the wall, you can send Momo into the Library to open the door from the inside, but why bother? The front door is now open, so return to it and enter.

The Ocean Spirit Statue is found on a pedestal at the East end of the Library. Grab it and make your way down the stairs to the West. Continue to the far West end of the Library and grab the Moon Spirit Statue from the pedestal. You now have the two artifact pieces that Zi is looking for.

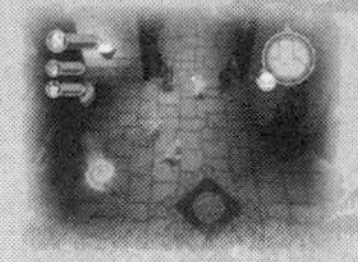

There is a SAVE POINT inside the Library. Break the vases nearby to obtain items. The guards won't let you pass and will stop you if they see you. So, don't let them see you! Use stealth to walk between them and into the next area.

Let your stealth recharge before attempting to pass the guards on the stairs. There are two of them blocking your way. At the bottom of the room you'll end up on a pier above the water. Walk across it to the East and enter the next area.

FORCIBLY REMOVED

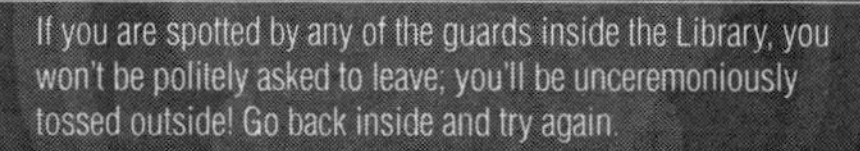

If you are spotted by any of the guards inside the Library, you won't be politely asked to leave; you'll be unceremoniously tossed outside! Go back inside and try again.

Two guards block the bottom of the stairs. Use stealth to sneak between them and walk to the far side of the room. There is a group of vases blocking a small passage. Break the vases to clear the path. On a pedestal in this passage is the information you need to retrieve for the scholar.

After reading about the shrinking crystal (i.e. Minimite), stealth past another pair of guards on the stairs and descend to the ground level. Hide behind the bookcases to recharge your stealth while waiting for the guards to pass by. Make your way to the South when the coast is clear and run up the stairs. You can save your progress at the SAVE POINT here.

Fortunately for you, there are no guards upstairs. A cinema scene shows the group finding a book about the machines. You'll automatically exit the Library with the Battle Records after reaching this point.

Quest 1: Machine Research - Update

Discuss the information found about the machines with King Bumi.

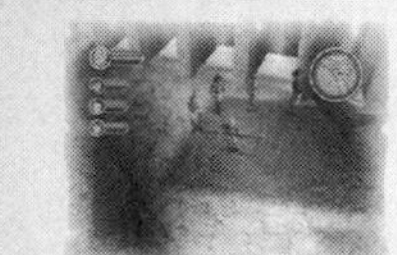

Haru meets up with you on your way back down from the Library. Return to the lifts and ride them down. You are on your way back to the Palace to speak with Bumi. Battle the Bandits and Feral Cats along the way.

Talk to the Confounded Scholar outside of the Palace and share the information you learned. She gives you a Purity Hat for your troubles. Continue up the stairs into the Palace.

Quest 6: Completed

Speak to King Bumi about the hidden island you learned of at the Library. He needs Mollifying Paste to help show you where it is. The Royal Merchant can make it for you, but the merchant is out on business. Meanwhile, King Bumi has sent the Stable Master to see Appa; he's going to make the Bison a new saddle.

Quest 1: Completed

QUEST 10: APPAS NEW SADDLE

Craft 5 hardened leather strips for Appa's new saddle.

QUEST 11: MOLLIFYING PASTE

Talk to the Stable Master while you wait for the Royal Merchant to return.

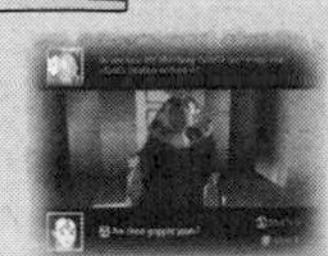

Before leaving the Palace, talk to King Bumi about the goggles. Sure enough, they belong to him. As a reward for finding them, the King gives you a Core Amulet.

QUEST 9: COMPLETED

Follow the path from the Palace back to the central marketplace. Zi is still waiting near the stairs. Speak to her and give her the two artifacts found in the Library. Although she offers you copper as a reward, you should refuse it. Instead, Zi presents you with a Soulband.

QUEST 4: COMPLETED

While in the central marketplace, locate the old woman Herbalist. She can craft the five Hard Leather Strips needed by the Stable Master. For each strip, you must give her 1 Honey and 1 Leather Strip. If you need additional materials, you can buy Honey from her first.

Take the stairs past the Four Nations Player up to Appa. The Stable Master is standing nearby. He wants to take Appa to the stables for a bath. He also asks you for 5 Hard Leather Strips to create a new saddle. Having made them in advance, you can give them to him right now.

QUEST 10: APPA'S NEW SADDLE - UPDATE

The Stable Master has taken Appa back to his stables. Go and see him to receive the new saddle.

After the Stable Master leaves, it is time to explore the area to the South of where you began the Chapter. South of the fountain is a chest. Open it and take the goodies. The nearby villagers don't have anything important to tell you.

Hidden Chest: 5 of 6

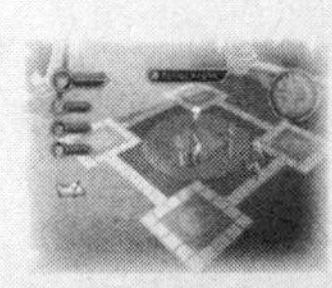

To the East of the fountain, your senses indicate the presence of a Hidden Chest. Take control of Haru and use Focus to reveal and open the chest. You don't need to explore that side of town any farther; there is only a single merchant on the path between the city and the Mail Center.

Momo Objects 7 of 8

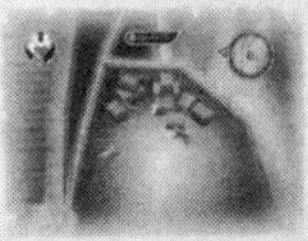

As you head West from the fountain area you'll encounter a group of Feral Cats. Take care of them and, switching to Momo mode, inspect the nearby hay bales. You'll find another Pumpkin there.

Follow the path to the Southwest and then West past a large tree. It continues to the North through a large gate. The market where you destroyed the cabbage vendor's cart is to the West; you probably don't want to show your face around there again! Head to the North.

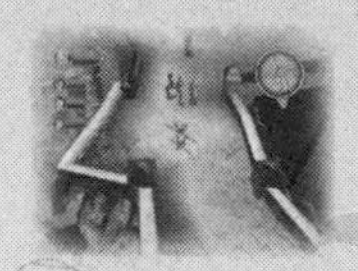

When the path splits, take a left turn and follow the path back to the Southwest and past the large lanterns (heading towards the lifts). At the next intersection, instead of traveling North to the lifts, head to the South.

Area Five: ROYAL STABLES

You may encounter a Bandit or two before you reach the Royal Stables. There is a SAVE POINT here, so take advantage of it. Look for Stable Master with a green icon over his head and speak to him. True to his word, he has crafted a new saddle for Appa.

quest 10: completed

Hidden Chest: 6 of 6

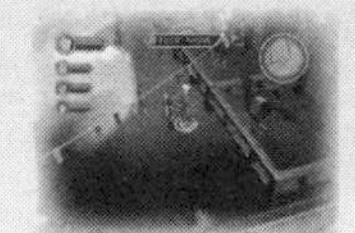

Open the normal chest at the far South end of the stable. There is also a Hidden Chest nearby. Use Sokka's Focus to reveal it.

quest 11: mollifying paste - update

The Royal Merchant has returned! Find him and buy some Mollifying Paste for Bumi.

As you leave the Royal Stables, you'll be informed that the Royal Merchant has returned. Speak to the villagers and they'll tell you that the Royal Merchant can be found at a small market in the Southern part of the city.

Head East at the intersection, then South and East to return to the fountain area. Look for a set of steps on the West side of the fountain area, right next to the Feral Cats where you found the last Pumpkin, and ascend.

Momo Objects 8 of 8

The path curves into a small marketplace area off of the fountain circle. Switch to Momo mode one final time and search the area until you find the last Pumpkin. Before talking to the Royal Merchant, return to the central marketplace and speak to the Merchant who asked for the Pumpkins. He gives you the Crane Pendant as a reward.

quest 3: completed

ENDGAME

Do not approach the Royal Merchant until you have completed the rest of your Quests! Once you obtain the Mollifying Paste, you will be unable to access certain areas of the city.

Now return to the market where the Royal Merchant is located. There is a SAVE POINT here; you'll definitely want to save your progress before continuing.

Speak to the Royal Merchant and let him know that you are working for the King. He'll give you the Mollifying Paste. However, as he does, the city comes under attack. A cinema scene shows the arrival of the Firebenders. Haru volunteers to fight them off while the others head to the Palace.

QUEST 11: MOLLIFYING PASTE - UPDATE

Help thin the Fire Nation's numbers as you make your way to the palace. Fire Nation to defeat: 15

When the cinema ends, you are in control of Haru all alone, fighting the Firebenders. Although there are many of them, you only need to defeat 15 Firebenders to continue the storyline.

Battle the nearby Firebenders before making your way back to the fountain area and North to the tower where you began this Chapter. Multiple Firebenders may await you there. With each one you defeat, you'll be given a message letting you know how many (of the required 15) remain.

HARU'S POWER

Haru's attacks work best at short or long range. Keep your distance from the Firebenders, holding the target lock button before launching an attack. If you get too close, you won't be able to throw rocks or perform special moves before they strike you.

Clear the tower and walk down the steps towards the central marketplace. The merchants have fled, and the market is on fire, but you can still break crates to find items. Haru isn't the strongest of your party, so you'll need to refill your Health (and Chi) frequently.

At some point, possibly on the landing, you'll face two Firebenders and a Mounted Captain riding a beast. You are only required to defeat 15 Firebenders in total, so choose your targets wisely! If you don't want to face the Mounted Captain, run away from the battle. There are plenty of Firebenders left to fight.

Use the SAVE POINT atop the stairs. If you fail this Quest, you can load your game from this point instead of having to replay the prior battles.

Additional Firebenders are located near the intersection where you met the guard. On your way back to the Palace, you will encounter even more Firebenders. Some Omashu guards may try to assist you. Stay alive by running past larger skirmishes and stopping to battle Firebenders only when you aren't heavily outnumbered.

QUEST 11: MOLLIFYING PASTE - UPDATE

The Fire Nation's numbers are too great! Get back to the Palace and help Aang escape!

After you have defeated 15 Firebenders, you'll see a message modifying your Quest. Now you can ignore the Firebenders altogether as you head for the Palace. Use stealth to pass large groups of enemies if necessary.

Back at the Palace, your companions are eagerly awaiting your arrival. Give the Mollifying Paste to King Bumi as he requested. To your surprise, it turns out to be merely lip balm! You almost got yourself beaten for that?!?

Quest 11: Completed

During a cinema scene, the King tells you about the island you seek: Four Paws Island. Although it is undocumented, Bumi knows where it is and points it out on a map.

Quest: Escape Omashu

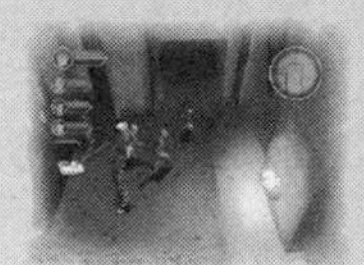

Escape through the Secret Palace Exit

King Bumi opens up a secret exit, allowing you to leave the Palace. As you do, you'll be prompted to save your game before meeting up with the Boss. Any Quests you failed to complete before talking to the Royal Merchant cannot be returned to.

Quest: Escape Omashu - Update

The Consul is working against the King and has blocked off the exit! He must be defeated!

As you make your escape, the path is suddenly blocked by an Earthbender. The King's Consul is responsible, and he has no intention of letting you leave. The Consul is part of a plan that will keep the Earth Kingdom safe—at the expense of destroying all Benders such as yourselves!

When control is returned to you, you'll find yourself in control of Haru. You don't have to keep control of him, however—press the D-pad in the appropriate direction to select Aang, Sokka, or Katara instead.

The Consul is able to disappear into holes in the ground and reappear elsewhere. He can also summon the earth to grab the feet of your companions. If he traps you this way, quickly switch to another character.

Keep moving to avoid being targeted by the Consul's rocky projectiles. Get in close enough to use a long-range attack; if you get too close, he'll usually burrow away.

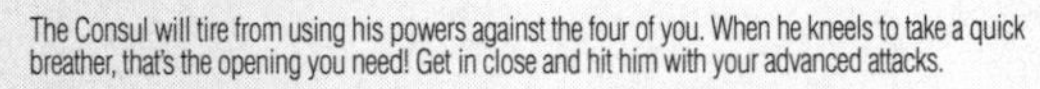

The Consul will tire from using his powers against the four of you. When he kneels to take a quick breather, that's the opening you need! Get in close and hit him with your advanced attacks.

Katara is able to heal the other characters as long as she remains in good health. She can take care of herself, so concentrate on the Consul. Haru's attacks can cause significant damage, but so do Aang's attacks.

Keep running around the arena trying to avoid the Consul's projectiles. Wait for him to pause before going on the offensive. When you've finally beaten him down, he'll collapse in a heap. A cinema scene shows our heroes leaving Omashu and closing the passage behind them. Zuko is right on their tail!

Chapter 5: The Hidden Island

The uncharted island of Four Paws is just where King Bumi said it would be. Is this where the Fire Nation is secretly building the Machines? You aren't sure exactly what you will find, but hopefully the inhabitants can help.

CHAPTER CHECKLIST

Hidden Chests	8
Momo Objects	8
Set Items	5

AREAS

1	ISLAND VILLAGE
2	RUINED SHRINE
3	NORTHERN RUINS
4	ARENA RUINS
5	ANCIENT PILLARS

QUESTS

1	MYSTERY OF THE PAST
2	FROZEN TOAD
3	THE CRAFTER
4	COCONUT COLLECTION
5	MAKESHIFT DAM
6	ANCIENT TREASURE
X	THE SACRED CAVERNS

Area One: Island Village

Quest 1: Mystery of the Past (Main Objective)

The book in Omashu's library showed a statue on the island. Find the statue and search around it.

The village is a short distance to the North of the water where you landed. Speak to any villagers you come across. They'll tell you that the statue you are looking for might be found in the ruins to the Northeast.

Continue exploring the village and talking to the inhabitants. You'll learn that, as a result of their isolation, the people are no longer sure what nation they belong to. The village Elder, however, is interested in artifacts and history, so you should talk with him.

Note the SAVE POINT near the village Elder. You don't have to use it just yet, as you haven't completed any tasks. The Elder explains that their history has been lost in the ruins, and tells you to travel North to find the statue.

Hidden Chest: 1 of 8

Before leaving the area, look for a stairway in the ruins near the Elder. Walk up to the top and use Sokka's Focus to reveal a Hidden Chest.

On the West side of the village you'll meet an Herbalist. She sells items such as medicines and is able to craft other items for you. At the moment, you don't need her services. A villager named Onn is right next to her. He's got a blue symbol over his head. Talk to him and he'll tell you that he needs a Frozen Toad as a cure for his sick son. He thinks you might find one in a pond East of here.

Quest 2: Frozen Toad

Find and freeze a toad for Onn so he can cure his sick son.

Don't leave the village yet—there are still more people to talk to. Just South of Onn and the Herbalist is an Artisan. He tells you that he can create a strong set of boots for you, but first you must bring 3 strips of palm bark and 5 smooth stones to him. You can find the stones in the ruins; palm bark is found on almost every beach.

Quest 3: The Crafter

Find 5 smooth stones and 3 bark pieces for the Artisan's crafting.

One of the Merchant sells the Inner Mind and an Evening Shadow Robe—two items you haven't seen before. Another Merchant on the East side of the village is represented by a blue dot on your radar. Talk to him and he'll ask you to find eight coconuts. Looks like another job for Momo!

Quest 4: Coconut Collection

8 coconuts remaining for Momo to collect

There is also a Four Nations player in the village not far from your starting position. It costs 30 copper to play against him, and the prizes for winning include an Avatar Tile and Ammas.

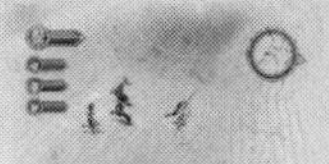

Since the Elder and villagers mentioned ruins to the Northeast, head that direction first. Look for the footprints on the beach to the East of the village and cross the sand bar over the shallow water. On the other side, you'll encounter a pack of wolves on the trail as it leads to the Northeast. Fight them off and continue on your journey.

Area Two: Ruined Shrine

You'll find the first Smooth Stone near a fountain straight ahead as you enter the Ruined Shrine. Two Platypus Bears are wandering around just South of that fountain. These guys are big, but they aren't the most dangerous creatures on the island. Eliminate them and move on.

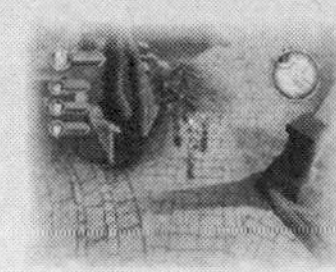

Walk around the East side of the Ruined Shrine and you'll spot two more Smooth Stones. Don't forget to break the piles of firewood for a chance to obtain copper and items.

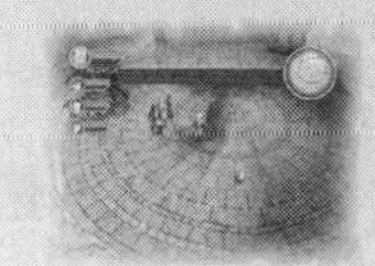

The final two Smooth Stones are found in the central area of the Ruined Shrine. You'll also find something called the 2nd Keystone Piece here. You aren't sure what it is for, but it must be important.

On the West side of the Ruined Shrine, and to the North, you can find additional Smooth Stones (although you don't need them). Leave the Ruined Shrine to the North, but watch out for a Platypus Bear at the edge overlooking the jungle.

If you thought the Platypus Bear was tough, you haven't seen the Shirshu! It's a giant lizard creature with sharp claws and a long tongue that can temporarily paralyze you. One of them is here in the jungle connecting the Ancient Ruins to the Northern Ruins. It isn't easy running past it, since it is so large. If you've been upgrading your weapons and trinkets along the way, however, you should be able to take it down without too much effort.

Area Three: Northern Ruins

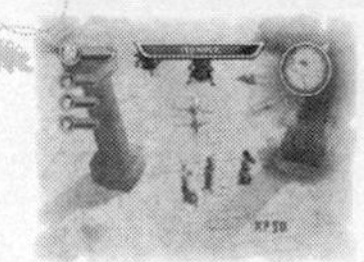

You are welcomed at the Ruins by a trio of Stompers. Greet them back with an advanced move! As usual, keep your distance while they are spinning. After defeating them, look for a SAVE POINT to the East and save your progress.

The dog statue near the SAVE POINT looks a lot like the one from the picture in Omashu's Library. Search behind it and you'll spot a large rock slab. Use Haru's Focus power to move it out of the way, revealing steps leading below ground.

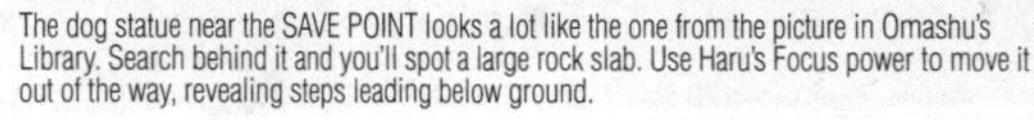

Quest 1: Mystery of the Past - Update

There's a hidden passage behind the statue! Enter and investigate the secret underground room.

A floor mechanism lowers the spikes as you walk over it. Activate the lever on the right side to turn one of the nearby statues. The spikes ahead are triggered as you walk across the floor mechanism, blocking your path.

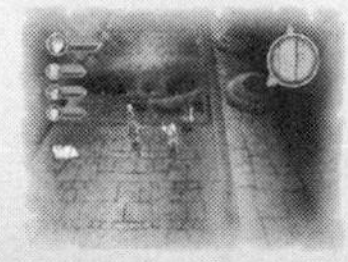

To reset the spikes, walk back over the first floor mechanism. Each time that you move forward, however, you'll trigger the spikes. How can you keep the first mechanism depressed? Why not knock a statue over onto it? Take control of Haru and use Focus to bring it down.

Now you can move ahead without triggering the second set of spikes. Yet there are more spikes blocking the path—and the floor mechanism is on the other side. Not a problem! Haru can use Focus to bring down a second statue, activating the floor mechanism and allowing you to pass.

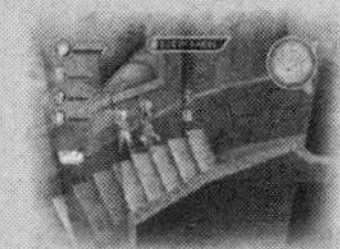

A spiral staircase leads to the top of the next room. Unfortunately, sections of the stairs are missing. Fortunately, you've got Haru with you. He can use his earthbending skills to bridge the gaps. Use Focus when prompted.

At the top, you'll spot a carving of a large water drop. Take control of Katara, the Waterbender, and use her Focus power to change the carving to water. A beam of light shines through both drops and activates the map below. (Aang is also a good choice here.)

Quest 1: Mystery of the Past - Update

Collect the Keystone that has risen up from the center of the huge map.

As you descend, battle the Stompers that entered the underground room in search of you. When you reach the map's level, walk over to it and grab the Keystone Centerpiece before descending to the ground floor.

Quest 1: Mystery of the Past - Update

Show the keystone to the Elder. He may know what to do with it.

There are more Stompers waiting for you below. Fight them or ignore them as you make your way over the deactivated spikes and out of the underground room. Save your progress at the SAVE POINT just outside.

Two Tempests are floating above the beach to the North. After taking care of them, look for a piece of Palm Tree Bark. Don't forget to break the pots and piles of firewood in search of items.

Hidden Chest: 2 of 8

The 1st Keystone piece is at the foot of the steps leading into the Ruins. Grab it and then climb the steps to the top of the Ruins. Here, you can use Aang's Focus to reveal a Hidden Chest.

Hidden Chest: 3 of 8

Walk out to the end of the pier just North of the Ruins. You can sense another Hidden Chest nearby. Take control of Katara and use her Focus to reveal the chest.

Two additional pieces of Palm Tree Bark can be found on the beach to the West of the ruins, along with a regular chest near the water. Five Stompers are hanging out in this area. Battle them for experience points (and items) or simply run away as there is nothing else here of importance.

Having retrieved all that you came for, you can now leave the Northern Ruins. Unfortunately, you'll have to battle your way back through the same creatures you encountered before—namely, the Shirshu, Platypus Bears, and Wolves. Use stealth to pass by unnoticed if you choose not to fight.

Make your way through the Ancient Ruins, heading West towards the village. Instead of crossing the sand bar at the water's edge, travel South at the intersection. There's another piece of Palm Tree Bark here if you need to collect it. Hear that? Sounds like a toad! Sure enough, you spot one near a small pond.

The toad jumps from rock to rock. You want to capture it, not kill it. Take control of Katara and quickly move to the rock the toad lands upon. Use Focus to freeze the toad in place before it jumps away again.

Hidden Chest: 4 of 8

Before returning to the village with the Frozen Toad, explore the area. Near a statue to the East you'll sense a Hidden Chest. Take down the pack of wolves before attempting to find it. Switch to Haru and use his Focus to reveal the Hidden Chest at the feet of the statue.

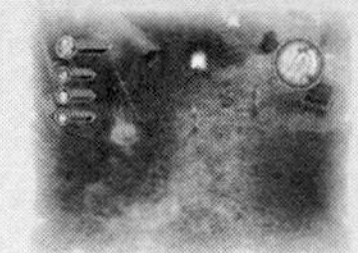

South of the toad pond you'll encounter numerous Stompers. The path encircles some sort of encampment. No one appears to be home, but there is a SAVE POINT nearby.

A man named Tai is standing here where the path crosses the water. He is trying to figure out a way to make a dam to block the water during the rainy season.

Quest 5: Makeshift Dam

Find something large to create a dam with, then return to Tai.

A Platypus Bear attacks as you cross the stream. Take care of it and follow the path up the slight hill to the North. There's a large rock formation here. With his earthbending skills, Haru can easily knock it down into the stream.

Return to Tai and speak with him. He thanks you for your assistance and gives you a Heavenly Charm for your efforts. Now return across the water and continue following the path to the West.

Quest 5: Completed

If you don't want to battle the wolves blocking the path, use stealth to sneak past them. The path ends at the Arena Ruins where you'll find the 4th Keystone piece—and more Wolves and Platypus Bears!

Area Four: Arena Ruins

Hidden Chest: 5 of 8

After defeating the nearby enemies, search the Arena Ruins area. You'll spot a handful of water wells along the beach. Where the beach comes to a dead end at the East, you'll find a piece of Palm Tree Bark. An archway on the East side of the ruins leads to a small grass area. There, you'll find the 3rd Keystone Piece. Your senses also suggest the presence of a Hidden Chest nearby. Use Aang's Focus to reveal it.

Momo Objects 1-2 of 8

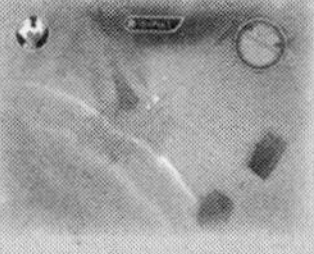

If you walk along the beach to the West of the Arena Ruins, you'll battle multiple enemies on the way to the Ancient Pillars. You don't need to go there yet. You only want the coconuts! Switch to Momo mode and send him to the West. At the edge of the water are multiple coconut trees. Inspect the trees until you've found two coconuts, then return to the Arena Ruins.

Momo Objects 3 of 8

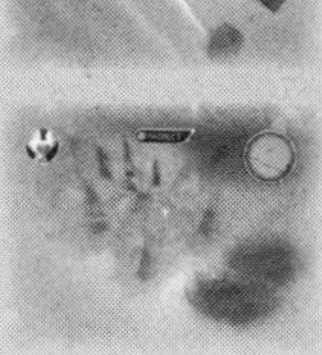

Before exiting Momo mode, search a set of three coconut trees on the beach due South of the Arena Ruins. You'll find another coconut there. Exit Momo mode and head North, battling any Platypus Bears who might be in your way.

Hidden Chest: 6 of 8

Stop and save your progress at the SAVE POINT before continuing North on the path away from the Arena Ruins. When you end up at the water, look for a pier and use Katara's Focus to reveal the Hidden Chest located there.

Momo Objects 4-5 of 8

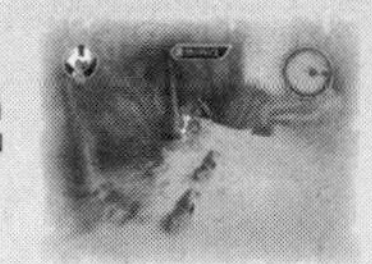

Travel to the Northwest as the path curves around the water. Fight off any Wolves who get in the way. Switch to Momo mode and inspect the trees lining the path back to the village. You can obtain two coconuts from the trees just before the first waterfall.

Momo Objects 6-8 of 8

Another coconut is found in the tree between the two waterfalls. Remain in control of Momo and continue around the water's edge, inspecting the trees near the campfire and huts to find the final two coconuts. That's all of them!

Exit Momo mode and return to the Island Village. Find the Merchant who asked you to collect all the coconuts in the first place. He gives you a trinket or armor as a reward.

Quest 4: Completed

While at the village, talk to the Artisan. He creates a pair of boots using the Palm Tree Bark and Smooth Stones you collected for him. The Artisan tells you that he can create an even better boot, but he needs a rare Iron Ore. Fortunately, you were given this as a reward back in Chapter 3. Give the Dark Iron Ore to the Artisan and he'll craft the Soul Iron Boots II for you.

Quest 3: Completed

Remember Onn, the villager who needed the Frozen Toad? Find him on the West side of the village and give him what he asked for. He gives you a trinket as thanks.

Quest 2: Completed

Talk to the Elder about the Keystone Centerpiece found in the Northern Ruins. He tells you that there are four more pieces to this key, which is said to open the caves to the North. If you already have the other pieces (and you should), the Elder will take them from you right now and give it back to you as a Completed Keystone.

The Elder tells you that the ancient inscriptions on the Keystones tell of a test of strength and spirit. They also mention the cavern entrance on the Northwest side of the island. He gives you a Core Raiment (for Haru) and wishes you luck.

Quest 1: Completed

Quest 6: The Sacred Caverns

Find the location in the Western part of the island that the keystone points to.

Locate the SAVE POINT near the Elder and save your progress before moving on. There is one more area you have yet to visit, so leave the Island Village to the West. Packs of Wolves guard a bridge over the water. Fight them off and continue to the West.

You can collect a piece of Palm Tree Bark at the intersection. Although the Ancient Pillars area is North of here, there is one important item to collect first. For now, head South. Battle the Wolves and fight or use stealth to pass by the Shirshu.

Hidden Chest: 7 of 8

Just off the West side of the path is a Hidden Chest. Use Haru's Focus to reveal it, and after grabbing the goodies inside, return to the North the way you came. Don't forget the Shirshu. If you didn't defeat it moments ago, it is still here!

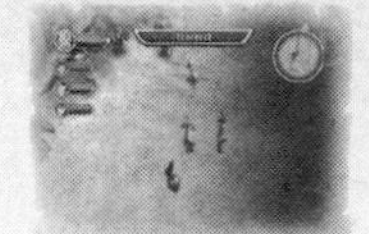

You'll encounter four Tempests North of the intersection. These flying Machines can generate a debilitating whirlwind. Use your advanced attacks against them and keep moving ahead.

Area Five: Ancient Pillars

Hidden Chest: 8 of 8

As you enter the Ancient Pillars area, you'll be accosted by multiple Stompers. There are additional Stompers amidst the ruins, so don't let your guard down. Your senses indicate that a Hidden Chest is in the corner of the ruins. Use Sokka's Focus to reveal it.

More Stompers frequent the beach to the Northeast of the ruins. Northwest of the ruins you'll find two Tempests. To the far West are a regular Chest and a SAVE POINT. Go ahead and save your progress if you wish.

Look for a pedestal where you can use the Completed Keystone. When you do so, four glyphs rise from the ground. They read (from left to right): Courage, Spirit, Strength, and Integrity.

The Elder mentioned a test of "strength and spirit," so stand in front of each of those pillars and activate them. Now take control of Haru and use Focus on the Central Keystone itself. The Strength Pillar and the Spirit Pillar land on either side of the cave entrance, causing it to open.

Quest 6: The Sacred Caverns - Update

The keystone revealed a secret cavern entrance. Explore the passages and see where they lead.

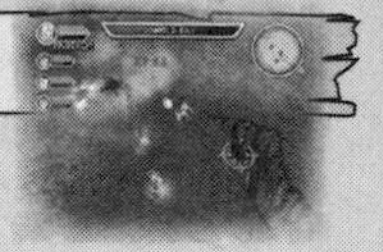

As you head South into the underground cavern, you are immediately attacked by a swarm, a pack, whatever you call a bunch of Wolfbats!

Defeat the Wolfbats and look for a large badger to the North. He's very easy to spot! He wants to know why you are here. The Badger is the guardian of treasure belonging to the island's inhabitants, although they have apparently forgotten it. Only children of the Earth may pass. Haru, the Earthbender, qualifies as such and is allowed to pass.

Quest 7: Ancient Treasure

Find a way to uncover the ancient treasure in the Sacred Caverns.

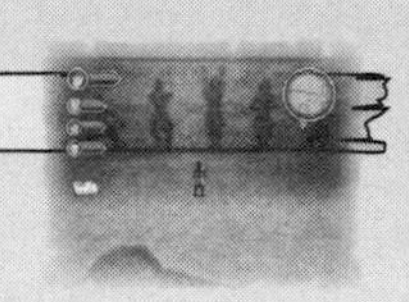

There are six figures on the sides of this room—three to the West and three to the East. On the back wall is a picture of six human figures. Take a good look at the picture first.

You'll notice that each figure in the room corresponds to one of the figures in the picture. Stand near a figure and activate it in the order that they appear in the picture.

If you activate a figure correctly, it will glow blue. If you activate a figure in the incorrect order, it will glow red. Fortunately, you won't have to start the puzzle over from the beginning but can simply locate the correct figure. Activate the figures in this order: Southeast, Northeast, East, Northwest, Southwest, and West.

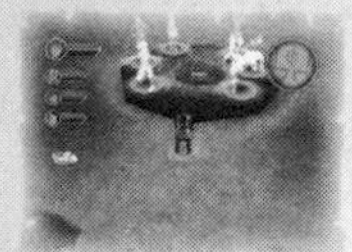

After activating all the figures in the proper order, Haru must use Focus to knock them into place. The structure in the center of the room breaks open, revealing a chest containing an Ancient Tablet.

Quest 7: Ancient Treasure - Update

Take the ancient tablet to the Village Elder for inspection.

Exit the Northwestern caves at the Ancient Pillars and make your way back to the Island Village. The Elder examines the ancient tablet and confirms that his people are descendants of Earthbenders. He also gives you a token of his appreciation.

Quest 7: Completed

Before proceeding, make sure that you have completed all Quests (except for The Sacred Caverns). Return to the Ancient Pillars area and enter the underground caverns. The Badger is still here. Ignore him and head to the Southeast until you find two glyph-covered rocks. One rock reads "Spirit is the essence of the soul." The other rock, slightly to the North, reads "Only those with true strength may pass."

STRENGTH OR SPIRIT?

From here on out, the path will split into two. At each intersection, you'll need to decide whether to follow the Strength or Spirit path. The Strength path involves battling multiple enemies, but may reward you with items and experience. The Spirit path is the easier route, only requiring you to use Focus.

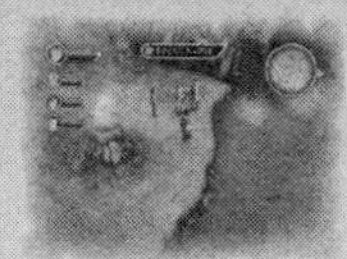

If you take the "spirit path" to the Southeast you'll notice small geysers just before the path ends at a molten river. Haru's Focus creates a rock bridge, allowing you to pass.

If you take the "strength path" to the East, it leads to an open area with several Tempest and new machines known as Guarders. The Guarders burrow into the earth and spring up underneath you, so watch out!

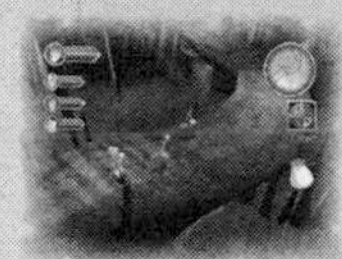

A regular Chest is found where the two paths rejoin. Continue to the East, crossing the rock structure over the water and defeating the Wolfbats atop it. On the other side, you'll spot two more glyph-covered rocks.

If you take the "spirit" path to the Northwest, you'll find it blocked by a large boulder. Haru's Focus sinks the rock into the ground, allowing you to pass.

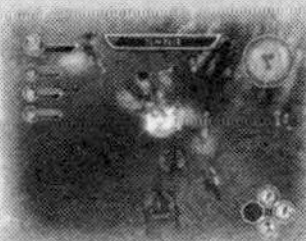

If you take the "strength" path to the Northeast, you'll encounter another group of Tempests and Guarders.

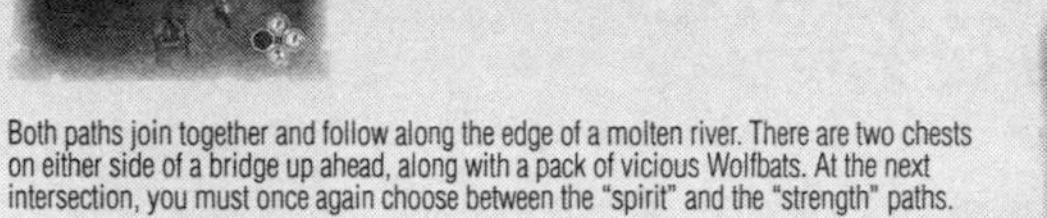

Both paths join together and follow along the edge of a molten river. There are two chests on either side of a bridge up ahead, along with a pack of vicious Wolfbats. At the next intersection, you must once again choose between the "spirit" and the "strength" paths.

The "spirit" path leads to a large lake. Katara must use Focus to create ice bridges connecting the tiny islands. On the last island, she can create two bridges—one to the treasure chest, and the other to the far shore of the lake.

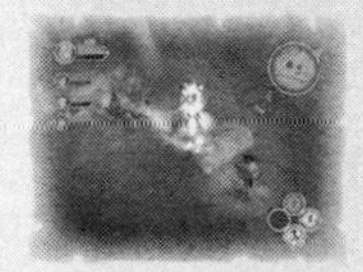

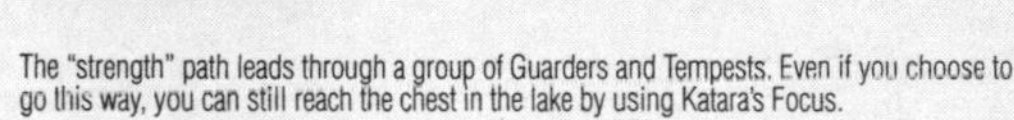

The "strength" path leads through a group of Guarders and Tempests. Even if you choose to go this way, you can still reach the chest in the lake by using Katara's Focus.

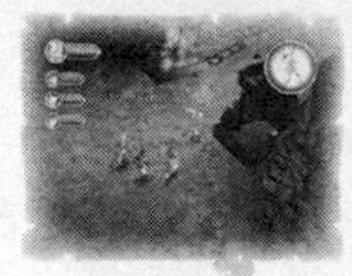

The paths reconnect just before the pre-Boss SAVE POINT. As usual, you should not proceed unless you've done everything else first. There is no going back! You'll be prompted to save your game before continuing.

Quest 6: Completed

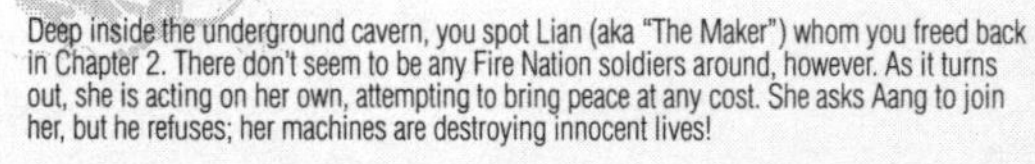

Deep inside the underground cavern, you spot Lian (aka "The Maker") whom you freed back in Chapter 2. There don't seem to be any Fire Nation soldiers around, however. As it turns out, she is acting on her own, attempting to bring peace at any cost. She asks Aang to join her, but he refuses; her machines are destroying innocent lives!

Quest: The Sacred Caverns

Defeat Lian's prototype Machine!

Lian summons a giant machine, the Prototype Dreadnaught, from the depths of the cavern. This machine has an ice ray that will freeze anyone caught in the blast. It can also hover, landing upon anyone caught underneath it. Finally, the machine is able to launch ice projectiles into the air, raining them down on opponents. This battle won't be easy!

As usual, don't stand still or you'll be an easy target. Instead, immediately circle around the machine to avoid its ice ray. If you find yourself frozen by the ray, take control of another character that is still running free.

Run away from the Dreadnaught when it hovers in the air. Keep your distance and hold the Block button to avoid being knocked over when the machine comes crashing back down. It does this twice before shooting projectiles.

You'll notice that the back of the Dreadnaught is lowered whenever it fires ice projectiles. The red glow indicates a target—move in close and attack the rear of the machine with a advanced move.

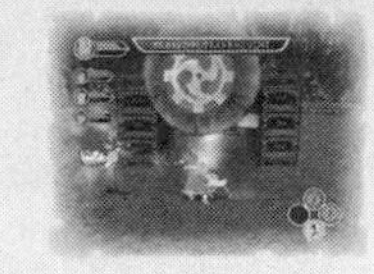

When the rear end of the Dreadnaught rises up again, run away from it. Keep away from the ice ray at the front by running to face the back. Hold block when the machine hovers and slams into the ground. As soon as the Dreadnaught starts firing ice projectiles, attack it once again.

You'll need to repeat this process until the Dreadnaught's energy gauge is emptied. A cinema scene shows the mechanical behemoth falling over the edge of a cliff. Good riddance! But what of Lian? You'll need to stop her, and Aang thinks he knows where she has gone.

STORYBOARD GALLERY

By successfully completing this Chapter, you have unlocked the Storyboard Gallery from the Extras Menu. Select it to view character sketches for the animated cinema scenes. Good job!

Chapter 6: The Air Temple

Aang is convinced that Lian's next targets are the Avatar statues in the Sanctuary. She'll destroy them in an attempt to break his connection with the spirits.

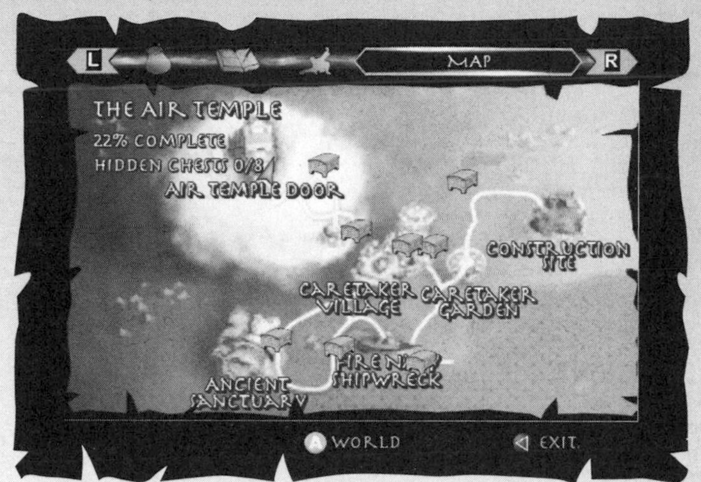

CHAPTER CHECKLIST

Hidden Chests	8
Momo Objects	8
Set Items	5

AREAS

1	CARETAKER VILLAGE
2	CARETAKER GARDEN
3	FIRE NAVY SHIPWRECK
4	ANCIENT SANCTUARY
5	CONSTRUCTION SITE
6	AIR TEMPLE

QUESTS

1	PROTECT THE STATUES
2	FIND FLOWERS
3	BROKEN STATUE
4	OLD WRONGS
5	VILLAGE FLAG
6	BROKEN WINDMILL
7	NEW PLANTINGS
8	BAD HOME COOKING
9	THE SOLSTICE
10	THE SCARLET TRADER
X	SEPARATED

Area One: Caretaker Village

Quest 1: Protect the Statues (Main Objective)

Warn the Village Elder about the machines before heading up to the Air Temple.

You've landed on a platform in the center of the Caretaker Village. As usual, Appa will wait here while you explore the area. There is a Merchant on this platform who sells a Treasure Map as well as an Ether Headband. Speak to him and he'll ask you to collect wildflowers for him.

QUEST 2: FIND FLOWERS

8 wildflowers left for Momo to collect

Cross over the bridge to the next platform. A Four Nations player is found on the left side. It costs 40 copper to challenge him. Prizes may include a Dragon Robe, Lemur Headband, and Ether Headband.

Another Merchant nearby sells a Malrize, Karmic Amulet, Moon Pendant, Rain Amulet, and Durzi. A villager next to a broken statue has a blue symbol over his head. Talk to Huan Yue and he'll tell you that he needs pure metal to repair the statue.

QUEST 3: BROKEN STATUE

Find some pure metal so Huan Yue can repair the statue.

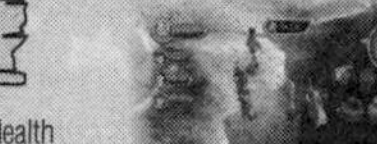

There is also an Herbalist on this platform—speak to her if you need to purchase Health or Chi medicine. The remaining villagers tell you that the Elder can be found South of the windmill near the flagpole. The Chest here can be opened, but it is empty. Break the jars and sacks for items.

Hidden Chest: 1 of 8

To the East, a path winds up to a smaller platform with a pagoda. Your senses tell you that a Hidden Chest is here. Use Aang's Focus to reveal it.

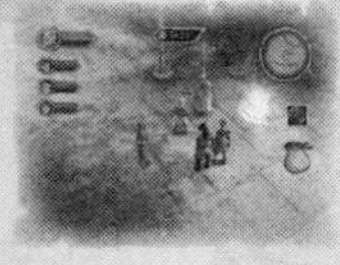

Head up the stairs to the North of the platform with all the Merchants and you'll spot a SAVE POINT. The Village Elder is standing just next to it, with a Blue symbol over her head. As you warn her about the Machines, she tells you that they have already infested the Sanctuary. The Villagers are afraid to clear them out, because they think the Sanctuary is haunted.

QUEST 1: PROTECT THE STATUES - UPDATE

Help the Village Elder before heading to the Air Temple.

QUEST 4: OLD WRONGS

Find and restore the Sacred Sanctuary in the South-west.

Hidden Chest: 2 of 8

Your senses indicate the presence of a Hidden Chest. Use Sokka's Focus move to open it. The Elder still has a blue symbol over her head; does she need something else from you? Speak with her, and she tells you of a village flag that was stolen by the Fire Nation years ago. Their ship was wrecked on the Southern coast.

Quest 5: Village Flag

Search for the village flag in the Fire Nation shipwreck on the Southern coast. Beware of booby traps!

A set of steps leads up to the North. There, you'll find a broken windmill being tended to by a villager named Ming Yue. He tells you that special bamboo is needed to repair it—and that only an Airbender can start it up again. After speaking with him, look for a chest on the far side of the windmill.

Quest 6: Broken Windmill

Momo Objects 1 of 8

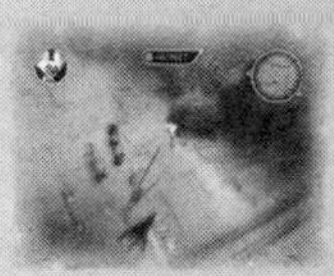

Now that you've got enough quests to keep you busy, it is time to leave the village. Before you go, switch to Momo mode and inspect the leafy green bush near the Elder. You'll find the first of the eight Wildflowers here. Keep an eye out for more bushes similar to this one.

Momo Objects 2 of 8

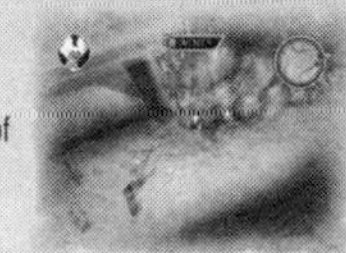

Return to the main platform with all the Merchants, and exit the village to the South. After passing through the final archway, switch to Momo mode and inspect the bush to the right of it for another set of Wildflowers.

The path leads South or East from here. For now, make your way to the East. Fight off any Hog Monkeys that block the path as it curves to the North. There is a SAVE POINT here if you wish to save your progress.

Area Two: Caretaker Garden

Cross the small bridge to the West to enter the Caretaker's Garden and speak with Aiyu. He is sad because the cherry blossoms will no longer grow in the garden. After you offer to help him, he gives you the Blossom Seeds.

Quest 7: New Plantings

Help the Caretaker plant cherry blossom ferns in his garden.

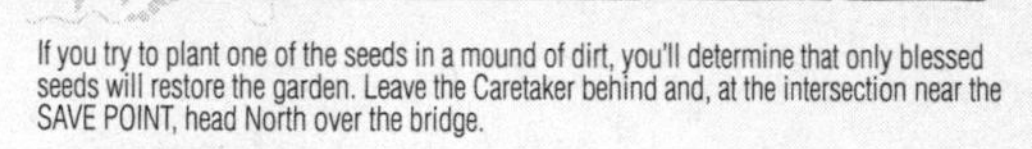

If you try to plant one of the seeds in a mound of dirt, you'll determine that only blessed seeds will restore the garden. Leave the Caretaker behind and, at the intersection near the SAVE POINT, head North over the bridge.

On the other side of the bridge you'll enter a bamboo forest. The path splits to the North and East. At the intersection, a trio of new enemies awaits. Infernos are miniature tanks capable of shooting fire. Use stealth to avoid a fight, or use advanced attacks against them.

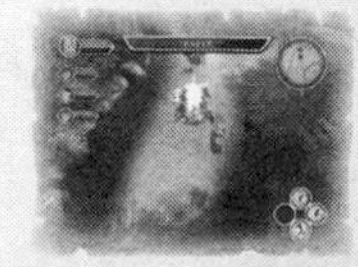

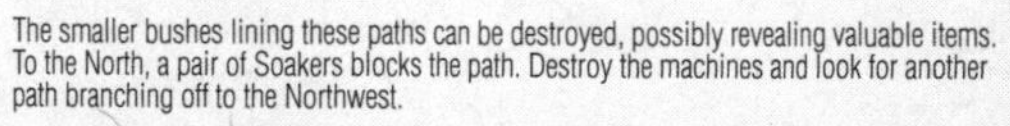

The smaller bushes lining these paths can be destroyed, possibly revealing valuable items. To the North, a pair of Soakers blocks the path. Destroy the machines and look for another path branching off to the Northwest.

Hidden Chest: 3 of 8

There are four Guarders in the small clearing. After destroying them, grab the Bamboo Part from the central plant. Haru can also reveal a Hidden Chest here using Focus.

Quest 6: Broken Windmill - Update

Use the special bamboo to fix the broken windmill.

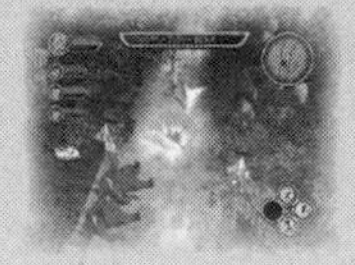

Leave the clearing and return to the South. Although the path also leads East to a Construction Site, you do not need to go there yet. Machines will likely have reappeared along the trail, so be prepared to do battle. You'll also encounter Platypus Bears on the bridge and Hog Monkeys on your way back to the Village.

Since you've found the bamboo, you might as well complete this quest while you are still here. Make your way to the far North side of the Village and talk to Ming Yue. Take control of Aang and stand in front of the windmill to repair it. Use your Focus to start it spinning again.

Quest 6: Completed

Leave the Village behind, once again exiting via the bridge to the South. This time, instead of heading East, continue South. Up ahead, you'll spot a woman named Lin on the path. She's got a blue symbol overhead, so speak with her. Lin needs someone to take her husband's dinner to him.

Quest 8: Bad Home Cooking

Take Lin's husband his dinner.

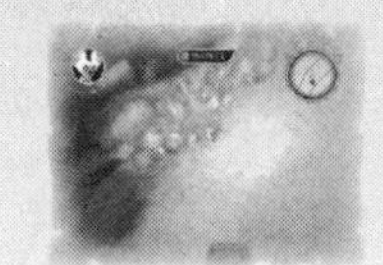

Momo Objects 3 of 8

On the North side of the path, near some rocks, you'll spot a leafy green bush. Switch to Momo and inspect the bush to find Wildflowers.

Hog Monkeys and a Platypus Bear guard the path to the Southwest, but at your power level, they shouldn't present much of a challenge. Take care of them and continue following the path to the beach. Let the green arrow on the side of the radar be your guide.

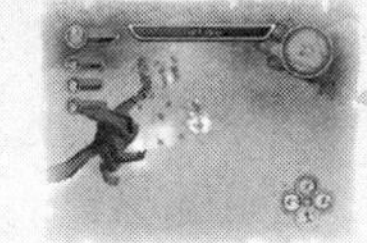

The Shirshus on the beach, however, are more challenging. Stay away from their tongues, circling around them using advanced attacks. Wide range attacks, such as Aang's air twirl, are particularly effective.

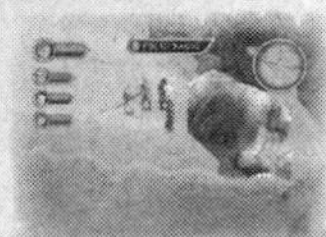

Hidden Chest: 4 of 8

Where the beach comes to a dead-end at a pile of rocks to the East, Katara can use her Focus to reveal a Hidden Chest. Open it and grab the goodies before turning around and heading West along the beach.

Area Three: Fire Navy Shipwreck

Use the SAVE POINT outside the Fire Navy Shipwreck to save your progress before entering the hole in the hull. As the Elder told you, the ship is full of booby traps, so watch your step! It is also inhabited by Hog Monkeys.

From the entrance, make your way to the left (west) side of the ship. To the North, guarded by Hog Monkeys, is a group of barrels and a regular chest which someone already opened. You'll spot some crates to the South. Break them and look for the piece of Pure Metal nearby (represented by a green dot on the radar).

The door here is the first of many booby traps. Although it looks like you can open it, if you try to do so, the vents on the side will blast you with fire. Having tripped the trap, you can use Katara's Focus to freeze the fire before opening the door—or you can simply avoid the door by walking South and following the passage to the West.

On the opposite side of the door, you can only head to the North. Hog Monkeys attack you here near some barrels. See the blue trip wire here? Use Aang's Focus to break it, allowing you to reach the chest. If you trip the wire, you'll first have to use Aang's Focus to blow away the steam.

Make your way down the passage to the West, then follow it to the South. Defeat the Hog Monkeys and follow the passage back to the West. In this next area, you'll spot a chest and several barrels. A rope connects the chest to a door to the South—opening the chest will close the door. Fortunately, you can get around it to the North.

To the North, you'll spot a colored temperature gauge on the wall of the ship. Don't enter the area to the North, as a door will close behind you! You'll have to quickly use Aang's Focus to extinguish the furnace flames.

Continue through an open door to the West, battling additional Hog Monkeys near a set of crates. More Monkeys, and barrels, can be found to the South, where the passage leads to the other side of the closed door.

Another trip rope crosses the passageway to the West. Stand in front of it and use Aang's Focus to break the rope before attempting to cross. On the other side, open the hatch to find the Village Flag. Break the barrels for items before retracing your steps back to the entrance.

TRAP SPRUNG

If you forget about the trip wire here, you'll fall through a trapdoor into a passageway at the bottom of the ship. Don't panic! Follow the passage up to the North, where it leads to the ship's entrance.

Quest 5: Village Flag - Update

Return the village flag to the elder

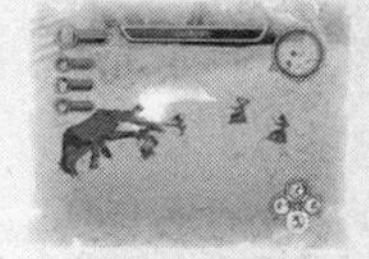

Save your progress at the SAVE POINT on the beach outside the ship. Continue to the Northwest around the ship, where you'll encounter a trio of Hog Monkeys. Up ahead, where stairs lead away from the beach, you'll face two Shirshus. Kill them and take the stairs to the North.

Momo Objects 4 of 8

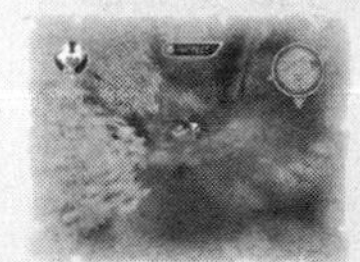

Switch to Momo mode when the path splits to the Northwest and Northeast. Take the right path and look for a leafy green bush near a tree. Inspect the bush to obtain Wildflowers. Exit Momo mode and lead your party to the Northwest.

Momo Objects 5 of 8

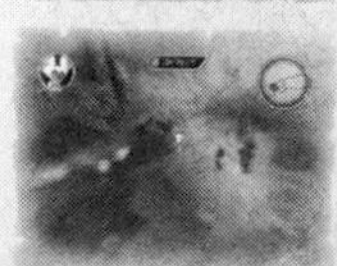

As the path straightens out, look for another leafy green bush to the North side of the path. You might want to defeat the nearby Hog Monkeys before switching to Momo mode to inspect and obtain the Wildflowers.

Watch for more Hog Monkeys on the path ahead. Where the path temporarily splits in two, a smaller path leads North to a house. There is a SAVE POINT here as well as a man named Dexu. He tells you that his mother went missing during the last Solstice—a time when the spirit and normal worlds intersect.

Quest 9: Solstice

Reunite Dexu with his lost mother

Momo Objects 6 of 8

Return to the main path and look for a leafy green bush just to the West of Dexu's house. Switch to Momo mode to obtain the Wildflowers, then exit Momo mode and continue following the path.

Hidden Chest: 6 of 8

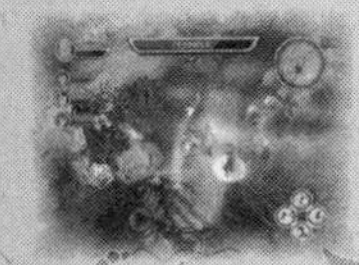

The path is temporarily split once again by a group of rocks. Your senses indicate the presence of a Hidden Chest. Defeat the trio of Stompers first, then use Haru's Focus to reveal the Chest near the rocks.

Area Four: Ancient Sanctuary

The path curves South to the Ancient Sanctuary. A Tempest is here near the SAVE POINT. Defeat it and enter the Sanctuary near the Forest Spirit Owl. He's not in the mood to talk. Clear the Machines out of the Sanctuary first. There are two Guarders and a Soaker remaining.

Quest 4: Old Wrongs - Update

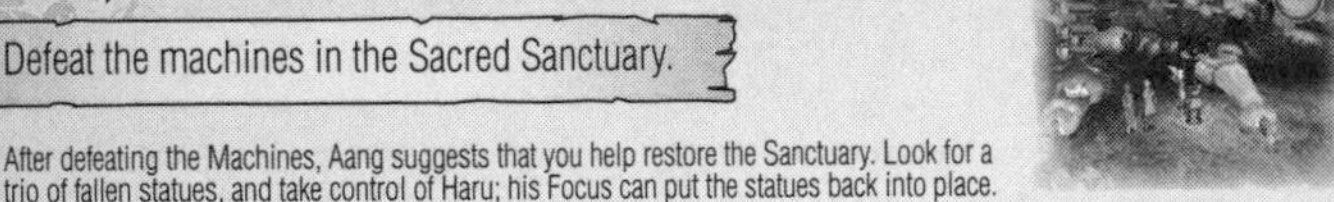

Defeat the machines in the Sacred Sanctuary.

After defeating the Machines, Aang suggests that you help restore the Sanctuary. Look for a trio of fallen statues, and take control of Haru; his Focus can put the statues back into place.

RESTORING THE SANCTUARY

If you forget what you are supposed to be doing, pause the game and check your journal under the "Old Wrongs" quest. Each time you do something to help restore the Sanctuary, the quest will be updated with your next task.

Having replaced the statues, take control of Katara and make your way to the back side of the Sanctuary. Aang tells you that there used to be water here. Use Katara's Focus to restore the water flow.

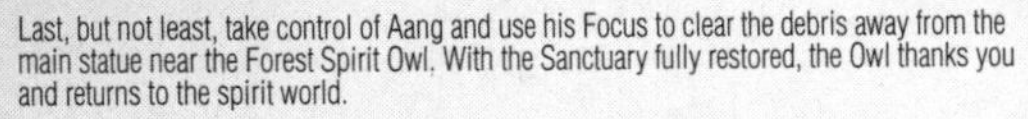

Last, but not least, take control of Aang and use his Focus to clear the debris away from the main statue near the Forest Spirit Owl. With the Sanctuary fully restored, the Owl thanks you and returns to the spirit world.

Quest 4: Completed

Aang suggests meditating at the statue. Take him there and then enter Spirit Mode when the game prompts you to do so. Aang's spirit can now walk freely away from his body. You can see the Forest Spirit in this mode. Approach him and tell him about the seeds.

Quest 7: New Plantings - Update

The Forest Spirit has blessed your seeds. Return to the natural world and plant them in the Caretaker's Garden.

You have two more tasks to perform while in the Spirit World. Walk back up the path to the Northeast, making your way to Dexu's house. Don't worry about the enemies, as they cannot see you and you cannot interact with them. Dexu's mother is standing outside right next to him. Speak to her and she will follow you back to the Sanctuary.

Talk to the Forest Spirit Owl, who tells you that you can bring Dexu's mother back to the normal world by concentrating upon her as you meditate. Stand near your body and meditate to leave the spirit world behind. Sure enough, Dexu's mother is here. She thanks you before returning to her son.

Quest 9: Completed

Even though you've already received credit for completing the Solstice quest, you should return to Dexu's house and speak with him. He thanks you for reuniting him with his mother, and gives you Core Sandals as a token of his appreciation. Leave the house behind and return to the Sanctuary once again.

There's another reason to return to the spirit world. Remember the empty chest back at the village, and the villagers talking about ghosts? Meditate to enter the spirit world and return to the village. On the platform with the Merchants, you'll spot a ghostly figure who is able to see you. Speak to him and he'll tell you that he has been trying to help his people from the spirit world.

Quest 10: The Scarlet Trader

Place some copper in the chest to receive an item.

Money has no value in the spirit world, so you must return to the natural world before you are able to place copper in the chest. Make your way back to the Sanctuary and meditate to leave the spirit world. Don't forget to try the chest the next time you are in the village.

Use the SAVE POINT before moving on. Follow the path away from the Sanctuary to the Southeast. There are three Guarders on the path, and you may also encounter three Soakers as the path leads East to the beach. Yoku is here, standing near an empty chest. Give him lunch courtesy of his wife. Apparently, he left it home for a reason!

Quest 8: Completed

Momo Objects 7 of 8

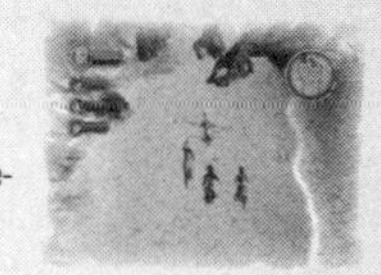

Follow the beach to the North. You'll spot a leafy green bush on the left side. Switch to Momo mode and inspect it for Wildflowers. Two Platypus Bears are here on the beach, and you might also encounter two Shirshus at the same time. Use Aang's Tornado or other wide-range attack to damage multiple enemies.

Hidden Chest: 6 of 8

Before continuing, take control of Katara and check out the rocks along the shore. Where your senses tingle, use her Focus to reveal a Hidden Chest. Make your way Northeast along the beach once again. If you encounter another Shirshu, you can use stealth to avoid a fight.

Momo Objects 8 of 8

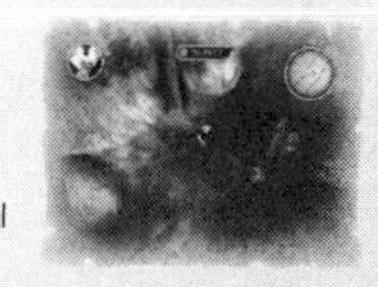

Take the stairs North away from the beach, but this time turn right (east) at the intersection. Battle the Hog Monkeys along the way, keeping an eye out for a leafy green bush on the North side of the path. After defeating the enemies, switch to Momo mode to obtain the final bunch of Wildflowers.

Eliminate any remaining Hog Monkeys as you follow the path across a bridge back to the village. You'll end up near the Village Elder. As you arrive, she spots a flock of birds in the sky. Those aren't birds—they're machines!

quest 1: protect the statues - update

Take Appa and fly to the Air Temple

Before you head to the Air Temple, you have other business to attend to. Talk to the Village Elder and give her the Village Flag recovered from the Fire Navy Shipwreck. She thanks you and gives you the Kata Mastery sandals as a reward. Tell her that you've also restored the Sanctuary.

quest 5: completed

Walk to the South and look for Huan Yue on the platform with the Merchants. He was trying to repair a statue, remember? Give him the Pure Metal that you found in the Fire Nation Shipwreck. That does the trick! He gives you the Soul Iron Helmet as a reward.

quest 3: completed

Look for the empty chest on the South side of the platform. Having first spoken with the Scarlet Trader in the spirit world, you may now place copper in the chest. When you open the chest back up again, an item will appear. Do this three times, and you'll eventually receive an Avatar Tile.

quest 10: completed

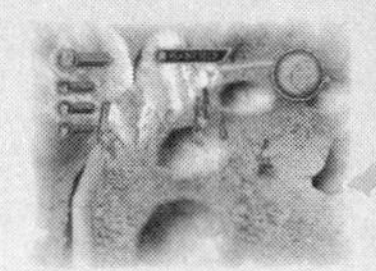

Leave the village across the bridge to the South, then head East to the Caretaker Garden. Now that the Forest Spirit has blessed the seeds, you will be able to plant them in the eight mounds. The Caretaker gives you his thanks.

quest 7: completed

It's a good idea to save your progress at the SAVE POINT near the Caretaker's Garden before continuing. Return to the village and follow the green arrow to the platform where you left Appa. The Merchant was looking for Wildflowers, remember? Give him the Wildflowers you collected, and accept the Vigard as a reward.

quest 2: completed

While facing Appa, choose to fly to the Air Temple when prompted. A cinema scene shows Katara arguing to come with you, but she, Haru, and Sokka need to stay behind to protect the villagers.

quest 1: protect the statues - update

Find a way inside the Air Temple.

Appa lands on a circular platform. On your way North, take out the two Stompers. Break the plants for items and continue along the path until you reach a four-way intersection.

Hidden Chest: 7 of 8

Turn right and head East. The path curves South to a cul-de-sac where two Tempests are stationed. Defeat them and use your senses to pinpoint the location of a Hidden Chest. Use Focus to reveal the chest and take the items inside.

Back at the intersection, take the path to the North. Two Guarders are here, just up the steps. Take care of them and continue on until you spot a small path leading North off the main path.

Hidden Chest: 8 of 8

Two Soakers are stationed in this cul-de-sac. It appears empty otherwise, but your senses tell you differently. Search for the Hidden Chest at the far North and use Aang's Focus to reveal its location.

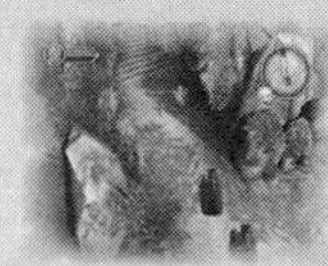

Return to the main path and follow it to the left (west). It eventually connects with the path that you could have taken West of the four-way intersection. There are multiple enemies along the path as it leads to the Air Temple. If you aren't in the fighting mood, use stealth to pass by them.

The path curves to the North, up some steps and through an archway to the Air Temple Door. Save your progress at the SAVE POINT here. Aang is unable to open the door, so switch to Momo mode and climb inside.

Quest 1: Protect the Statues - Update

The door to the Air Temple won't open! Send Momo in to find out what's blocking it.

You cannot unlock the door until you find a key. As Momo, follow the green arrow as it leads you down passageways to the West side of the temple. You'll spot Lian up ahead—and near her, the Locking Device Key. Get close enough to grab it and then quickly return to the door. When you unlock it, you will automatically exit Momo mode and take control of Aang.

Quest 1: Protect the Statues - Update

Find the Avatar Statue room before its too late!

Inside the Temple you can ignore or battle the Stompers, Guarders, and Tempests. Follow the path that Momo took (to the West). Lian is no longer here, but the door is open. Head down the hallway until it ends at a circular platform with a Fire emblem.

The circular platform automatically rises with Aang on top of it. On the upper level, inspect the picture on wall. It shows the four elements in a specific sequence: Air, Water, Earth, and Fire. This is your road map!

Starting from the Fire symbol on the floor, take the path represented by the first element on the picture: Air (yellow). This path leads West to a large Air floor symbol. Walk across it to activate it.

The next element in the picture was Water (blue). Starting from the large Air symbol on the floor, head North over the blue Water icon. The passage leads to a large Water floor symbol which is activated when you step on it.

Earth is next, so take the West passage indicated by the green Earth icon. It leads to a large Earth symbol on the floor. Stepping on it opens a door to the North, in the direction of the red Fire icon. That's your destination!

In the corridors, you'll encounter Guarders and Tempests. A green dot appears on your radar, indicating the location of the statues. There is a SAVE POINT here—use it before doing battle with the machines.

Quest 1: Protect the Statues - Update

Protect the Avatar Statues from the destructive Machines!

There are eight machines in all. The easiest way to defeat them is to use Tornado, Air Twirl, or another wide-range attack. Refill your Health and Chi immediately with the medicine you have collected, then continue the battle. Don't worry about accidentally hitting the statues. When you've destroyed all of the machines, a cinema scene shows Aang closing up the Air Temple.

Quest 1: Completed

Quest: Separated

A bunch of machines were seen heading Northeast. Find out what they're up to while you wait for Aang to return.

Meanwhile, Sokka, Katara, and Haru remain at the village. They spot some machines heading to the Northeast and decide to investigate. Take control of any of the three, and lead your party out of the village to the South. Head East and follow the path to the North past the Caretaker's Garden.

Area Six: Construction Site

You'll have to battle or avoid the Hog Monkeys along the way. If you aren't comfortable fighting, use stealth to avoid the Platypus Bears. You'll encounter multiple Inferno tanks inside the bamboo forest. Continue East as the path splits, and you'll reach the Construction Site. Before you can react, something very big arrives...

Quest: Separated - Update

Katara, Haru, and Sokka are missing! Find out what happened to them!

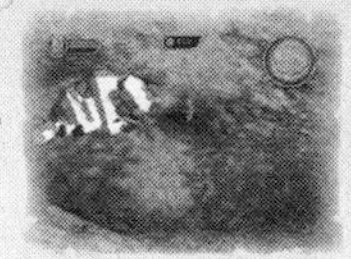

Meanwhile, back at the Air Temple, Aang notices all the flying machines heading back to the village. He knows his friends need his help! Save your progress at the SAVE POINT outside the Temple before taking the path back to Appa. You'll face multiple machines - Inferno tanks, Guarders, Stompers, and Tempests - on the way back.

Approach Appa and choose to fly back to the village when prompted.

Back at the Village, leave the villagers behind and follow the green arrow adjacent to the radar. Take the path past the Caretaker's Garden and across the bridge towards the bamboo forest. Defeat the machines on your way to the Construction Site. As you reach it, you will be prompted to save your game before battling the Boss.

Quest: Separated - Update

Defeat the massive Geo-Tunneler Machine guarding the construction site.

A cinema scene shows the Geo-Tunneler rising out of the ground. It has an arm that knocks rocks along ground as well as a drill that knocks Aang backwards. The Geo-Tunneler also slams the ground and fires boulders. All in all, it appears to be a formidable foe!

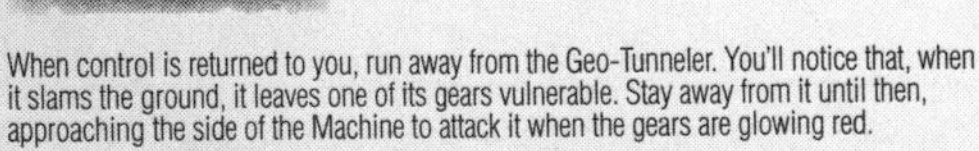

When control is returned to you, run away from the Geo-Tunneler. You'll notice that, when it slams the ground, it leaves one of its gears vulnerable. Stay away from it until then, approaching the side of the Machine to attack it when the gears are glowing red.

Aang cannot block the shockwave from the Geo-Tunneler's ground pound, so don't bother trying. Instead, remain in motion, running away from its deadly drill! Once it's beaten, watch the cutscene and get ready for the next chapter!

Chapter 7: The Fortress

At a construction site near the Air Temple, Momo and Aang have discovered an underground passage leading to an isolated society. Could this be where Sokka, Katara, and Haru have gone?

CHAPTER CHECKLIST

Hidden Chests	8
Momo Objects	8
Set Items	1

AREAS

1	SETTLER'S VILLAGE
2	FARMER'S FIELDS
3	LUSH OASIS
4	FIRE NATION CAMP
5	FORTRESS

QUESTS

1	RESCUE FRIENDS
2	LADY LUCK
3	GATHER GEMS
4	POISONED HUSBAND
5	HOME IS WHERE THE HEART IS
6	BAD WATER
7	INFESTATION
8	A MACHINE-FREE WORLD
X	REIGN MUST END!!!

Area One: Settler's Village

Quest 1: Rescue Friends (Main Objective)

Talk to the Village Elder. He might have seen Katara, Sokka, and Haru.

Appa can go no farther, but fortunately you can travel the rest of the way on foot. Make your way down the path and speak to the villager at the intersection. He tells you to rest at his village to the West. Break the mushrooms to find items before following the green arrow.

Take the curving path down to the buildings you see below. A villager named Leanne wants to speak with you. She dropped a necklace and wants you to retrieve it from a Fire Nation Camp to the North.

Quest 2: Lady Luck

Retrieve Leanne's necklace. It was stolen by one of the Fire Nation soldiers from the Northern camp.

Walk around the left side of the buildings and you're your way down towards the rest of the village. A Merchant is here on the left side of the path. He can craft robes such as the Transient Emperor, and sells the Warrior's Mark (among other items).

The Village Elder's hut is on the West side of the village. Look for a SAVE POINT nearby. He thinks he saw your friends brought down by the Fire Nation, but they have sealed the passage with rocks. He recommends that you speak to a farmer named Jedd for help.

Quest 1: Rescue Friends - Update

It seems farmer Jedd has earthbending skills! Find him and see if he can remove the blockage on the Western path.

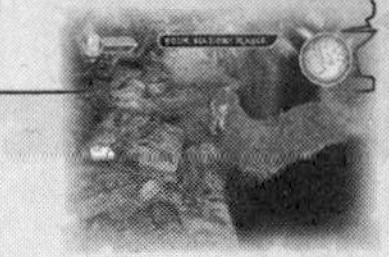

Before locating Jedd, look for a Four Nations player on the path near the Elder's hut. Challenge him to a game—for the entrance fee of 50 copper, you might win a Heavenly Headband, Heavenly Charm, or the Four Winds Headband.

Down the path from the Four Nations player are two villagers with Blue symbols over their heads. Talk to the first, a Merchant, and he'll ask you to gather gems for him.

Quest 3: Gather Gems

8 Gems left for Momo to collect

Quest 4: Poisoned Husband

Find 1 Honey, 1 Bai Don Kon Herb, and 1 Shi Take Herb.

The second villager, Chin, needs ingredients to make a healing potion for her husband. You should already have more than enough of them in your inventory. If not, purchase them from the Herbalist. Give them to her to complete the Quest.

Quest 4: Completed

Hidden Chest: 1 of 8

Continue North down the hill. At the intersection, your senses tell you that a Hidden Chest is nearby. Look around the statue and use Focus to reveal it. To the North of the intersection is another SAVE POINT if you want to use it.

Before venturing North to look for the lost necklace, find Jedd the farmer. Head back up the path to the South, leaving the village behind. Look for an intersection and follow the green arrow adjacent to your radar. It is pointing to the South.

There is a lost deer here, along with its child. Try talking to it. Although you might not understand what it is saying, you do know that it is lost—and it seems to know that you are here to help.

Quest 5: Home Is Where The Heart Is

Lead the lost deer back to their herd.

Hidden Chest: 2 of 8

On the South side of the intersection where you found the deer, you'll sense another Hidden Chest. Use Focus to reveal it and take the treasure. You are pretty sure that the deer don't belong anywhere near here, so return to the path above the village. At the intersection where you met the first villager, continue straight across to the East.

Area Two: Lush Oasis

Now this looks more like deer habitat! Take a right turn at the split and pass the SAVE POINT. Up ahead, the path descends to an area inhabited by more deer. Your friends seem happy to be home.

Quest 5: Completed

Hidden Chest: 3 of 8

Before leaving the Oasis area, search for a regular chest. A Hidden Chest can be found nearby. As usual, use Focus to reveal its location.

On your way out of the Oasis, you might want to save your progress at the SAVE POINT. Retrace your steps back to the intersection where you found the deer at the Southern edge of the map. At the intersection, head to the West.

Take either path across the river and look for a villager named Fang with a blue symbol over her head. She wants you to check on their water supply. After speaking with her, open the Chest nearby.

Momo Objects 1-2 of 8

Switch to Momo mode and inspect the rocks near the mushrooms. You'll find a Gem there. There's a second Gem in the rocks behind Fang.

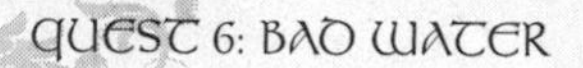

Quest 6: Bad Water

The village water supply has dried up. Follow the creek upstream, and see if there's a blockage.

Area Three: Farming Fields

Leave Fang behind and follow the path across the intersection and down to the East. You'll encounter Jedd, the farmer and Earthbender, on the path. He will gladly help you, but cannot leave his farm while it is infested by Crawlers.

Quest 7: Infestation

Defeat the Canyon Crawlers: Northern farm (5), Eastern farm (5), and Southern farm (6).

There is a SAVE POINT behind Jedd. Use it before entering the farm. The three areas are designated by purple-colored gateways. It doesn't matter which area you enter first. Start with a full Chi supply, and you'll be able to take out a group of Crawlers with a single Tornado attack.

Six Canyon Crawlers infest the Southern Farm. Break the mushrooms for items, and search the farm for a Chest after destroying the Crawlers. The villager at the house thanks you for helping.

Hidden Chest: 4 of 8

There are five Canyon Crawlers on the terraced Eastern Farm. Use the steps to reach the upper levels, and break mushrooms for items. Your senses pinpoint a Hidden Chest next to the main house. Use Focus to reveal it.

On the Northern Farm, you'll face five Canyon Crawlers. There aren't any chests here, but you can break mushrooms for items.

Quest 7: Infestation - Update

Tell Farmer Jedd he can safely return to his fields.

Speak to Farmer Jedd outside the fields and let him know that the Crawlers have been vanquished. He thanks you and asks if he can return the favor. Ask him to help clear the blockage, and he'll follow you. Save your progress at the SAVE POINT here before continuing.

Quest 7: Completed

Lead Jedd to the trail above the village and follow it to the West until the rocks block your path. He'll automatically use his earthbending powers to move the boulders out of your way. Now you can investigate the areas West of the village.

Quest 1: Rescue Friends - Update

Continue West in search of Katara, Sokka, and Haru.

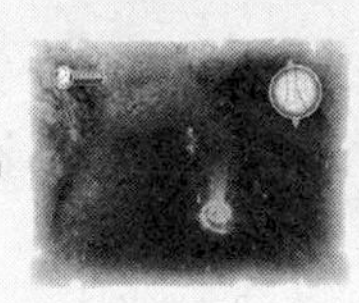

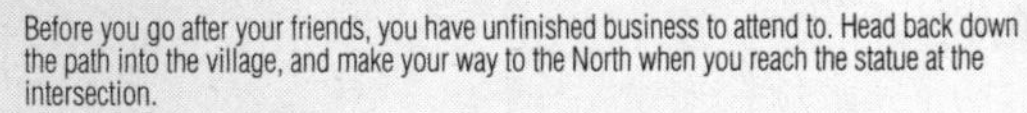

Before you go after your friends, you have unfinished business to attend to. Head back down the path into the village, and make your way to the North when you reach the statue at the intersection.

Momo Objects 3 of 8

As the path turns sharply to the East, switch to Momo mode and inspect the Northern side of the path. The sparkling rocks indicate the presence of a Gem.

Area Four: Fire Nation Camp

Hidden Chest: 5 of 8

The path passes by the Fire Nation Camp, where two soldiers are standing guard to the North. Defeat them and explore the area. To the far West you'll find two soldiers stationed on a narrow ledge. Perhaps they are here to protect the Hidden Chest that your senses can detect. After defeating them, use Focus to reveal the Chest.

Momo Objects 4 of 8

Make your way back to the East. Switch to Momo mode and inspect the rock formation to obtain another Gem.

Momo Objects 5 of 8

Remain in Momo mode and use the little guy to scout ahead. Not only does this give you a better idea of what you are about to face, but you will also be able to obtain a Gem at the far Northwest side of the Fire Nation Camp.

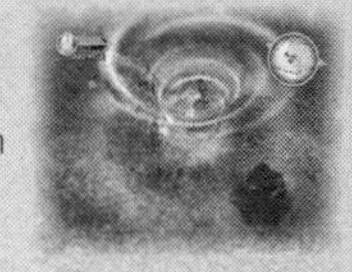

Back as Aang, follow the path to the Camp, battling the soldiers along the way. When you see the mounted soldier, use a wide range attack such as Tornado or Air Twirl to damage him from a distance.

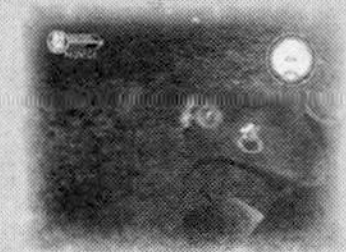

One of the Admirals is carrying Leanne's necklace. He's represented by a green dot on your radar. Target him and grab the necklace after he's eliminated.

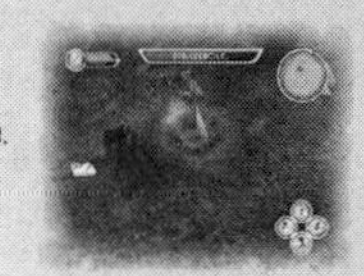

There are a handful of soldiers remaining in the Fire Nation Camp, but nothing else of value. Battle them for the experience and items if you wish; otherwise, leave the Camp the way you came in.

Return to the West and then South into the village.

Wind your way up the paths on the East side of the village and look for Leanne. She's represented by a green dot on the radar. Give her the necklace you recovered from the Fire Nation Camp. In return, she gives you an old coin.

Quest 2: Lady Luck - Update

Find a place to use the lucky coin

Momo Objects 6-7 of 8

There is a SAVE POINT right on the other side of where the blockage used to be. Use it before continuing down the path. Switch to Momo mode and inspect the rocks near the SAVE POINT to find another Gem. Continue down the path as Momo, where it curves to the North, inspect the rocks for another Gem.

Momo Objects 8 of 8

You might as well find the last Gem and return to the village before going after your friends. As Momo, follow the path to the West and ignore the Machines. Underneath a tree on the right side of the clearing you'll find the final Gem. Grab it and take control of Aang.

Walk down the curved path past the Elder into the village, looking for the Merchant who asked you to obtain the Gems. He gives you a trinket called Meld as payment.

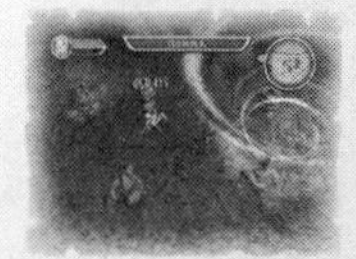

Quest 3: Completed

Return to the path and make your way West past the SAVE POINT. As you reach the clearing where Momo found the final Gem, you'll be attacked by a multitude of Machines. It is time to end this once and for all!

Quest 8: A Machine-Free World

Defeat all the Machines inside, and outside, the Fortress!

Use your advanced attacks against the Tempests, Guarders, and Soakers here. There are 66 Machines in all, scattered throughout the area.

Quest 6: Bad Water - Update

Find a way to destroy The Maker's Dam.

At the water's edge, you'll see why the village water supply has run dry: Lian has dammed the stream! Find the proper location and use your Focus power to destroy the blockage. Don't bother returning to Fang. Although she thanks you, there is no reward involved.

Quest 6: Completed

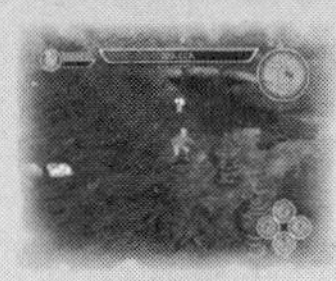

Explore the area on the other side of the stream, searching for more Machines to destroy. At the far South end, you'll sense a Hidden Chest. Aang isn't able to locate it, so don't forget to return here with a companion later on. Destroy the remaining Machines.

The steps lead up to an overlook, where two Tempests circle around a Chest. Defeat them and open the Chest to recover more items. At the edge of the overlook, facing the waterfall, you'll find the perfect place to toss your Lucky Coin. Make a wish! When you throw it over the edge, an Avatar Tile returns to you. That's some Lucky Coin!

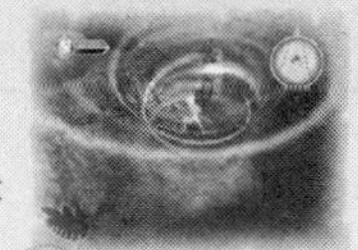

Quest 2: Completed

Make your way back down the steps and across the stream. You've got a lot of Machines left to destroy. Start with these Inferno tanks to the right of the waterfall. Your senses tell you that there is a Hidden Chest behind the water, but Aang is unable to locate it.

Area Five: Fortress

Continue to the North down the path. Up ahead, you can see the Fire Nation Fortress. This must be where your friends are being held captive! Use a advanced move against the Inferno tanks at the corner, but don't let them catch you in a crossfire.

Continue to the bottom of the path, destroying any remaining Inferno tanks. The Chest to the left of the main gate cannot be opened by Aang. You can, however, enter the Fortress itself.

Quest 1: Rescue Friends - Update

Destroy all the Machines while searching the Fortress for Katara, Sokka, and Haru.

There's a SAVE POINT just inside the Fortress. You had better use it before continuing the battle. In a room to the East you'll spot Haru locked in a giant cage. You can open the nearby chest, but you cannot open the lock.

EMPTYING YOUR POCKETS

Having played as Aang for such a long time, you might have collected enough armor and trinkets to completely fill your inventory! If you see a red line through the bag icon, you'll be unable to pick up anything else. Since you aren't able to sell items to a Merchant at this point in the game, go into the inventory screen and drop unwanted items.

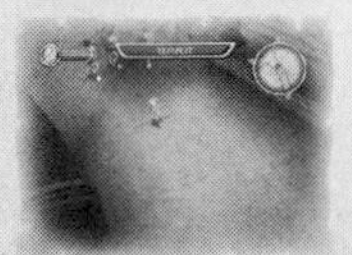

The passageway to the West comes to an end at a stream of lava. Aang is unable to cross it. Don't bother with it now. Instead, head to the North and battle a trio of Tempests.

Sokka is being held in a flying cage in a small alcove to the West. Approach him and use your Focus to send the cage (and Sokka) flying. Now that you've managed to free him, you can now take control of Sokka.

Quest 1: Rescue Friends - Update

Sokka is free! But Katara and Haru are still being held.

With Sokka in tow, return to the Fortress' entrance hall and enter the room to the East. Take control of Sokka and use his Focus to break the lock on Haru's cage. Two down, one to go!

Quest 1: Rescue Friends - Update

Katara is the last remaining captive. Free her!

None of the three can cross the lava, so head North into the Fortress. In the hallway, you'll encounter a handful of Machines. Destroy them and continue to the East until you see Katara on the other side of the lava.

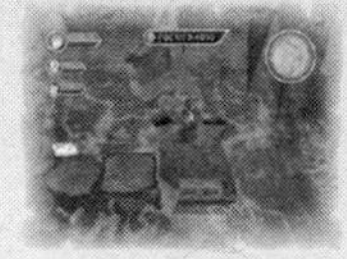

It is too dangerous for all three of you to cross, so take control of Haru and use his Focus to knock the stalactites down into the lava, creating a makeshift bridge. Think she'll mind if you create a bridge to the Chest before rescuing her?

Quest 1: Completed

After Haru reaches Katara, the pair automatically crosses the lava to rejoin the others. Now the team is back in business! Head back down the hallway and South to the Fortress' main entrance. You might want to save your progress here at the SAVE POINT.

Quest: Reign Must End!!! (Main Objective)

It's time to confront Lian, The Maker, once and for all! Search the Fortress until she is found!

Hidden Chest: 6 of 8

You still have a three Hidden Chests to find. Leave the Fortress and look for the Chest on the West side of the main steps. Take control of Sokka and use his Focus to open it.

Hidden Chest: 7 of 8

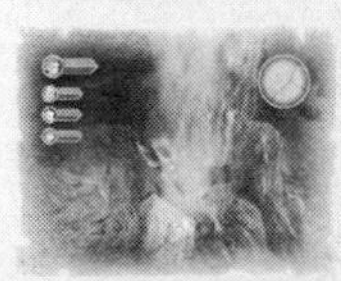

Continue up the path to the South and make your way to the waterfall outside. Take control of Katara and stand behind the falls, using her Focus to reveal the Hidden Chest.

Hidden Chest: 8 of 8

The final Hidden Chest is on the West side of the stream where you destroyed the dam. Take control of Haru, as only his Focus can reveal the Chest.

You've found all the Hidden Chests and all the Momo Objects, having completed 7 of the 8 Quests. Your final challenge is to destroy the remaining Machines and stop Lian. Time to head back to the Fortress! Once inside, take the hallway leading to the West. Katara's Focus can cool down the lava long enough to allow you to cross it.

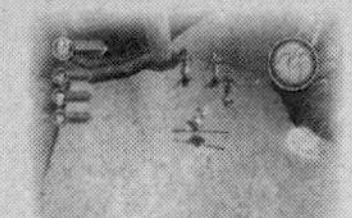

Defeat the Soakers and follow the hallway as it curves to the South. There is a SAVE POINT here if you want to use it.

As you make your way deeper into the Fortress, you spot Zuko stranded next to a waterfall. Aang takes pity on his nemesis and decides to help. Zuko, however, isn't grateful for the assistance. He tries to attack and ends up falling into the water despite Aang's efforts to save him.

There's no shortage of enemies in the next room! Inferno tanks, Soakers, Tempests, and Guarders—the gang's all here! Make your way around the room using your radar to locate and destroy the remaining enemies.

Quest 8: Completed

Follow the hallway that leads to the South until it ends at a SAVE POINT. You'll be prompted to save your game prior to the Boss battle.

Quest: Reign Must End!!! - Update

It's a trap! Defeat the Maker's fearsome Dreadnaught Machine!

Lian has you where she wants you, and unleashes a Dreadnaught Machine. It isn't much different than the last one you fought—except that it is bigger. Oh, and it also drops Machine enemies down on you while hovering—

As before, hold the block button to protect yourself from the Dreadnaught's shockwave and run around to the back of it. Hit the glowing area at the rear with your advanced attacks.

You and your party should be at Level 20 at this stage in the game. At that level of power, it won't take you very long to destroy the Dreadnaught.

Quest: Reign Must End!!! - Update

The Maker escaped through the Western door! Find a way to open it and follow her.

It's not over yet! Lian herself is making a break for it. Inspect the book and the plaque on the Northern wall before following her to the West. Use Haru's earthbending power to open the door.

Quest: Reign Must End!!! - Update

Follow The Maker!

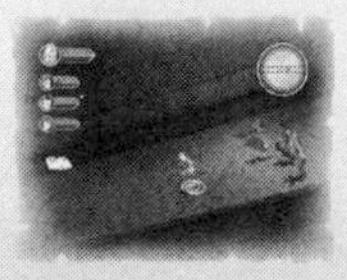

Head down the long ramp to the West until you reach the SAVE POINT. Once again, you'll be prompted to save your progress before the Boss battle.

Quest: Reign Must End!!! - Update

Defeat The Maker once and for all!

Inside the next room, your party confronts Lian, The Maker. She explains that Benders have created an imbalance in the world which has led to war. Her Machines will level the playing field. This final machine, the Ultimaton, uses the powers of several Benders who have chosen to assist Lian. Aang, Sokka, Katara, and Haru refuse her offer to join forces.

The Ultimaton has spinning blades that create a vortex, spinning blades that tear up the earth, a cannon that shoots ice projectiles, and another that spits flame. The curved dome on top lets you know what attack is coming next by projecting an image of the element it is about to use (earth, fire, air, water).

Fortunately, all of its weapons are designed to aim forward. Quickly circle around to the sides of it, avoiding the front. If you become encased in ice, quickly take control of another member of your party and continue the attack.

After the Ultimaton has launched several attacks, it begins to overheat. You'll notice some of its tread gears glowing red. That's your cue to move in and launch an attack of your own. Hit it as hard as you can, as quickly as possible.

It takes patience to wait for the proper moment to attack. Continue running around the room until that moment comes. When you've depleted its energy, a cinema scene shows the characters attending to a wounded Haru.

The Machine is still active, however, and is about to strike Aang when Katara pushes him out of the way, taking the blow herself. As Lian gloats, Aang undergoes a dramatic transformation. He has invoked the power of the Avatar! Three "ultimate" moves have now been assigned to the Quick Panel.

The Dreadnaught now uses all four elements at once, but in Avatar mode it is no match for Aang. You are fast enough to easily avoid its attacks, circling around it without getting hit.

You don't need to wait for the Dreadnaught to overheat this time. Instead, run around behind it or to the side and use the Waterbender ultimate attack to freeze it.

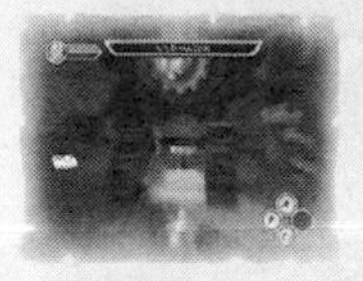

When the Dreadnaught turns white, hit it with the Airbender or Earthbender ultimate attack. Repeat this process until the machine is destroyed for good!

Lian is unable to escape and is crushed beneath the fallen Dreadnaught. At last, her reign of terror is over! Katara is unharmed, and together with Aang, Sokka, Haru, and the surviving Benders, the group leaves the Fortress. Appa whisks our heroes off to an uncertain but hopeful future.

Meanwhile, somewhere in the distance, Zuko crawls out of the water—battered, but still alive! Sit back and watch the credits roll. Congratulations on completing the game!

GALLERY

By successfully completing this Chapter, you have unlocked the Gallery and Character Gallery from the Extras Menu. Select it to view production artwork for the game's various Chapters. Good job!

NICKELODEON AVATAR: THE LAST AIRBENDER

PSP® system Version

PSP system

Chapter 1: Characters & Skills

Aang

Air Wave

This move shoots a wave of air to the front that can inflict damage. It can be used rapid-fire until Aang runs out of Chi.

Power

Rank	CP Cost	Chi Cost
Rank 1	0	5
Rank 2	200	+2
Rank 3	300	+2
Rank 4	400	+2
Master	500	+2

Speed

Rank	CP Cost	Chi Cost
Rank 1	0	5
Rank 2	300	+3
Rank 3	550	+3
Master	800	+3

Gale

Aang is surrounded by a rushing wind that can hit nearby opponents up to twice. The second hit is always more powerful than the first and tends to knock most opponents over. Great when surrounded, but it can be interrupted by an enemy attack.

Power

Rank	CP Cost	Chi Cost
Rank 1	—	12
Rank 2	450	+6
Rank 3	650	+6
Rank 4	850	+6
Master	1,050	+6

Air Scooter

Aang rides on a ball of air bowling enemies over. He falls off when the he rams into something solid like a rock, wall, or a large machine. This is great in large areas with numerous enemies. The move can be maintained until Aang runs out of Chi.

Power

Rank	CP Cost
Rank 1	—
Rank 2	100
Rank 3	200
Master	300

Duration

Rank	CP Cost	Duration (Chi per second)
Rank 1	—	18
Rank 2	500	-1.5
Rank 3	650	-1.5
Rank 4	800	-1.5
Master	950	-1.5

Hand to Hand

This increases the damage caused by Aang's basic physical attack and the speed at which the blows are delivered. The basic attack combo is a five-hit ⊗ ⊗ ⊗ ⊗ ⊗ command.

Power

Rank	CP Cost
Rank 1	—
Rank 2	150
Rank 3	250
Rank 4	350
Rank 5	450
Master	550

Speed

Rank	CP Cost
Rank 1	—
Rank 2	250
Rank 3	400
Rank 4	550
Master	700

Bending Combo

Aang can put a twist on his basic physical attack by throwing in a few bending moves. The basic combo is a four-hit attack, ⊗ ⊗ ▣ ▣, but increases to five-hits, ⊗ ⊗ ▣ ▣ ▣, when mastered.

Combo No. Up

Rank	CP Cost
Rank 1	—
Master	600

Power

Rank	CP Cost	Chi Cost
Rank 1	—	5
Rank 2	200	+3
Rank 3	350	+3
Master	500	+3

Air Shield

This skill increases Aang's resistance to enemy airbending moves. The bonus is passive, so it's always active once purchased with no Chi consumption.

Passive Effect

Rank	CP Cost	Air Resistance
Rank 1	—	0%
Rank 2	100	2%
Rank 3	200	4%
Rank 4	300	6%
Rank 5	400	8%
Rank 6	500	10%
Rank 7	600	12%
Rank 8	700	14%
Rank 9	800	16%
Rank 10	900	18%
Master	1,000	20%

Tornado

Tornado is a powerful airbending move that creates a large wind vortex. It strikes everyone around Aang and can hit enemies multiple times if they're able to remain standing after the initial blow. Works best against bosses.

Power

Rank	CP Cost
Rank 1	—
Rank 2	500
Rank 3	650
Rank 4	800
Rank 5	950
Master	1,100

Meditate

Increase Aang's Chi restoration by increasing this skill's level. Though expensive, this skill is critical as Aang's attacks grow in power and consume large amounts of Chi.

Effect

Rank	CP Cost	Duration (Chi per second)
Rank 1	—	1.8
Rank 2	1,000	2.1
Rank 3	1,250	2.4
Rank 4	1,500	2.7
Master	1,750	3

Katara

Freeze

Freeze locks an opponent in ice upon contact (unless the attack is blocked) leaving the enemy defenseless for a short amount of time.

Power

Rank	CP Cost	Chi Cost
Rank 1	—	6
Rank 2	200	+1.5
Rank 3	300	+1.5
Rank 4	400	+1.5
Master	500	+1.5

Speed

Rank	CP Cost	Chi Cost
Rank 1	—	6
Rank 2	200	+3.5
Rank 3	400	+3.5
Master	600	+3.5

Water Strike

Creates an arc of water in front of Katara that can strike multiple opponents.

Power

Rank	CP Cost	Chi Cost
Rank 1	—	8
Rank 2	150	+2
Rank 3	400	+2
Master	650	+2

Range

Rank	CP Cost	Chi Cost
Rank 1	—	8
Rank 2	350	+4
Master	1,100	+4

Maelstrom

This skill surrounds Katara with swirling water that can strike enemies up to two times. The second hit is always more powerful than the first. This attack can be interrupted by an enemy attack.

Power

Rank	CP Cost	Chi Cost
Rank 1	—	12
Rank 2	400	+6
Rank 3	550	+6
Rank 4	700	+6
Master	850	+6

Hand to Hand

This skill increases the damage caused by Katara's basic four-hit combo ⊗ ⊗ ⊗ ⊗ and the speed at which the blows are delivered.

Power

Rank	CP Cost
Rank 1	—
Rank 2	150
Rank 3	250
Rank 4	350
Rank 5	450
Master	550

Speed

Rank	CP Cost
Rank 1	—
Rank 2	250
Rank 3	400
Rank 4	550
Master	700

Bending Combo

Buying into this skill increases Katara's Bending Combo from three-hits, ⊗ ■ ■, to four-hits, ⊗ ■ ■ ■. It also increases the power of her attacks making her more effective at close range.

Combo No. Up

Rank	CP Cost	Hits
Rank 1	—	3 Hits
Master	600	4 Hits

Power

Rank	CP Cost	Chi Cost
Rank 1	—	5
Rank 2	200	+3
Rank 3	350	+3
Master	500	+3

Water Shield

The Water Shield skill increases Katara's resistance to enemy waterbending. This skill is passive, so it's always in effect once purchased with no Chi cost.

Effect

Rank	CP Cost	Water Resist
Rank 1	—	0%
Rank 2	100	2%
Rank 3	200	4%
Rank 4	300	6%
Rank 5	400	8%
Rank 6	500	10%
Rank 7	600	12%
Rank 8	700	14%
Rank 9	800	16%
Rank 10	900	18%
Master	1,000	20%

Power

Rank	CP Cost	Chi Cost
Rank 1	—	25
Rank 2	300	+15
Rank 3	600	+15
Rank 4	900	+15
Rank 5	1,200	+15
Master	1,500	+15

Single Heal

Katara can use this skill to heal herself and a nearby ally. This skill is a great way to save gold throughout the game, since it reduces the need for healing items. The Chi cost grows quickly, so build the Meditate skill along with this one.

Meditate

Increase the speed at which Katara recovers consumed Chi by purchasing this skill. This is critical as Katara's skills grow in power and consume additional Chi.

Effect

Rank	CP Cost	Duration (Chi per second)
Rank 1	—	1.8
Rank 2	1,000	2.1
Rank 3	1,250	2.4
Rank 4	1,500	2.7
Master	1,750	3

Mass Freeze

Katara freezes all enemies within range for a short time leaving them defenseless and unable to act. It's a great way to slow down a powerful boss.

Power

Rank	CP Cost
Rank 1	—
Rank 2	500
Rank 3	650
Rank 4	800
Rank 5	950
Master	1,100

Sokka

Power Attack

Use this skill by holding ⊗ to build power then releasing it near an enemy. Sokka's movement speed is greatly reduced while charging, which makes this skill difficult to use at times.

Load Time

Rank	CP Cost
Rank 1	—
Rank 2	250
Rank 3	450
Rank 4	650
Master	850

Power

Rank	CP Cost
Rank 1	—
Rank 2	150
Rank 3	300
Rank 4	450
Rank 5	600
Master	750

Rapid Attack

Rapidly tap ■ to pound an enemy into submission. This is a great way to pin down monsters that move quickly.

Power

Rank	CP Cost	Chi Cost
Rank 1	—	3
Rank 2	350	4.5
Rank 3	450	6
Rank 4	550	7.5
Rank 5	650	9
Master	750	10.5

Boomerang

Toss a boomerang at an enemy. The boomerang may bounce between several enemies causing damage to everyone it touches.

Power

Rank	CP Cost	Chi Cost
Rank 1	—	7
Rank 2	200	9
Rank 3	300	11
Rank 4	400	13
Rank 5	500	15
Rank 6	600	17
Master	700	19

Hand to Hand

Sokka has the longest physical attack combo, ⊗⊗⊗⊗⊗⊗⊗, at seven-hits. Get the most out of it by spending points on this skill. Speed is especially important due to the length of the move.

Power

Rank	CP Cost
Rank 1	—
Rank 2	300
Rank 3	550
Rank 4	800
Master	1,050

Speed

Rank	CP Cost
Rank 1	—
Rank 2	400
Master	700

Auto Block

This skill increases the odds that Sokka will automatically defend when an enemy attacks him. This is especially useful when allowing the CPU to control his actions, since it reduces the need for healing items. This skill is passive, so it's always in effect at no Chi cost.

Effect

Rank	CP Cost	Auto-defense Rate
Rank 1	—	10%
Rank 2	200	16%
Rank 3	400	22%
Rank 4	600	28%
Rank 5	800	34%
Master	1,000	40%

Meditate

Meditate tends to be less important for Sokka than other characters unless he's using Boomerang often. Invest in it if you notice he's running out of Chi too quickly.

Effect

Rank	CP Cost	Chi Restored (per second)
Rank 1	—	1.8
Rank 2	1,000	2.1
Rank 3	1,250	2.4
Rank 4	1,500	2.7
Master	1,750	3

Special Boomerang

Sokka bombards any enemies within range with a cloud of boomerangs. This attack can inflict multiple hits on enemies if they remain on their feet after the first blow.

Power

Rank	CP Cost
Rank 1	—
Rank 2	500
Rank 3	650
Rank 4	800
Rank 5	950
Master	1,100

Haru

Wall of Earth

Summon a rock from the ground and shoot it forward with a solid punch. This is a powerful, but somewhat slow ranged attack.

Power

Rank	CP Cost	Chi Cost
Rank 1	—	6
Rank 2	200	+2
Rank 3	300	+2
Master	400	+2

Speed

Rank	CP Cost	Chi Cost
Rank 1	—	6
Rank 2	200	+3
Rank 3	400	+3
Rank 4	600	+3
Master	800	+3

Ground Wave

Create a wall of earth around Haru that can temporarily stun its victims. Range is extremely important with this attack. Invest in it early.

Power

Rank	CP Cost	Chi Cost
Rank 1	—	10
Rank 2	300	+4
Rank 3	500	+4
Master	700	+4

Range

Rank	CP Cost	Chi Cost
Rank 1	—	10
Rank 2	600	+6
Master	1,200	+6

Shoot Rocks

Haru tends to use this attack the most, so buy into both range and power early when partnering with him. It's a quick ranged attack that's great for bowling enemies over from a distance.

Power

Rank	CP Cost	Chi Cost
Rank 1	—	8
Rank 2	200	+3
Rank 3	400	+3
Master	600	+3

Speed

Rank	CP Cost	Chi Cost
Rank 1	—	8
Rank 2	500	+5
Mater	1,000	+5

Hand to Hand

Haru's three-hit combo, ⊗ ⊗ ⊗, is slow but powerful. Invest in speed early in the game.

Power

Rank	CP Cost
Rank 1	—
Rank 2	150
Rank 3	250
Rank 4	350
Rank 5	450
Master	550

Speed

Rank	CP Cost
Rank 1	—
Rank 2	250
Rank 3	400
Rank 4	550
Master	700

Bending Combo

Haru has one of the most powerful Bending Combos in the game. The basic attack is three-hits, ⊗ ■ ■, but it can be increased to four-hits ⊗ ■ ■ ■. Buy heavily into this skill when performing Haru lead quests.

Combo No. Up

Rank	CP Cost	Hits
Rank 1	—	3 Hits
Master	600	4 Hits

Power

Rank	CP Cost	Chi Cost
Rank 1	—	5
Rank 2	200	+3
Rank 3	350	+3
Master	500	+3

Earth Shield

Increase Haru's natural earthbending resistance with this skill. The shield is passive, so it's always in effect at no Chi cost.

Effect

Rank	CP Cost	Earth Resist
Rank 1	—	0%
Rank 2	100	2%
Rank 3	200	4%
Rank 4	300	6%
Rank 5	400	8%
Rank 6	500	10%
Rank 7	600	12%
Rank 8	700	14%
Rank 9	800	16%
Rank 10	900	18%
Master	1,000	20%

Meditate

Haru relies heavily on earthbending, so he always needs additional Chi. Purchasing into this skill increases the rate at which his Chi recovers making him infinitely more useful.

Effect

Rank	CP Cost	Chi Restored (per second)
Rank 1	—	1.8
Rank 2	1,000	2.1
Rank 3	1,250	2.4
Rank 4	1,500	2.7
Master	1,750	3

Giant Boulder

This attack delivers a single powerful strike to all enemies within range. This is the best of the super moves for wiping out a large group of lesser enemies.

Power

Rank	CP Cost
Rank 1	—
Rank 2	500
Rank 3	650
Rank 4	800
Rank 5	950
Master	1,100

Equipment

Armor and accessories can be purchased from artisans, found in chests, and occasionally dropped by defeated foes. Body and waist armor can be fortified by artisans using common materials that are found during combat for a fee. Fortification only increases the item's defense rating. Other stats and resistances are unaffected. Items found later in the game can be upgraded more than those seen at the beginning. Rings and amulets cannot be fortified, but sometimes drop from enemies with a '+1' or greater status attached, which increases the items defensive bonus by the number of points indicated in the name. These rare finds are worth the same amount of gold as a normal ring or amulet. Likewise fortifying body or waist armor does not increase its resale value.

Armor (Body)

Name	Buy	Sell	Defense	Other	Air Resist	Earth Resist	Fire Resist	Water Resist	Fortifying Materials
Bear Wrap	330	165	+3	+1 PWR	+0%	+0%	+0%	+0%	Tattered Cloth x2, Bone Chip x1, Tattered Fur Skin x1
Bear Robe	720	360	+7 (+12)	+3 PWR	+0%	+0%	+0%	+0%	Silk Cloth x2, Beast Bone x1, Beast Hide x1
Bear Vest	1500	750	+12	+5 PWR	+0%	+0%	+0%	+0%	Flax Cloth x2, Beast Fangs x1, Beast Fur x1
Bear Dogi	3000	1500	+18	+8 PWR	+0%	+0%	+0%	+0%	Embroidered Cloth x2, Old Bones x1, Mystic Beast Fur x1
Sun Wrap	330	165	+3	+1 MND	+0%	+0%	+0%	+0%	Tattered Cloth x2, Cord x1, Amber x1
Sun Robe	720	360	+7	+3 MND	+0%	+0%	+0%	+0%	Silk Cloth x2, Silk Rope x1, Jade x1
Sun Vest	1500	750	+12	+5 MND	+0%	+0%	+0%	+0%	Flax Cloth x2, Strong Rope x1, Tiger's Eye x1
Sun Dogi	3000	1500	+18	+8 MND	+0%	+0%	+0%	+0%	Embroidered Cloth x2, Charm String x1, Diamond x1
Dragon Wrap	330	165	+3	+1 VIT	+0%	+0%	+0%	+0%	Tattered Cloth x2, Bone Chip x1, Bronze Sheet x1
Dragon Robe	720	360	+7	+3 VIT	+0%	+0%	+0%	+0%	Silk Cloth x2, Beast Bone x1, Iron Sheet x1
Dragon Vest	1500	750	+12	+5 VIT	+0%	+0%	+0%	+0%	Flax Cloth x2, Beast Fangs x1, Silver Sheet x1
Dragon Dogi	3000	1500	+18	+8 VIT	+0%	+0%	+0%	+0%	Embroidered Cloth x2, Old Bones x1, Gold Sheet x1
Panda Wrap	330	165	+3	—	+5%	+5%	+0%	+0%	Tattered Cloth x2, Tattered Fur Skin x1, Cord x1
Panda Robe	720	360	+7	—	+5%	+5%	+0%	+0%	Silk Cloth x2, Beast Hide x1, Silk Robe x1
Panda Vest	1500	750	+12	—	+5%	+5%	+0%	+0%	Flax Cloth x2, Beast Fur x1, Strong Rope x1
Panda Dogi	3000	1500	+18	—	+5%	+5%	+0%	+0%	Embroidered Cloth x2, Mystic Beast Fur x1, Charm String x1
Moon Wrap	330	165	+3	—	+0%	+0%	+5%	+5%	Tattered Cloth x2, Amber x1, Bone Chip x1
Moon Robe	720	360	+7	—	+0%	+0%	+5%	+5%	Silk Cloth x2, Jade x1, Beast Bone x1
Moon Vest	1500	750	+12	—	+0%	+0%	+5%	+5%	Flax Cloth x2, Tiger's Eye x1, Beast Fangs x1
Moon Dogi	3000	1500	+18	—	+0%	+0%	+5%	+5%	Embroidered Cloth x2, Diamond x1, Old Bones x1
Tortoise Wrap	330	165	+3	+2 DEF	+0%	+0%	+0%	+0%	Tattered Cloth x2, Bronze Sheet x1, Tattered Fur Skin x1
Tortoise Robe	720	360	+7	+3 DEF	+0%	+0%	+0%	+0%	Silk Cloth x2, Iron Sheet x1, Beast Hide x1
Tortoise Vest	1500	750	+12	+5 DEF	+0%	+0%	+0%	+0%	Flax Cloth x2, Silver Sheet x1, Beast Fur x1
Tortoise Dogi	3000	1500	+18	+7 DEF	+0%	+0%	+0%	+0%	Embroidered Cloth x2, Gold Sheet x1, Mystic Beast Fur x1
4 Element Robe (*)	—	2500	+20	—	+10%	+10%	+10%	+10%	Diamond x3, Gold Sheet x3, Old Bones x3
Master's Dogi	—	1250	+3	+10 PWR, +10 MND, +10 VIT	+0%	+0%	+0%	+0%	Embroidered Cloth x2, Gold Sheet x2, Charm String x2
Metallic Vest	—	578	+15	—	-30%	-30%	-30%	-30%	—
White Dogi (**)	—	50	+1	—	+0%	+0%	+0%	+0%	Embroidered Cloth x1, Charm String x1, Mystic Beast Fur x1
Wise Man's Robe	—	390	+5	+5 MND	+0%	+5%	+5%	+0%	Beast Bone x2, Beast Hide x2

	+1 Cost	+2 Cost	+3 Cost	+4 Cost	+5 Cost	+6 Cost	+7 Cost	+8 Cost	+9 Cost	+10 Cost	+11 Cost	+12 Cost	+13 Cost	+14 Cost	+15 Cost	Chapters
	48	57	67	—	—	—	—	—	—	—	—	—	—	—	—	2 & 3
	146	175	204	233	262	—	—	—	—	—	—	—	—	—	—	4 & 5
	220	264	308	352	396	440	484	—	—	—	—	—	—	—	—	6 & 7
	346	415	484	553	622	692	761	830	899	968	1038	1107	1176	1245	1314	7
	58	69	81	—	—	—	—	—	—	—	—	—	—	—	—	2 & 3
	152	182	212	243	273	—	—	—	—	—	—	—	—	—	—	4 & 5
	222	266	310	355	399	444	488	—	—	—	—	—	—	—	—	6 & 7
	336	403	470	537	604	672	739	806	873	940	1008	1075	1142	1209	1276	7
	52	62	72	—	—	—	—	—	—	—	—	—	—	—	—	2 & 3
	152	182	212	243	273	—	—	—	—	—	—	—	—	—	—	4 & 5
	224	268	313	358	403	448	492	—	—	—	—	—	—	—	—	6 & 7
	356	427	498	569	640	712	783	854	925	996	1068	1139	1210	1281	1352	7
	42	50	58	—	—	—	—	—	—	—	—	—	—	—	—	2 & 3
	134	160	187	214	241	—	—	—	—	—	—	—	—	—	—	4 & 5
	208	249	291	332	374	416	457	—	—	—	—	—	—	—	—	6 & 7
	280	336	392	448	504	560	616	672	728	784	840	896	952	1008	1064	7
	64	76	89	—	—	—	—	—	—	—	—	—	—	—	—	2 & 3
	164	196	229	262	295	—	—	—	—	—	—	—	—	—	—	4 & 5
	234	280	327	374	421	468	514	—	—	—	—	—	—	—	—	6 & 7
	402	482	562	643	723	804	884	964	1045	1125	1206	1286	1336	1447	1527	7
	56	67	78	—	—	—	—	—	—	—	—	—	—	—	—	2 & 3
	158	189	221	252	284	—	—	—	—	—	—	—	—	—	—	4 & 5
	228	273	319	364	410	456	501	—	—	—	—	—	—	—	—	6 & 7
	330	396	462	528	594	660	726	792	857	924	990	1056	1122	1188	1254	7
	1122	1346	1570	1795	2019	2241	2469	2692	2971	3141	3366	3590	3841	4039	224-225 per level	7
	448	537	627	716	806	896	985	—	—	—	—	—	—	—	—	7
	—	—	—	—	—	—	—	—	—	—	—	—	—	—	—	5
	214	256	299	342	385	428	470	513	556	599	642	684	727	770	+42-43 per level	7
	Silk Rope X3	214	256	299	—	—	—	—	—	—	—	—	—	—	—	3

Armor (Waist)

Name	Buy	Sell	Defense	Other	Air Resist	Earth Resist	Fire Resist	Water Resist
Bear Strap	192	96	+2	+1 PWR	+0%	+0%	+0%	+0%
Bear Belt	558	204~279	+5	+3 PWR	+0%	+0%	+0%	+0%
Sun Strap	192	96	+2	+1 MND	+0%	+0%	+0%	+0%
Sun Belt	558	214~279	+5	+3 MND	+0%	+0%	+0%	+0%
Dragon Strap	192	96	+2	+1 VIT	+0%	+0%	+0%	+0%
Dragon Belt	558	208~279	+5	+3 VIT	+0%	+0%	+0%	+0%
Panda Strap	192	96	+2	—	+5%	+5%	+0%	+0%
Panda Belt	558	200~279	+5	—	+5%	+5%	+0%	+0%
Moon Strap	192	96	+2	—	+0%	+0%	+5%	+5%
Moon Belt	558	218~299	+5	—	+0%	+5%	+5%	+5%
Tortoise Strap	192	96	+2	+2 DEF	+0%	+0%	+0%	+0%
Tortoise Belt	558	212~279	+5	+5 DEF	+0%	+0%	+0%	+0%
4 Element Belt (*)	—	2400	+10	—	+10%	+10%	+10%	+10%
Black Belt	—	278	+6	+5 VIT	+0%	+0%	+0%	+0%
Fire Nation Belt	—	92~187	+1	—	+0%	+0%	+10%	+0%
Monk's Rope	—	360	+1	+5 MND	+0%	+0%	+0%	+0%
Multi-color Braid	—	700	+9	—	+7%	+7%	+7%	+7%

* Can be refined to +30 ** Can be refined to +99

Jewelry (Neck)

Name	Buy	Sell	Defense	Other	Air Rst	Earth Rst	Fire Rst	Water Rst	Chapters
Flame Amulet	118	59	+1	—	+0%	+0%	+5%	+0%	1, 2 & 3
Fire Amulet	354	177	+2	—	+0%	+0%	+7%	+0%	4, 5, 6 & 7
Blaze Amulet	—	531	+3	—	+0%	+0%	+10%	+0%	7
Pebble Amulet	118	59	+1	—	+0%	+5%	+0%	+0%	1, 2 & 3
Rock Amulet	354	177	+2	—	+0%	+7%	+0%	+0%	4, 5, 6 & 7
Boulder Amulet	—	531	+3	—	+0%	+10%	+0%	+0%	7
Drop Amulet	118	59	+1	—	+0%	+0%	+0%	+5%	1, 2 & 3
Water Amulet	354	177	+2	—	+0%	+0%	+0%	+7%	4, 5, 6 & 7
Flood Amulet	—	531	+3	—	+0%	+0%	+0%	+10%	7
Breeze Amulet	118	59	+1	—	+5%	+0%	+0%	+0%	1, 2 & 3
Wind Amulet	354	177	+2	—	+7%	+0%	+0%	+0%	4, 5, 6 & 7
Gale Amulet	—	531	+3	—	+10%	+0%	+0%	+0%	7
3-Holed Amulet	—	91	+3	—	+0%	+5%	+5%	+5%	4
4 Element Amulet	—	720	+7	—	+10%	+10%	+10%	+10%	7
Air Amulet	—	180	+2	—	+8%	+0%	+0%	+8%	5
Gyatso's Amulet	—	322	+5	—	+12%	+0%	+0%	+0%	6
Obsidian Pendant	—	29	+0	+3 MND	+0%	+0%	+0%	+0%	3

Fortifying Materials	+1 Cost	+2 Cost	+3 Cost	+4 Cost	+5 Cost	+6 Cost	+7 Cost	Chapters
Cord x2, Bone Chip x1, Tattered Fur Skin x1	40	48	56	—	—	—	—	2, 3, 4
Strong Rope x2, Beast Fangs x1, Beast Fur x1	204	244	285	326	367	408	448	5, 6, 7
Cord x2, Tattered Cloth x1, Amber x1	54	64	75	—	—	—	—	2, 3, 4
Strong Rope x2, Flax Cloth x1, Tiger's Eye x1	214	256	299	342	385	428	470	5, 6, 7
Cord x2, Bone Chip x1, Bronze Sheet x1	44	52	61	—	—	—	—	2, 3, 4
Strong Rope x2, Beast Fangs x1, Silver Sheet x1	208	249	291	332	374	416	457	5, 6, 7
Cord x2, Tattered Fur Skin x1, Tattered Cloth x1	38	45	53	—	—	—	—	2, 3, 4
Strong Rope x2, Beast Fur x1, Flax Cloth x1	200	240	280	320	360	400	440	5, 6, 7
Cord x2, Amber x1, Bone Chip x1	56	67	78	—	—	—	—	2, 3, 4
Strong Rope x2, Tiger's Eye x1, Beast Fangs x1	218	261	305	348	392	436	479	5, 6, 7
Cord x2, Bronze Sheet x1, Tattered Fur Skin x1	48	57	67	—	—	—	—	2, 3, 4
Strong Rope x2, Silver Sheet x1, Beast Fur x1	212	254	296	339	381	424	466	5, 6, 7
Diamond x3, Gold Sheet x3, Mystic Beast Fur x3	1044	1252	1461	1670	1878	2086	+208-209 per level	7
Silk Rope x3, Beast Hide x2, Beast Bone x2	214	256	299	—	—	—	—	4
Amber x3, Bronze Sheet x3	156	187	218	249	—	—	—2	
Jade x1, Bone Chip x2, Tattered Fur Skin x2	114	136	159	182	205	—	—	4
—	—	—	—	—	—	—	—	7

Jewelry (Finger)

Name	Buy	Sell	Defense	Other	Air Rst	Earth Rst	Fire Rst	Water Rst	Chapters
Flame Ring	125	62	+1	—	+0%	+0%	+5%	+0%	1, 2 & 3
Fire Ring	375	177~187	+2	—	+0%	+0%	+7%	+0%	4, 5, 6 & 7
Blaze Ring	—	562	+3	—	+0%	+0%	+10%	+0%	7
Pebble Ring	125	62	+1	—	+0%	+5%	+0%	+0%	1, 2 & 3
Rock Ring	375	177~187	+2	—	+0%	+7%	+0%	+0%	4, 5, 6 & 7
Boulder Ring	—	562	+3	—	+0%	+10%	+0%	+0%	7
Drop Ring	125	62	+1	—	+0%	+0%	+0%	+5%	1, 2 & 3
Water Ring	375	177~187	+2	—	+0%	+0%	+0%	+7%	4, 5, 6 & 7
Flood Ring	—	562	+3	—	+0%	+0%	+0%	+10%	7
Breeze Ring	125	62	+1	—	+5%	+0%	+0%	+0%	1, 2 & 3
Wind Ring	375	177~187	+2	—	+7%	+0%	+0%	+0%	4, 5, 6 & 7
4 Element Ring	—	1340	+7	—	+10%	+10%	+10%	+10%	7
Gale Ring	—	562	+3	—	+10%	+0%	+0%	+0%	7
Hermit's Ring	—	132	+7	—	+0%	+0%	-20%	+0%	6
Jaeger Ring	—	10	+0	Increases gold drops	+0%	+0%	+0%	+0%	7
Omniscient Ring	—	98	+4	+2 PWR, +2 MND, +2 VIT	+0%	+0%	+0%	+0%	7
Yin-Yang Ring	—	220	+3	+2 PWR, +2 MND	+0%	+0%	+0%	+0%	4

Usable Items

Name	Buy	Sell	Effect	Chapters
Exploding Bomb	36~57	18~28	Damage from explosion.	All
Freeze Bomb	36~57	18~28	Damage and effect from freezing.	All
Flash Bomb	36~57	18~28	Damage and effect from the flash.	All
Bison Whistle	100~160	50~80	Call Appa to return to town.	All
Health Remedy 30	52~83	26~41	Honor Point 30 point recovery.	All
Health Remedy 100	183~244	91~122	Honor Point 100 point recovery.	3, 4, 5, 6 & 7
Health Remedy Full	712~760	356~380	Honor Point full recovery.	6 & 7
Chi Remedy 30	38~60	19~30	Chi Point 30 point recovery.	All
Chi Remedy 100	148~198	74~99	Chi Point 100 point recovery.	3, 4, 5, 6 & 7
Chi Remedy Full	594~633	297~316	Chi Point full recovery.	6 & 7
Recovery Potion	1952	976	Honor points and Chi points will be fully restored.	7
Revival Potion	360~480	180~240	Revitalize your team mates who are exhausted and can't move.	2, 3, 4, 5, 6 & 7

Materials

Name	Sell	Description	Chapters
Cord	3	Weak cord that has been twined together.	2, 3, 4, 5
Silk Rope	11	Rope made of supple silk.	4, 5, 6
Strong Rope	22	Durable rope which has been strengthened with chemicals.	6, 7
Charm String	27	Mysterious string that can be used for fortune telling.	7
Tattered Cloth	5	A tattered piece of cloth.	2, 3, 4, 5
Silk Cloth	18	Supple cloth woven of silk.	4, 5, 6
Flax Cloth	26	Strong cloth made of flax.	6, 7
Embroidered Cloth	33	Cloth embroidered with some sort of pattern.	7
Bronze Sheet	10	Bronze pressed into a sheet.	2, 3, 4, 5
Iron Sheet	23	Steel pressed into a sheet.	4, 5, 6
Silver Sheet	32	Silver pressed into a sheet.	6, 7
Gold Sheet	52	Gold pressed into a sheet.	7
Tattered Fur Skin	8	Degraded piece of fur skin.	2, 3, 4, 5
Beast Hide	20	Processed hide of a beast from the surrounding area.	4, 5, 6
Beast Fur	30	Fur from a wild beast.	6, 7
Mystic Beast Fur	47	Rugged fur taken from a legendary wild beast.	7
Bone Chip	6	A broken bone from something.	2, 3, 4, 5
Beast Bone	17	A bone from some beast.	4, 5, 6
Beast Fangs	28	Sharp fangs from a wild animal.	6, 7
Old Bones	60	Mystical bones used in astrology readings.	7
Amber	16	An amber colored jewel.	2, 3, 4, 5
Jade	29	A green colored jewel.	4, 5, 6
Tiger's Eye	37	Amber colored gem that reflects light like a cat's eye.	6, 7
Diamond	75	A very hard, expensive jewel.	7

Event Items

Name	Buy	Description	Chapters
Fishing Pole	—	High end fishing rod that won't let any fish get away.	1
Metal Shard	—	A metal shard found at the scene of a battle	1
Scented Bait	—	Bait designed to attract fish by its special scent.	1
Waterbender's Skin		A water skin typically used by Waterbenders.	1
Jewel	—	A valuable jewel kept by a woman in town. Shines in 7 colors when light is shone on it.	2
Prison Cell Key	—	Open up a cell door within the prison.	2
Soldier's Uniform	—	Worn by Fire Nation soldiers. A bit stinky...	2
Widow's Ring	—	Husband's keepsake ring lost by a widow.	2
Beautiful Necklace	—	A necklace found in the forest. Did someone lose it there?	3
Earth Talisman	—	A talisman that Earthbenders keep on themselves to ward off bad luck.	3
Moonpeach	—	A very sweet and delectable peach.	3
Broken Urn	—	Shattered urn fragment.	4
Bumi Fake Ring	—	A fake ring made to look just like Bumi's. It has no value whatsoever.	4
Bumi's Paste	—	Medicine requested by King Bumi. It seems to be a cream of some sort.	4
Bumi's Ring	—	An expensive ring made of Jennamite. Borrowed from Bumi.	4
Cabbage	—	Cabbage dropped by the cabbage merchant.	4
Clay	224	Clay to fix an urn.	4
Earthbender Stone	—	A stone with the Earth Kingdom symbol. An Earthbender was looking for this.	4
Earthbending Scroll	—	A scroll detailing earthbending forms.	4
Fake Crystal	800	An ore that has the same color as Jennamite. But it has no value as a metal.	4
Luxurious Urn	—	An urn restored by an artisan	4
Spirit Statue	—	A carved wooden statue of a bear. Enshrined in the village shrine.	4
Ancient Chest	—	Something seems to be inside the box but it won't open.	5
Blue Keystone	—	Blue ore with writing carved into it. Looks like some sort of key.	5
Keystone	—	Stone with writing carved into it. Can't make out the writing.	5
Merchant's Bag	—	A bag dropped by the merchant.	5
Red Keystone	—	Red ore with writing carved into it. Looks like some sort of key.	5
Air String	—	A special process gives this string the power of air.	6
Crystal	—	Mineral necessary to repair the windmill.	6
Quality Bamboo	—	A very flexible yet sturdy bamboo.	6
Haru's Cell Key	—	Opens the cell door where Haru is kept	7
Herb Dictionary	—	Text describing the effect of various herbs.	7
Super Crystal	—	High-grade mineral used to make strong equipment	7

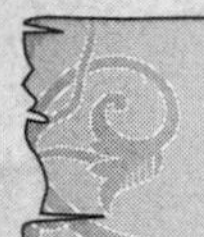

Chapter 1: Fire Navy Attack

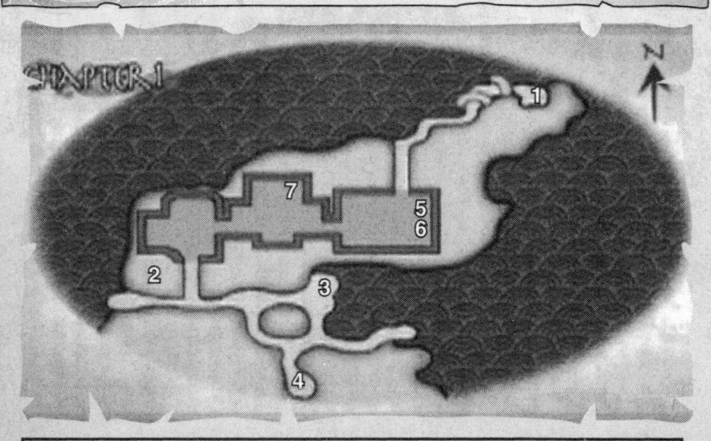

1. Health Remedy 30
2. Panda Strap
3. Moon Wrap
4. Chi Remedy 30
5. Merchant
6. Herbalist
7. Health Remedy 30

Merchant

Item	Cost
Exploding Bomb	36
Freeze Bomb	36
Flash Bomb	36
Bison Whistle	100
Flame Amulet	118
Pebble Amulet	118
Drop Amulet	118
Breeze Amulet	118
Flame Ring	125
Pebble Ring	125
Drop Ring	125
Breeze Ring	125

Herbalist

Item	Cost
Health Remedy 30	52
Chi Remedy 30	38

The Missing Waterbender

1. Speak to Master Pakku in the village
2. Collect the Metal Shard and Waterbender's Skin
3. Return to Master Pakku

REWARD: 350 Skill Points, 150 gold, Chi Remedy 30

This quest is available as soon as *Chapter 1* begins.

Seek **Master Pakku** in the middle of the village to learn about the missing Waterbender, Hiryu. He disappeared after heading west. Take the southwest road out of the village and head for the western edge of the map.

Some large icicles block the road south of the village. Destroy them with a Bending Move or a quick punch. Proceed to the west clearing and search the ground for a **Metal Shard** and a **Waterbender's Skin**. Return the items to Master Pakku to complete the quest.

Fish Bait

1. Speak to the wife on the west side of the village
2. Go to the merchant and herbalist to get fishing tackle
3. Deliver the fishing tackle to the husband
4. Use a Bending Move to cross the water

Reward: Chi: 850 pts, Health Remedy 30

This quest is available once *The Missing Waterbender* has been completed.

Speak to the wife on the far west side of the village. She asks Aang to pick up two packages and deliver them to her husband the fisherman.

The packages are found at the merchant and herbalist on the east side of the village. This event also signals the opening of the shops, so you can now purchase basic equipment and items. Gather the **Fishing Pole** and **Scented Bait** before leaving town.

The husband is found at the water's edge at the far southeast point of the map. Upon arriving head to the east edge and an airbending Icon appears. Press △ and Aang flies across the gap to the fisherman, which completes the quest.

Save the Northern Water Tribe

1. Return to town after the *Fish Bait* quest is completed
2. Meet up with Sokka at the west end of the village
3. Defeat the Fire Nation soldiers in the center of the village
4. Return to Master Pakku and Katara
5. Run to Appa to pursue the Fire Nation
6. Defeat the firebending machine

REWARD: 1,000 Skill Points, 300 gold

This quest begins as you return to the village after completing the *Fish Bait* quest.

As Aang enters the area just south of the village there's a large rumble and the Fire Nation appears. Travel to the west end of the village to meet Sokka, who joins the party.

Run to the center of the village and defeat the Fire Nation soldiers that appear there. Use Bending Moves to make it easier and don't forget to spend Skill Points and level up before the fighting. Press [R] if anyone is low on HP to use a Health Remedy.

Return to the west end of town to check on Master Pakku and Katara when the last of the soldiers is defeated. Master Pakku orders Aang to pursue the Fire Nation. Head to the east end of town and save before returning to Appa in the north.

The path north of the village is blocked by a pair of enormous ice blocks. Go behind the ice pillar during the attack animation and use the Gale Bending move. A huge firebending machine is blocking the road right before Appa and must be dealt with.

Firebending Machine

The boss uses two firebending attacks and a claw sweep. The area in the center is extremely dangerous, but the alcoves to either side of the boss are completely safe. The boss's attacks are easy to predict. Prior to shooting fire bombs a large fire burns in the center of the boss. The flamethrower is lead by the same fire animation, but the boss waggles back and forth before attack. The claw sweep is always preceded by the boss releasing from the icy arch that runs above it. Quickly move to either side when these animations occur and wait for the attack to pass.

Aang can handle this boss on his own. Put Sokka into 'don't attack' mode and stand to either side of the boss. Angle Aang so he can hit the boss with his Air Wave move without being in range of the boss's attacks. Unload on the enemy until Aang is out of Chi. Rest or use a Chi Remedy and begin the assault again.

Chapter 2:
Among the Enemy

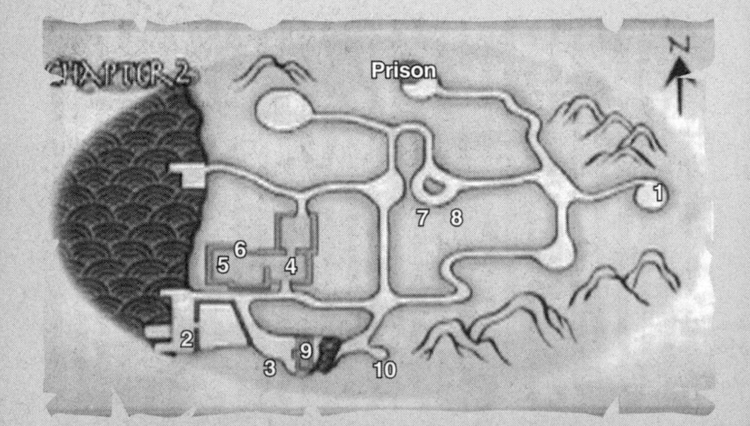

1. Tattered Fur Skin 2. Bronze Sheet 3. Tattered Cloth 4. Merchant	5. Herbalist 6. Artisan 7. Health Remedy 100 (requires an exploding bomb or earthbending)	8. Bone Chip 9. Amber 10. Fire Nation Belt

ITEMS INSIDE PRISON

Chi Remedy 30	Prison Cell Key x 3
Fire Nation Belt	Realth Remedy 100
Health Remedy	

Merchant

Item	Cost
Exploding Bomb	39
Freeze Bomb	39
Flash Bomb	39
Bison Whistle	110
Flame Amulet	118
Pebble Amulet	118
Drop Amulet	118
Breeze Amulet	118
Flame Ring	125
Pebble Ring	125
Drop Ring	125
Breeze Ring	125

Artisan

Item	Cost
Bear Wrap	330
Sun Wrap	330
Dragon Wrap	330
Panda Wrap	330
Moon Wrap	330
Tortoise Wrap	330
Bear Strap	192
Sun Strap	192
Dragon Strap	192
Panda Strap	192
Moon Strap	192
Tortoise Strap	192

Herbalist

Item Cost	
Health Remedy 30	57
Chi Remedy 30	41
Revival Potion	330

Disguise

1. Speak to the man near the town's southeast entrance
2. Cross the pond at the back of the Fire Nation's barracks
3. Retrieve the Soldiers' Uniforms from the bath area

REWARD: 1,200 Skill Points

This quest is available as soon as *Chapter 2* begins.

Begin the quest by speaking to the man near the town's southeast entrance. The party must enter the Fire Nation's prison to the northeast, but to do that they need a clever disguise. A pair of Fire Nation soldier uniforms should do the trick.

Travel south from the village to find the barracks. The front entrance is guarded and there's no way past the vigilant guard. Go around to the east side of the barracks to find a back door. Stand Aang at the edge of the pond and perform a Bending Move to cross the water.

Once inside the barracks, use the west door in the first room, then the southeast door in the second room. Pass through the southwest door in the third room to reach the bathing area. Pick up the **Soldiers' Uniforms** from the bench in the bathing area to complete the quest.

Exit the barracks by backtracking to the third room and using the north door to reach the first room and the rear entrance. Several soldiers discover the party in the bathing area before they can escape. Use Aang's Gale to mow them down quickly in the tight space. The base is on full alert now, so expect more resistance on the way out than on the way in.

Don't miss the chest in southeast soldier's room within the third area that contains **Amber**.

Help the Widow

1. Speak to the widow at the northeast dock
2. Defeat the monkeys in the northwest clearing and search the junk pile to find the Widow's Ring
3. Return the ring to the widow

REWARD: 450 Skill Points, Pebble Ring x1

This quest is available once *Disguise* has begun.

Seek out the widow at the dock northwest of the village. She has lost a precious ring and she isn't sure who took it. A little detective work around the village leads to clues about animals stealing shiny objects.

Enter the clearing due north of the village to find a group of troublesome monkeys. These creatures are fast and difficult to pin down, so be cautious. Defeat the monkeys with Bending Moves then search the junk pile in the northeast corner. Aang finds the **Widow's Ring** amongst the other trinkets. Return to ring to the widow for a reward.

The Captured Men

1. Talk to the man in then northeast corner of the village to learn about the prisoners
2. Complete the *Disguise* quest to get the Soldiers' Uniforms
3. Enter the prison and collect the four Prison Cell Keys
4. Release the prisoners from their cells

REWARD: 630 Skill Points, Bison Whistle

This quest can be taken once *Disguise* has begun, but it can't be completed until *Disguise* is completed and *Rescue Katara* has been initiated.

Speak to the man in the northeast corner of the village about the missing men and initiate the quest. Then complete the *Disguise* quest to collect the necessary items.

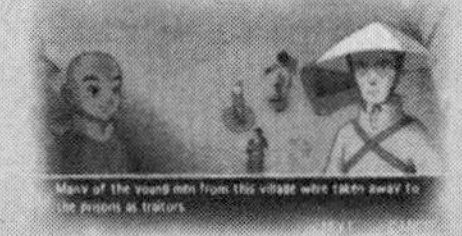

Use the **Soldiers' Uniforms** to sneak past the guards at the prison's front gate. Defeat the warden (see *Rescue Katara* quest) and head up the stairs in the southeast corner.

Enter the door at the top of the stairs. Defeat the soldiers in the hall that follows and search the top right room for a chest containing the first of four **Prison Cell Keys.**

Go up the stairs at the back of the hallway to reach the roof. Defeat the lone soldier to get the second **Prison Cell Key**.

Backtrack through the barracks to the curved hallway and go around to the north end and use the stairs to return to the main level. Enter the small alcove to the right of the staircase to find another chest and the third **Prison Cell Key**.

Follow the hallway around to the south end and go down the stairs to the dungeon. Bypass the prisoners for now and head into the room at the north end where Katara is being held captive. Defeat the Waterbender machines then check Katara's cell for the fourth **Prison Cell Key**.

Return to the prisoners and unlock their cell doors to complete the quest. Don't miss the **Health Remedy 100** in a chest in the top right cell.

The Sailor's Request

1. Talk to the sailor at the southwest dock
2. Give the sailor two pieces of Tattered Cloth

REWARD: 120 Skill Points, 32 gold

This quest is available once *Disguise* has begun.

Look for a sailor at the southwest docks. His clothing has taken a beating from the elements and he needs to fashion some new duds. Bring him two pieces of **Tattered Cloth** (this item may drop from any enemy in the area) to get the reward. This quest can be repeated infinitely until the story moves to *Chapter 3*. It's a good way to earn a few extra Skill Points if you don't plan on reinforcing the party's armor.

Stolen Jewel

1. Speak to the woman in the north portion of the village
2. Approach the barrack's rear entrance
3. Go around to the front of the barracks and use the main entrance
4. Defeat the soldiers and claim the Jewel
5. Return the Jewel to the lady in the village

REWARD: 520 Skill Points, 220 gold, Amber x1

This quest is available after completing the *Disguise* quest.

Speak to a woman at the north end of the village. A Fire Nation soldier has stolen a valuable jewel from her. She asks that Aang return the item to her.

Approach the barrack's rear entrance to find that security has been beefed up since Aang and Sokka last visited. Travel to the west side of the barracks where the main entrance is located. Aang distracts the guards while Sokka enter the barracks to retrieve the item.

Go through the front door then the southeast door to the sleeping quarters. The **Jewel** is in the chest in the northeast corner surrounded by three soldiers. Eliminate them and collect the item. Escape through the front and return the **Jewel** to its owner.

Rescue Katara

1. Complete the *Disguise* quest
2. Enter the prison and defeat the warden
3. Release Katara from her cell
4. Enter the secret passage and defeat the Fire Nation general

REWARD: 2000 Skill Points

Complete the *Disguise* quest to obtain the **Soldiers' Uniforms**, which allow Aang and Sokka to sneak past the prison guards and enter the main gate. Unfortunately, the prison warden and some of his guards are waiting just inside the door to thwart any rescue attempts.

Prison Warden

This fight involves the powerful prison warden and several guards. Eliminate the guards that surround the warden and two more join the battle. Defeat all five before focusing on the main threat. The warden primarily stands back and shoots fireballs at the party. They can be dodged by running back and forth while approaching him.

Occasionally, the warden grunts and turns bright red. In this enraged state the warden is far more dangerous than before. Up close he unleashes a powerful spinning flame kick that can be absolutely devastating. He also has a flame ring burst that can damage anyone standing around him. Back off and put your ally into 'don't attack' mode. Avoid the warden until he unleashes the flame ring and stuns himself. Quickly charge in and take advantage of his defenseless state by unleashing a Bending Combo.

Proceed through the southeast door after the battle. Don't pass up the **Chi Remedy 30** in the chest before the stairs. Enter the barracks at the base of the stairs and wage war on the soldiers in the room. Reinforcements pour through the door behind the party, so keep your guard up. Check the chest in the bottom left room to find a unique **Fire Nation Belt**. The chest in the center left room contains a **Health Remedy 30**. A **Prison Cell Key** is found in the top right room.

The Prison Cell Keys are part of *The Captured Men* quest.

Climb the stairs at the north end of the hall and defeat the soldier on the prison's roof. He drops a second **Prison Cell Key**. Backtrack through the barracks to the curved hallway. Go up and around to the next set of stairs.

Walk down the stairs and enter the alcove to the east where there's a chest containing a third **Prison Cell Key**. The door in the center of the area leads back to the prison's entrance. Ignore it and go down the stairs on the south end to find the prison cells.

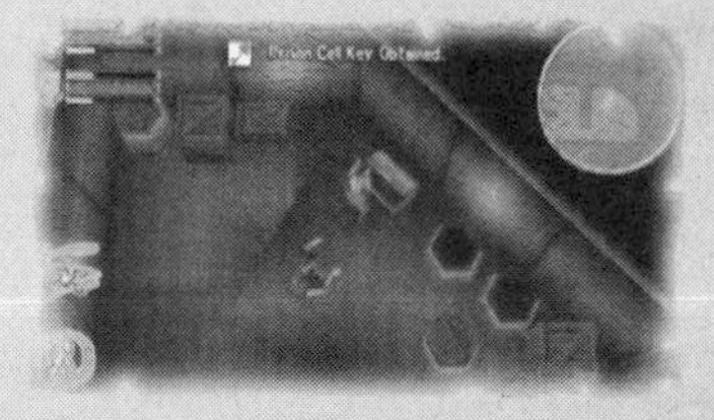

Bypass the cells and head to the end of the hall. Defeat the two waterbending machines to rescue Katara. Check her cell later to find a fourth **Prison Cell Key**.

Fire Nation General

The Fire Nation General's twirling fire staff is difficult to evade. Set your ally to 'don't attack' mode and run around the perimeter while the boss twirls his staff. He occasionally pauses, providing a tiny window for you to perform a quick attack. Don't linger. The general has several powerful attacks that he only uses when someone is standing too near to him.

The best strategy for this boss involves switching between Sokka and Aang. Begin with Sokka and use a Freeze Bomb to stun the boss from a distance. Immediately switch to Aang and charge the frozen enemy. Chances are the general will defrost before Aang can get to him, but there should be just enough time for Aang to reach the enemy and perform a full Bending Combo without being counterattacked. Back off and repeat. Sokka's Exploding Bombs also work well against this enemy. Those without either type of bomb should use ranged Bending Moves like Aang's Air Wave or Sokka's Boomerang to poke at the boss from a safe distance. Gale also works well when the boss pauses. Another option is to repeatedly use the Gale Bending attack. It knocks the General down and you can repeatedly use it as he stands up.

Do not enter the secret passage until you're ready to complete *Chapter 2*. This is a good time to save and finish any lingering quests. Take a moment to return to town and buy a few Exploding and Freeze Bombs if you're currently low on or out of either.

Katara opens a hidden passage in the east wall. Proceed through the passage to face a Fire Nation General.

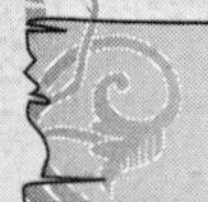

CHAPTER 3: THE FOREST

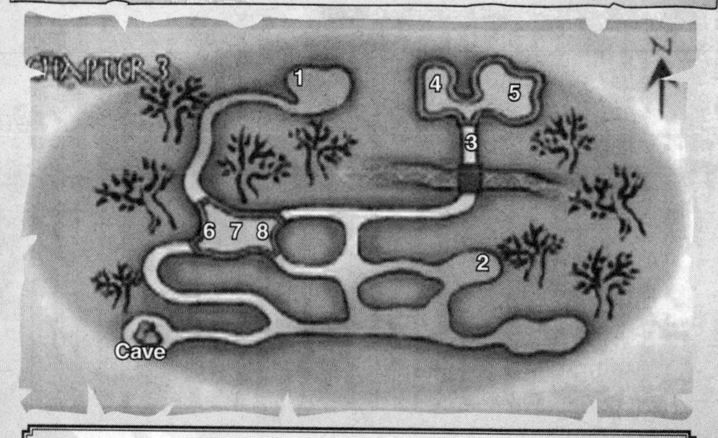

1. Bison Whistle
2. Exploding Bomb
3. Health Remedy 100
4. Beast Bone
5. Silk Cloth
6. Herbalist
7. Merchant
8. Artisan

CHESTS INSIDE HIDDEN CAVE INCLUDE

Wise Man's Robe (*requires an exploding bomb or earthbending)

Chi Remedy 100

Herbalist

Item	Cost
Health Remedy 30	62
Health Remedy 100	183
Chi Remedy 30	45
Chi Remedy 100	148
Revival Potion	360

Merchant

Item	Cost
Exploding Bomb	43
Freeze Bomb	43
Flash Bomb	43
Bison Whistle	120
Flame Amulet	118
Pebble Amulet	118
Drop Amulet	118
Breeze Amulet	118
Flame Ring	125
Pebble Ring	125
Drop Ring	125
Breeze Ring	125

Artisan

Item	Cost
Bear Wrap	330
Sun Wrap	330
Dragon Wrap	330
Panda Wrap	330
Moon Wrap	330
Tortoise Wrap	330
Bear Strap	192
Sun Strap	192
Dragon Strap	192
Panda Strap	192
Moon Strap	192
Tortoise Strap	192

Aid the Earthbenders

1. Heal the injured Earthbender
2. Fix the bridge leading to the Earthbender camp
3. Speak to Tyro
4. Rescue the four Earthbenders fighting in the woods

REWARD: 1,800 Skill Points

The chapter begins with the party next to an injured Earthbender. Use Katara's Bending Move to heal the man. He mentions that the Earthbender camp to the northeast is under attack by strange beings.

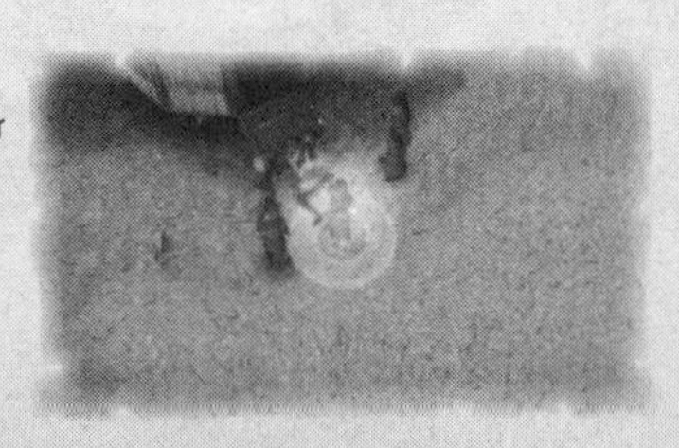

Exit the village using the northeast path and follow it to a bridge south of the Earthbender camp. Someone has destroyed the bridge leaving the river impassable. Stand Katara at the southern edge of the broken bridge and use her Bending Move to create a sheet of ice connecting the two broken ends.

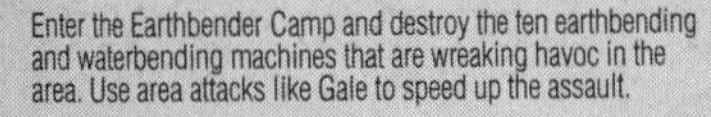

Enter the Earthbender Camp and destroy the ten earthbending and waterbending machines that are wreaking havoc in the area. Use area attacks like Gale to speed up the assault.

Enter the eastern section of the Earthbender camp when the machines are gone and speak to the leader, Tyro. He asks the party assist Earthbenders still fighting the machines in the woods.

Backtrack to the woods. The first Earthbender is in the clearing just south of the camp. The second Earthbender is found at the four-way crossroad in the center of the map. The third Earthbender is located at the three-way crossroad south of the village. The fourth and final Earthbender is trapped in the large clearing in the southeast corner of the map. The party automatically returns to the Earthbender camp when all four Earthbenders have been saved.

Find the Elder

1. Return to the village and speak to the elder
2. Go back to the Earthbender camp and talk to Tyro
3. Check the southeast clearing to find a new cave
4. Enter the cave and defeat the Forest Spirit

REWARD: 3,000 Skill Points, 530 gold

This quest can be taken once the *Aid the Earthbenders* quest has been completed.

Return to the village elder after completing the *Aid the Earthbenders* quest and speak to him. He points the party back to the Earthbender camp to speak with Tyro. Travel back to Tyro to learn more and initiate this quest.

Tyro mentions a hidden Forest Elder (Spirit). The mystical creature can be found somewhere around the clearing in the southeast. Travel to the large clearing in the southeast corner to find a hidden cave has appeared.

Enter the cave and take two lefts to reach a dead end with huge rocks surrounding a chest. Use either Sokka's Bomb or Haru's earthbending to destroy the giant boulders. The chest contains a unique **Wise Man's Robe**.

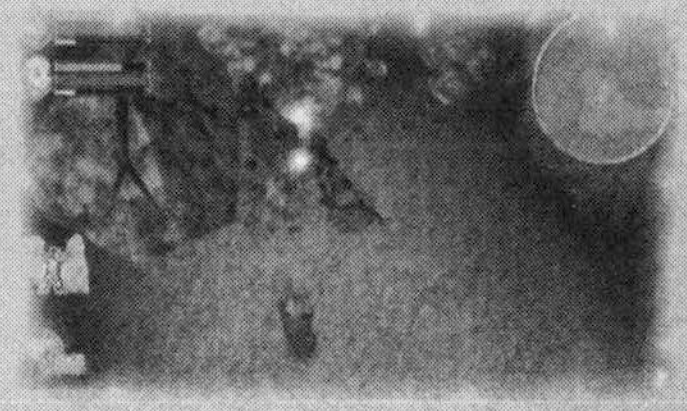

Backtrack into the previous hall and head straight east. Follow the curving hallway south to an intersection. Head down the east path and defeat the wolves in the next hall before collecting a **Freeze Bomb** from the chest in the southwest corner. Continue down the hallway until you come to a Save Point. Use it then enter the room to the north to find a chest containing a **Chi Remedy 100**. Return to the Save Point and go east to find the Forest Elder.

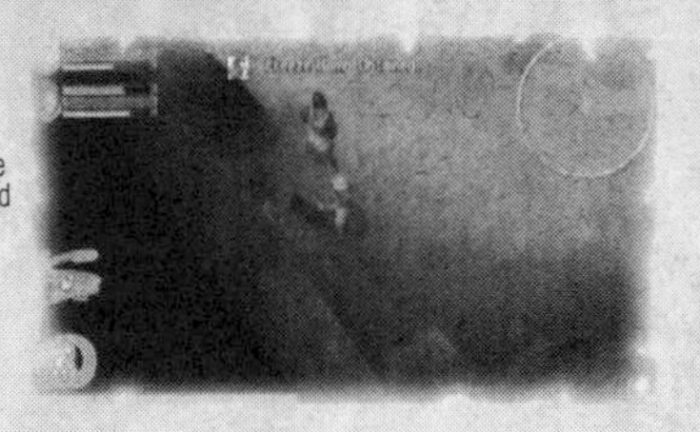

Take a moment to wrap up any unfinished quests before facing the Forest Spirit. The story automatically moves on to *Chapter 4* after the battle, so this is your last chance.

Forest Spirit

The party must deal with two things in this fight. First, there are falling rocks, which are nearly constant and can stun their victims. The avalanche is triggered any time the boss stomps on the ground or runs into a wall. Look for shadows on the ground and quickly get out of the way. The second is the Forest Spirit's charging attacks. Keep some space between the beast and the party so they have time to dodge when the monster charges.

Aang's Bending Combo is very effective against this enemy, but it isn't easy to pull off due to the constant boulder barrage. The best time to attack is after the boss charges and misses. Lure the boss into charging by pelting it with Air Wave between avalanches. Dodge the charge attack and the boss rams a wall, which triggers an avalanche, and stuns the beast. This gives Aang and company a few seconds to counterattack freely. This is important, since there's no way to knock the boss of its feet and it can counter most attacks easily. Any ally does well, but Katara's heals are the most useful. Katara is extremely helpful as the secondary character. She uses her freeze skill often.

Pass It On...

1. Talk to the man on the west side of the village
2. Retrieve the Moonpeach from the northern clearing
3. Return the Moonpeach to the man in the village
4. Take the Beautiful Necklace back to its owner in the Earthbender camp
5. Give the Earth Talisman to the girl in the southwest clearing

REWARD: 850 Skill Points, 180 gold, Obsidian Pendant

This quest is available after completing the *Aid the Earthbenders* quest.

Speak to a man located in the west end of the village. He mentions someone found a **Moonpeach** in the forest to the north.

Leave the village using the northwest exit and follow the path to the clearing at the far end. Defeat the monkeys hopping around the area and collect the Moonpeach from the center of the clearing. Return it to the man in the village to receive a **Beautiful Necklace**.

Travel to the Earthbender camp in the northeast and look for a woman near the camp's entrance. She's happy to have her necklace back and presents the party with an **Earth Talisman** as a reward.

Take the Earth Talisman to the clearing in the southwest corner of the map. Speak to the young person there and give her the talisman to complete the quest and earn the unique **Obsidian Pendant**.

Fixing Up the Camp

1. Give the worker in the Earthbender camp three Cords

REWARD: 160 Skill Points

This quest becomes available once the *Aid the Earthbenders* quest is complete.

Look for a man standing next to the field in the west section of the Earthbender camp. He's trying to repair the damage done by the machines. He asks for three **Cords**, which drop from any enemy in the area. Give them to him to receive a small reward. This quest can be repeated infinitely until the story moves on to *Chapter 4*. It's a great way to earn a few extra Skill Points if you don't need the Cords to fortify the party's armor.

Haru's Training

1. Speak to the visiting Earthbender in the southeast clearing with Haru leading the party
2. Defeat the man in one-on-one combat

REWARD: 630 Skill Points (+80 on later attempts)

This quest becomes available upon completion of the *Aid the Earthbenders* quest.

Speak to the man in the large hat in the southwest clearing while Haru is leading the party. He challenges Haru to a match. Enter this fight equipped with armor and accessories that boost Haru's earth defense.

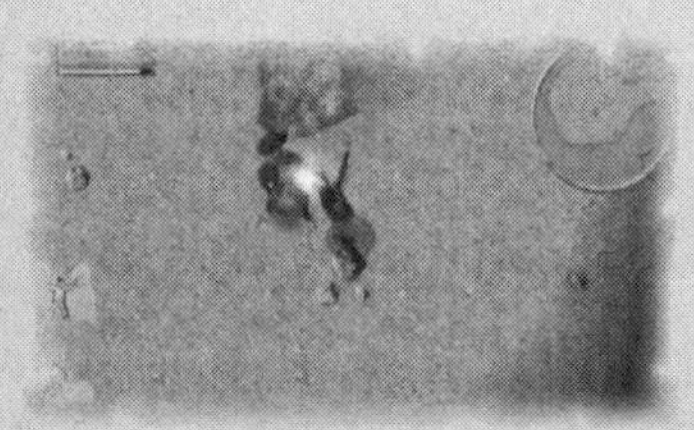

The challenger can slow Haru with a bit of quicksand, which causes Haru's legs to sink into the ground. He can still move (slowly), but can't use Bending Moves while trapped. The enemy typically follows the quicksand with a barrage of rocks. Stay back and walk back and forth to avoid the rocks until the quicksand wears off and Haru's movement returns to normal.

Charge the enemy and perform Haru's three-hit Bending Combo. The challenger sometimes teleports, disappearing into the ground, and reappears at a random location. This move is more of an evasive maneuver than an attack, but it can hurt Haru if the enemy reappears next to him. Haru's Ground Wave is less damaging, but knocks the man down.

The challenger remains in the clearing after losing the battle. Challenge him again with Haru at any time to earn more Skill Points.

CHAPTER 4: OMASHU

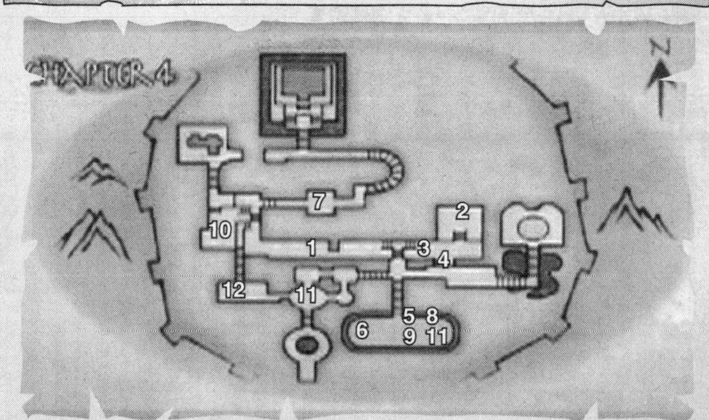

1. Bison Whistle
2. Silk Cloth
3. Health Remedy 100
4. Beast Bone
5. Tattered Fur Skin
6. Tattered Cloth
7. Tattered Cloth
8. Herbalist
9. Merchant
10. Merchant (Rare Goods)
11. Artisan
12. Black Belt

Herbalist

Item	Cost
Health Remedy 30	67
Health Remedy 100	198
Chi Remedy 30	49
Chi Remedy 100	161
Revival Potion	390

Merchant (Rare Goods)

Item	Cost
Exploding Bomb	46
Freeze Bomb	46
Flash Bomb	46
Bison Whistle	130
Fake Crystal	130
Clay	224

Merchant

Item	Cost
Exploding Bomb	46
Freeze Bomb	46
Flash Bomb	46
Bison Whistle	130
Fire Amulet	354
Rock Amulet	354
Water Amulet	354
Wind Amulet	354
Fire Ring	375
Rock Ring	375
Water Ring	375
Wind Ring	375

Artisan

Item	Cost
Bear Robe	720
Sun Robe	720
Dragon Robe	720
Panda Robe	720
Moon Robe	720
Tortoise Robe	720
Bear Strap	192
Sun Strap	192
Dragon Strap	192
Panda Strap	192
Moon Strap	192
Tortoise Strap	192

Discover the Mystery of the Machines

1. Go to the palace at the north end of the city and speak to Bumi
2. Use the supply cart to travel to the Royal Library and speak to the guard
3. Visit the tea house and speak to the owner
4. Destroy the crates within the time limit to get the Royal Library's password
5. Give the password to the Royal Library guard
6. Sneak past the guards within the Royal Library to reach the back room
7. Return to Bumi in the palace
8. Visit the royal supply merchant to get Bumi's Paste
9. Deliver the medicine to Bumi

REWARD:8,000 Skill Points (Unseen) OR 2,000 Skill Points (Seen); 2,500 Skill Points (All Guards Defeated)

This quest is available when the party enters *Chapter 4*.

Put your party members in don't attack mode. The party arrives at Omashu in search of information and the king, Bumi, might be the wealth of knowledge they seek. Travel to the palace at the top of the city and enter to initiate an audience with the king. He points Aang to the Royal Library in the northeast corner of the city. Haru won't be able to accompany Aang into the library, so head down to merchant town and pick up Katara or Sokka.

Speak to the guard standing in front of the Royal Library and he asks for a password. Only guards know the password, so you must find someplace where guards tend to gather. Talk to the locals and they mention the local tea house is infested with guards.

Visit the tea house south of the Royal Library. Speak to the owner out front about the password. She's only willing to reveal the password in exchange for a bit of manual labor. Agree and the party's leader appears in back of the tea house with a bunch of crates. Smash thirty crates in sixty seconds. Use an area attack like Aang's Gale and stand in the middle of a several crates to destroy multiple boxes with a single attack.

Upon completing the chore the owner presents the party with the Royal Library's password. Return to the library and give the password to the guard to gain access to the building. The library is full of security guards. Be cautious and don't get caught.

Pass through the first room to a hallway with two guards. They ask a question that only a true master would know (actually the answers come from the various quests in the area). The answer to the first question is "**Fine Works**."

The next hall is full of guards. Use the book stacks to sneak past the guards unnoticed. Pay less attention to the main screen and focus on the mini-map in the corner. It provides a better idea of where the guards are really located and what routes they patrol.

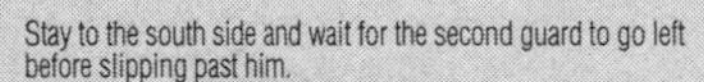

Wait for the first guard to turn and walk away, then quickly run past and hide between the next set of shelves. There's a chest hiding in the alcove next to the door. To reach it, wait for the first guard to walk near the door, then dart into the alcove and get the **Chi Remedy 30** from the chest. Rush back between the stacks or hide in the alcove until the guard passes and returns to the left side again.

Stay to the south side and wait for the second guard to go left before slipping past him.

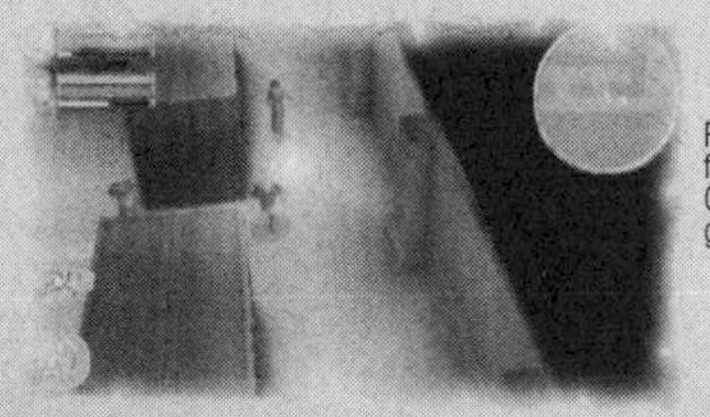

Remain back and well hidden from the third guard and wait for him to walk into the alcove on the east end of his path. Quickly run past him and around the stack to the west. Don't go too far! There's a fourth guard just ahead.

You may notice a chest in the alcove where the third Earthbender pauses. It's tricky, but you can reach the chest without alerting the guards. Wait for the third guard to walk between the stacks and the fourth guard to walk away to the west, so their backs are turned to the path leading to the chest. Quickly run behind the third guard and open the chest to get a **Health Remedy 30** and run back and to the exit before the guards turn around. Be fast but don't move too quickly, or the party may run right into the fourth guard.

There are two more guards with another question in the next hall. Answer "A jennamite ring" to bypass the guards and reach the next section.

This section is a little trickier, but the rewards are greater. Stand at the southeast corner and watch the southern guard and the guard pacing back and forth down the center of the room. Wait for the southern guard to face north as the center guard is walking east, then dash past the southern guard and around the west corner.

Pause before the north guard and wait for the center guard to walk back to the west end. Run by the north guard when he faces south and duck between the next set of book stacks on the south side. The north guard is a little tricky since you can't see his face to determine which way he's facing. Look for his shoes. His shoes are only visible from his front side.

One more guard is hiding in the northeast corner. Wait for him to go to the west end of his route then make beeline for the room in the northeast corner. The room contains a unique **Monk's Rope**.

Return to the main room and stay against the east wall until the center and northeast Earthbenders go to the west ends of their routes. Slip behind the stack south of the fourth guard and wait for him to walk back east before sneaking past him to the door in the northwest corner.

There's another question in the room that follows. Answer "Cabbage" this time to gain admittance to the final room of the Royal Library. There's a reward once the party leaves the Royal Library that's based on your performance. You receive 2,000 Skill Points if the party was detected or 8,000 Skill Points if they cleared the library without being noticed. Technically the quest is over at this point, but it won't be checked off in the journal until the following steps are completed.

Return to Bumi in the palace. He asks the party to get his mollifying paste from the royal supply merchant on the east side of town.

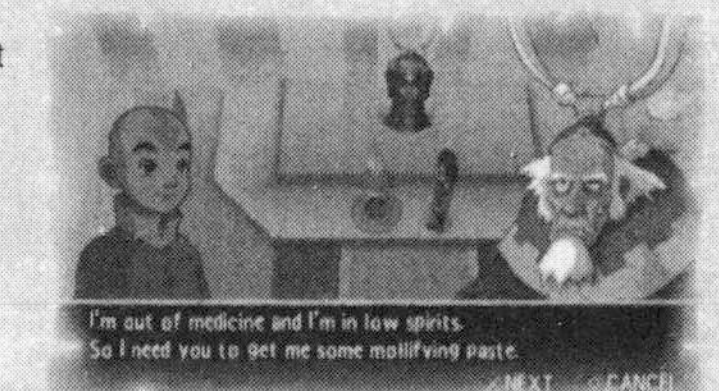

Hop on the cart headed for the center of town then travel east to find the royal supply merchant at the end of the road. She provides the party with **Bumi's Paste** and suggests it might be a good time to save. Listen to her.

Return the paste to Bumi in the palace. This is where the *Escape from Omashu* quest begins. The current quest ends upon your return to Bumi.

Escape from Omashu

1. Defeat 20 Fire Nation soldiers at the city gate
2. Deliver Bumi's Paste to the king
3. Rush to the secret exit from the city
4. Defeat the Consul
5. Guide Sokka and Katara to the secret exit too

REWARD: 5,000 Skill Points & 720 gold

This quest begins after the party picks up Bumi's Paste from the royal supply merchant during the *Discover the Mystery of the Machines* quest.

The Fire Nation is attacking. Katara and Sokka run off to slow the enemy soldiers at the city gates. Guide them to the city gates in the southwest section of the city. Defeat 20 Fire Nation soldiers with no time limit. Four Fire Nation soldiers attack at a time. You can retreat to the area to the north if Sokka and Katara get into trouble and need time to rest and restore. This may be difficult if you haven't spent Skill Points on either character. If so, stay close to the north edge and do your best with a barrage of Bending Moves.

The focus switches to Aang and Haru once 20 soldiers have fallen. Run to the palace defeating Fire Nation soldiers along the way. Make a quick detour to the stable in the southwest section of the city. A chest containing a unique Black Belt has appeared in front of the building.

Bumi tells Aang and Haru of a hidden exit on the east side of the city. Exit the palace and defeat the Fire Nation soldiers at the base of the stairs before using the carts to the west to ride back to the merchant town.

Exit merchant town and head east to the secret exit in the southeast corner. The area has been blocked by a guard until this point, so you may have noticed it before. Save in the middle of the stairs before heading to the bottom.

Consul

The Consul fights much like the Earthbender from ***Haru's Training*** in the previous chapter, but his skills are far more deadly. His attacks are much larger and his teleport moves are usually right on target when he pops out of the ground. However, he has one major weakness that can be exploited.

Control Aang and let Haru do his own thing. Switch to the Gale Bending Move and rush the enemy. Stand right next to him and attack with Gale to where it hits twice. Follow the boss as he's knocked back and stand next to where he lands. Wait for him to begin to stand back up and quickly use Gale again. It should hit him again before the Consul can counterattack. The only exception is when he uses his teleport to evade the second hit. No problem. Just run around until he reappears and repeat the attack. That's all it takes. The Consul is no match for a simple Gale assault.

The focus switches back to Sokka and Katara after the Consul is defeated. Run them to the secret exit and move on to the next chapter of the story.

The Misfortunes of the Cabbage Merchant

1. Watch as the merchant's cart is destroyed
2. Gather the three missing cabbages
3. Give the cabbages to the merchant OR the ostriches

REWARD: 2200 Skill Points & Chi Remedy Full OR 2000 Skill Points & Health Remedy Full

This quest begins the first time the party passes through the curve southeast of the palace.

Upon entering the curved area prior to the palace for the first time the party encounters a merchant with a cart full of **Cabbages**. An angry Earthbender smashes the cart and the Cabbages go flying. Search the city to collect the merchant's Cabbages.

There are three Cabbages in all. One can be found near the rare goods merchant on the west side of the city. Look for it near the stairs just east of the shop.

Another Cabbage is found between the stairs north of merchant town.

One more can be found near the city gates on the south side close to the gate guards.

Once you've collected all three you must make a decision. There are two ways to complete this quest. The obvious way is to return the Cabbages to the merchant, who is waiting a little to the north of merchant town. Doing so earns the party 2200 Skill Points and a **Chi Remedy Full**.

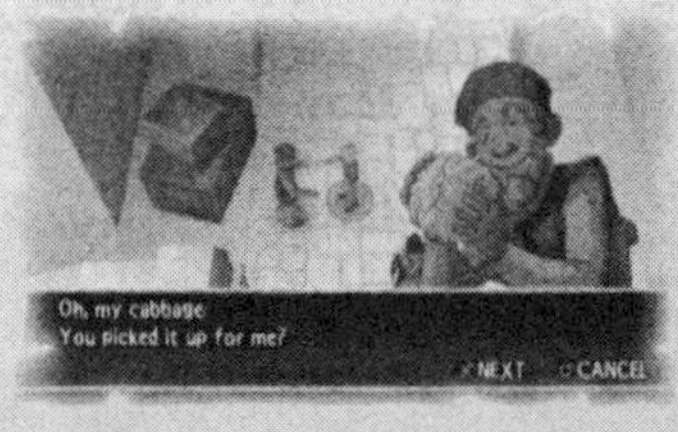

However you may have seen the ostrich stables on the west side of town. The owner mentions that his ostriches love to eat cabbage. Give each ostrich one Cabbage to get the alternate reward of 2000 Skill Points and a **Health Remedy Full**. You may only complete this quest in one of the two ways. *DO not* split the Cabbages between the ostriches and the merchant, or you won't be able to collect the full reward (it's only 500 Skill Points).

The Stolen Spirit Statue

1. Talk to the despairing man in the center of merchant town
2. Speak to the crooked merchant on the west end of merchant town
3. Enter the palace and ask Bumi for his ring
4. Find the master artisan north of the town gate
5. Purchase the Fake Crystal from the rare goods merchant
6. Deliver Bumi's Ring and the Fake Crystal to the artisan
7. Coax the crooked merchant into trading the statue for the fake ring
8. Return the Spirit Statue to the despairing man

REWARD: 1,230 Skill Points & Yin-Yang Ring

This quest can be taken at the start of *Chapter 4*.

Look for a man standing on the south side of the central portion of merchant town. A criminal has stolen a valuable **Spirit Statue** from his village and the he must find a way to get it back. The crook has a stand set up on the west side of the square and he's trying to sell the statue for an exorbitant price.

Find the crooked merchant and ask him about the Spirit Statue. He makes it clear his asking price is too much for Aang, but suggests he'd be willing to trade it for something of even greater value.

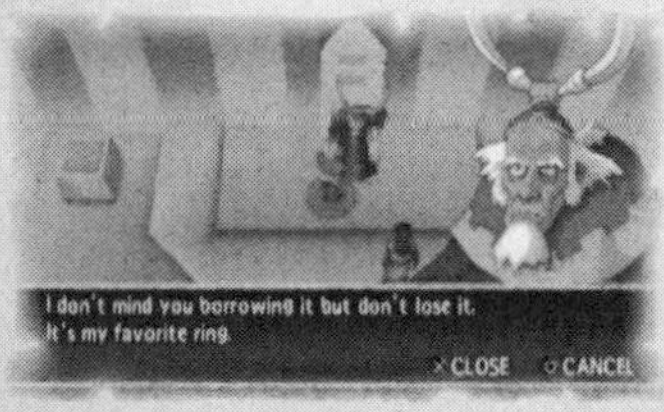

Visit Bumi in the palace and ask about his ring. The king is happy to loan his ring to the party temporarily.

Take the ring to the master artisan north of the village gate. He can make a copy, but needs materials.

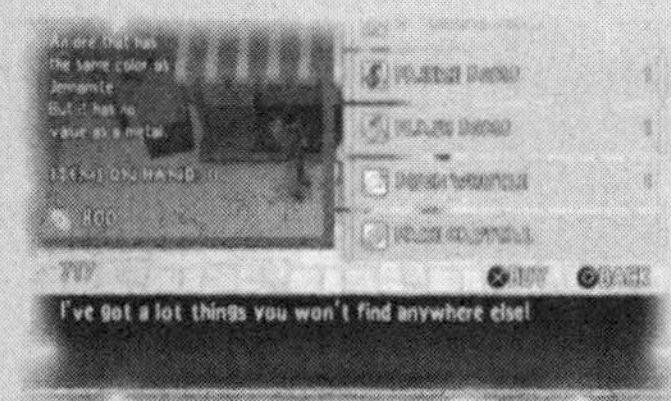

Go to the rare goods merchant northwest of the artisan. Check his store for a **Fake Crystal** that costs 800 gold. Short on cash? Run the 'Costumes for the Play' quest a few times to earn some extra money, or sell off duplicate items.

Return **Bumi's Ring** and the Fake Crystal to the artisan. He quickly fashions the **Bumi Fake Ring**. Visit the shady merchant once more and negotiate to get the Spirit Statue in exchange for the worthless fake.

Return the Spirit Statue to the man in the center of the merchant town to complete the quest and earn a unique **Yin-Yang Ring**.

Costumes for the Play

1. Speak to the guard at the Palace about the costumes
2. Pick up the Silk Cloth and Silk Rope from the rare goods merchant
3. Return the goods to the guard

REWARD: 200 Skill Points & 80 gold

This quest is available once the party has spoken to Bumi for the first time.

Bumi requests a play the first time you visit his Palace. Speak to the guard near the entrance afterward. He's in charge of costumes and needs some materials from the rare goods merchant on the west side of town.

Ride a cart to the stables and run to the vendor to retrieve the necessary materials. The merchant gives the party ten rolls of **Silk Cloth** and ten lengths of **Silk Rope**. These are normal materials that can be used to fortify armor or sold, but resist the temptation. The most you'd get for the Silk Cloth and Silk Rope is 290 gold. That's a decent sum, but you earn 200 Skill Points and 80 gold for returning the materials to the guard. The guard then asks for another shipment, so the quest can be completed over and over again until the story progresses to *Chapter 5* meaning there's no limit to the amount of gold and Skill Points that can be earned. However, selling the materials or using them interrupts the quest. The merchant won't replace the lost goods.

A Side Job at the Tea House

1. Speak to the owner of the tea shop
2. Destroy 30 crates in 60 seconds

REWARD: 150 Skill Points & 100 gold

This quest is available once the party has destroyed the crates at the tea house as part of the *Discover the Mystery of the Machines* quest.

Destroy the crates at the tea house during the ***Discover the Mystery of the Machines*** quest then speak to the owner again. She offers the chance to smash more crates for money. You have one minute to destroy thirty wooden crates. This is an easy way to earn a few Skill Points and some gold.

The key to this game is to use Aang's Gale Bending Move. It can smash four or more crates at a time if Aang is standing in the right spot. Try to get between several crates and use the attack. You may be surprised at how effective it can be. Destroy single crates with a quick punch. Sometimes it's best to leave a small group of crates alone while smashing single crates. New crates that drop into the area may land with the other crates creating a larger group that can be destroyed with a single move.

Any character can play this game. The party's leader at the time the game is initiated is who appears behind the building to smash crates. Give it a try with all four characters.

The Skilled Earthbender's Challege

1. Speak to the Earthbender on the west side of town
2. Locate the hidden door on the east side of town and open it with Haru's Bending Move
3. Collect the Earthbending Scroll and return it to the Earthbender

REWARD: 670 Skill Points & 3-Holed Amulet

This quest is available once the party has cleared the Royal Library during the ***Discover the Mystery of the Machines*** quest.

Talk to the Earthbender east of the rare goods merchant on the west side of town while Haru is leading the party. He has hidden an object somewhere in the town using his earthbending skills. Use Haru's skills to find it!

Venture to the east side of town and look for the outline of a door on the northeast wall next to the royal supply merchant's home. Use Haru's Bending Move to reveal a hidden passageway. Enter the passage and check the chest to find an **Earthbender Scroll**. Return to scroll to the Earthbender for a reward.

The Forgetful Earthbender's Wish

1. Speak to the forgetful Earthbender about his hidden treasure
2. Locate the secret passage north of the rare goods merchant and open it using Haru's Bending Move
3. Collect the Earthbender Stone from the hidden passage and return it to the Earthbender

REWARD: 790 Skill Points & 480 gold

This quest is available once the party has cleared the Royal Library during the *Discover the Mystery of the Machines* quest.

Speak to the Earthbender on the middle path between the palace and the front gate while Haru is leading the party. He's hidden an item in the city using his earthbending skills and needs help finding it.

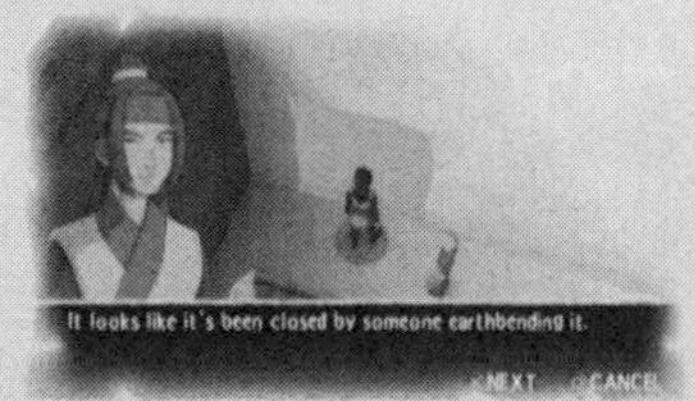

Look for a strange outline on the wall north of the rare goods merchant. You can see a hint of a door. Use Haru's Bending Move to remove the door and check the chamber behind it to find an **Earthbender Stone**. Return the stone to the Earthbender for a reward.

Restoration

1. Encounter the merchant and his urn on the path leading to the palace
2. Speak to the master artisan north of the village gate about repairing the urn
3. Purchase some Clay from the rare goods merchant
4. Return the Broken Urn and the Clay to the artisan to repair the urn
5. Give the Luxurious Urn back to the merchant

REWARD: 1,580 Skill Points

This quest is available after completing the Royal Library portion of the *Discover the Mystery of the Machines* quest.

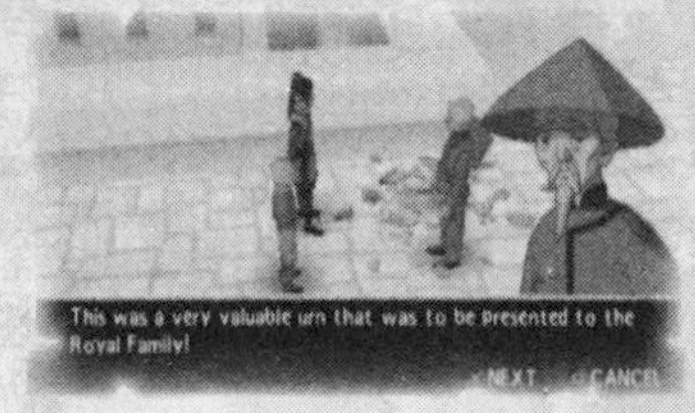

I can repair this with some clay, but THIS urn isn't worth much.
NEXT CANCEL

The party may encounter a merchant and his very valuable urn while returning to the palace. The urn is smashed and the merchant isn't happy about it.

Take the **Broken Urn** to the artisan north of the village gate (the same guy that made the Bumi Fake Ring earlier). He can fix the urn, but needs some **Clay** to do the job.

Travel northwest to the rare goods merchant and purchase some Clay for 224 gold. Return both the Clay and the Broken Urn to the artisan to receive the **Luxurious Urn**. Carry the urn back to the steaming merchant to complete the quest.

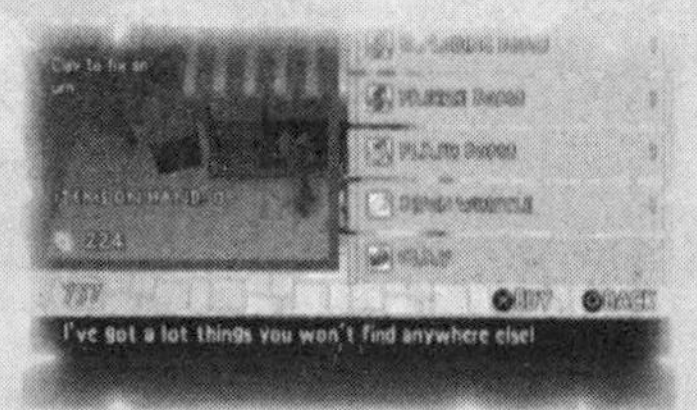

Chapter 5: The Sacred Caverns

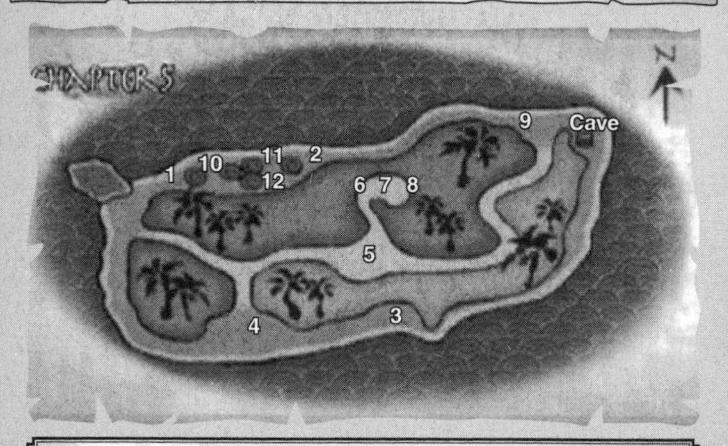

1. Health Remedy 100	5. Silk Rope	9. Freeze Bomb
2. Bison Whistle	6. Fire Ring	10. Herbalist
3. Silver Sheet	7. Chi Remedy Full	11. Merchant
4. Fire Amulet	8. Health Remedy Full	12. Artisan

ITEMS INSIDE HIDDEN CAVE

Chi Remedy 30	Red Keystone x2	Jade
Health Remedy 30 x2	(*Needs exploding	Health Remedy Full
Metallic Vest	bomb or earthbending)	Ancient Chest
Beast Bone	Bison Whistle	

Herbalist

Item	Cost
Health Remedy 30	72
Health Remedy 100	214
Chi Remedy 30	53
Chi Remedy 100	173
Revival Potion	420

Merchant

Item	Cost
Exploding Bomb	50
Freeze Bomb	50
Flash Bomb	50
Bison Whistle	140
Fire Amulet	354
Rock Amulet	354
Water Amulet	354
Wind Amulet	354
Fire Ring	375
Rock Ring	375
Water Ring	375
Wind Ring	375

Artisan

Item	Cost
Bear Robe	720
Sun Robe	720
Dragon Robe	720
Panda Robe	720
Moon Robe	720
Tortoise Robe	558
Bear Belt	558
Sun Belt	558
Dragon Belt	558
Panda Belt	558
Moon Belt	558
Tortoise Belt	558

The Closed Door

1. Speak to the village elder
2. Check out the huge rock on the west beach
3. Return to the village elder for more information
4. Use the stairs in the northeast ruins and defeat eight machines to acquire a Keystone from the backroom
5. Take the Keystone to the village elder
6. Use the Keystone to unlock the door in the huge rock

REWARD: 4000 Skill Points

This quest is available at the start of *Chapter 5*.

The village elder suggests that the party search the many ruins on the island. Talk to the villager southeast of the elder to learn of a big rock to the southwest.

The first time the party walks past the huge rock on the west beach they hear machines and observe what appears to be a sealed entrance to something. Go to the village elder to see if he has any information.

The elder has no idea how to enter, but suggests checking the ruins around the island. Travel to the ruins in the northeast and use the stairs on the east side. Defeat eight earthbending machines in the first chamber to open the interior door. Proceed to the backroom to get a **Keystone** then return to the elder in the village. Don't miss the chest at the top of the backroom, which contains unique **Air Amulet**.

The elder suggests the Keystone opens a passage into a cavern. Head to the huge stone where the whirring machines could be heard and use the Keystone to reveal a hidden entrance.

The Cavern of the Machines

1. Complete 'The Closed Door' and enter the huge rock on the west side of the island
2. Collect the first Red Keystone
3. Douse the fire and collect the second Red Keystone
4. Divert the lava flow
5. Gather the Ancient Chest
6. Return the chest to the village elder
7. Use the Blue Keystone to open the path to the boss
8. Defeat the waterbending machine

REWARD: 6000 Skill Points

This quest begins once the party completes *The Closed Door* and enters the huge rock.

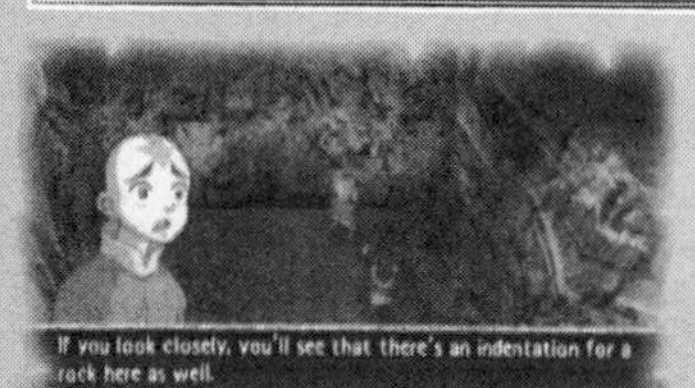

Entering the cave you find two closed passages dead ahead. One has a red indention and the other has a blue indention. Ignore these for now, but keep them in the back of your mind. Begin by searching the west end of the hall.

Take Sokka and Haru into the cave and make sure Sokka has at least two Freeze Bombs. Some of the obstacles require multiple allies.

The far left path is blocked by two huge boulders. Use Sokka's bomb or Haru's earthbending to destroy the boulders then continue west. Follow the hall until it splits. The south fork is blocked by more boulders. Destroy them and use the southern path to find three chests containing a **Chi Remedy 30**, **Health Remedy 30**, and **Health Remedy 30**.

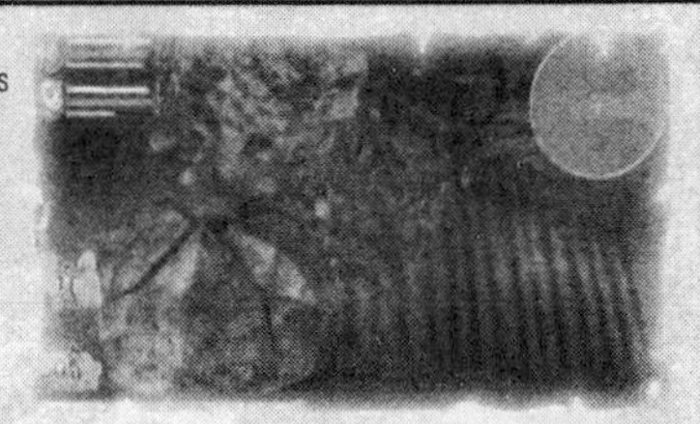

Continue north to a room with four machines. Defeat the machines and the door at the back opens. Follow the hallway to its end where a chest containing a **Red Keystone** sits.

Backtrack to the entrance and head straight east through the hall to a second room with four machines. Defeat all of the machines and the door at the back opens. The path beyond is blocked by a strip of fire that stretches from wall to wall. Use Katara's Bending Move or Sokka's Freeze Bomb to douse the flames.

The path to the west leads to a chest with a unique **Metallic Vest**. Follow the north path to its end. A large boulder is found in the final room. Destroy it with Haru's Bending Move or Sokka's Exploding Bomb to find a chest containing a second **Red Keystone**.

Return to the entrance and use one of the Red Keystones to open the door on the left. Follow the hallway north. Again the party enters a room with four machines. Defeat them to open the door at the back of the room. Continue up the hall and look for a huge boulder ahead. You can bypass the boulder on the left, but a chest containing a **Beast Bone** hides under the boulder.

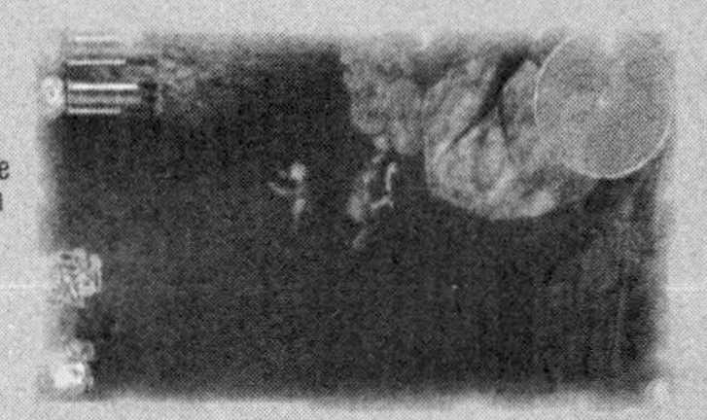

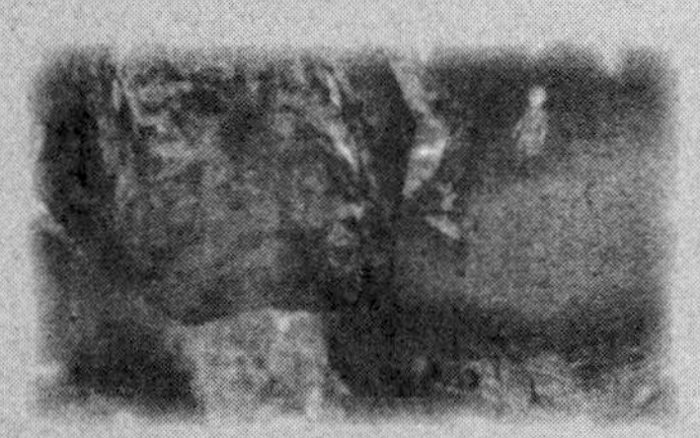

The path to the north is blocked by a lava flow, but there's a clear path to the east. Use the clear path to climb to the top of the rocks. A huge rock sits at the lava's edge. Use Haru's Bending Move to dislodge the rock and divert the lava flow, so the path to the north opens. Unfortunately, the change of direction blocks the path up the small rock formation, so the party must find a different route back.

Clear the chest at the top containing a **Bison Whistle** then follow the path to the east. Once again giant boulders block the path. Destroy them with Haru's earthbending. The path winds around to where there's a chest containing some **Jade** and a giant boulder on the left. Destroy the boulder to find a second chest containing a **Health Remedy Full**.

The path heads south to another room with four machines. Destroy them all to open the door on the south side. Return to the entrance and head back to the north to get to the west side of the lava flow. Use the second Red Keystone to open the door at the end. Collect the **Ancient Chest** and return to the village elder.

The elder opens the chest revealing a **Blue Keystone**. Return to the cavern and use the keystone on the door to the right. Save at the savepoint in the bend then prepare to meet the boss. *Be sure to complete any outstanding quests before proceeding.*

Waterbending Machine

Immediately place the ally in "don't attack" mode then run away from the boss moving clockwise around the oval. Continue running until the party ends up directly behind the boss. They're safe in this position, since the boss never turns around.

Switch the ally back to "attack mode" then start picking away at the enemy whenever it stops near a corner. Ranged moves like Aang's Air Wave work best, but simple combos also cause fair damage. Keep pursuing the boss around the circle and attacking when possible. It doesn't take too long to turn the boss into scrap.

The Artisan's Despair

1. Speak to the artisan's wife in the village
2. Defeat the monkeys on the mountain
3. Return to the artisan's wife

REWARD: 2400 Skill Points

This quest is available at the start of *Chapter 5*. (Can not be started while in the middle of *The Spirit's Grief*.)

Search near the savepoint to find the artisan's wife. She's concerned because some unruly monkeys have settled on the mountain where her husband travels frequently. She asks the party to do something about the menacing primates.

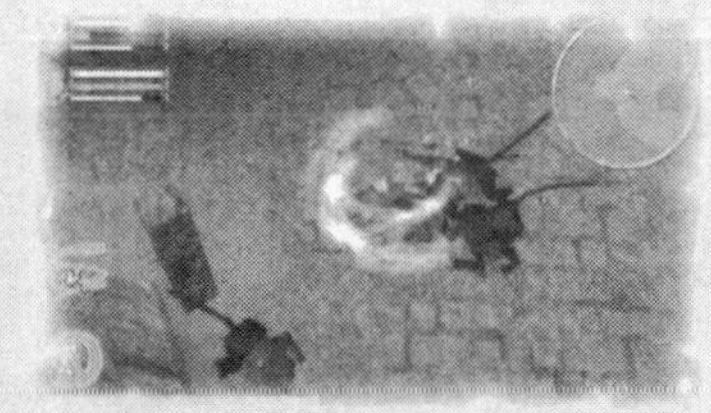

Leave the village and use any path toward the center of the island. The monkeys are dead center in a large clearing. There are ten monkeys in the clearing and a huge purple monkey seems to be the ringleader. This is tricky. The monkeys move around a lot and they're hard to pin down. Katara's Freeze can be helpful and so are most area attack's like Aang's Gale. Haru's quick 3-hit Bending Combo is also effective. Eliminate all of the monkeys then return to the village to claim the reward.

The Spirit's Grief

1. Speak to the turtle spirit
2. Defeat the seven machines on the southeast beach
3. Return to the turtle spirit

REWARD: 2240 Skill Points & Tiger's Eye

This quest is available before accepting of after completing *The Artisan's Despair*.

Climb the mountain in the center of the island and check the clearing north of where the monkey boss (The Artisan's Despair) was located. The party discovers an enormous turtle spirit, which is seeking someone to help rid the island of machines.

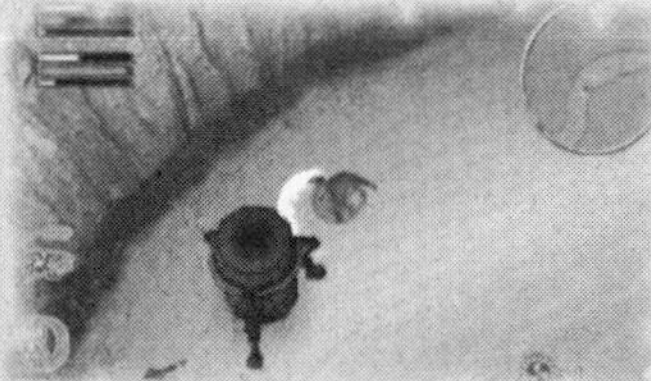

The machines are located in the southeast corner of the island. There are seven machines in all. Defeat them and return to the spirit for the reward.

The Spirit's Remedy

1. Speak to the herbalist
2. Place a Health Remedy 30, Iron Sheet, Jade, Beast Hide, and Beast Bone in the spirit's clearing
3. Leave and return later then claim the contents of the white chest

REWARD: 330 Skill Points

This quest becomes available once the party completes *The Spirit's Grief.*

Talk to the village herbalist after completing *The Spirit's Grief.* She mentions a spirit on the island, obviously pointing to the turtle spirit. She suggests leaving a **Health Remedy 30**, **Iron Sheet**, **Jade**, **Beast Hide**, and a **Beast Bone** in the spirit's clearing. She won't say why, but implies that something marvelous will happen.

Travel to the clearing in the center of the island and check the spot where the turtle spirit was located. Inspect the glowing light and a bag appears assuming you have the necessary items in your inventory. Exit and reenter the clearing and check on the bag. A large white chest has taken its place. Open the chest to find a **Health Remedy Full** and to gain a few Skill Points. This quest can be repeated over and over until the end of the chapter.

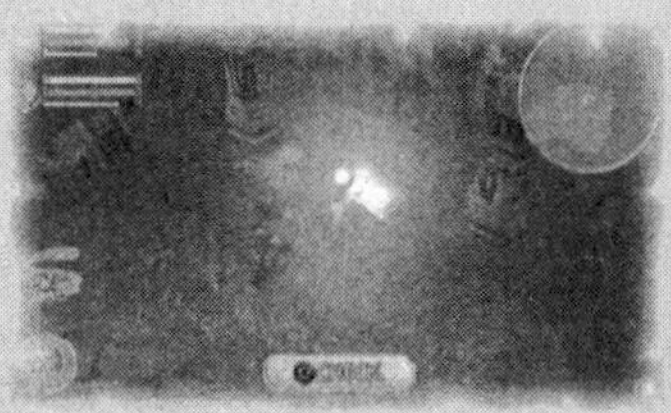

The Bumbling Merchant

1. Talk to the local merchant about his missing wares
2. Gather the missing bags
3. Return them to the merchant

REWARD: 1,560 Skill Points, 390 gold & Silver Sheet

This quest becomes available once the party has discovered the Keystone in the northeast ruins during the *The Closed Door.* Select "Converse" with the merchant to begin this quest.

Visit the village merchant. He lost some of his goods while exploring the island. There are three in all. He asks the party to locate them and return the lost goods.

A bag can be found in the junction within the hills just south of the village.

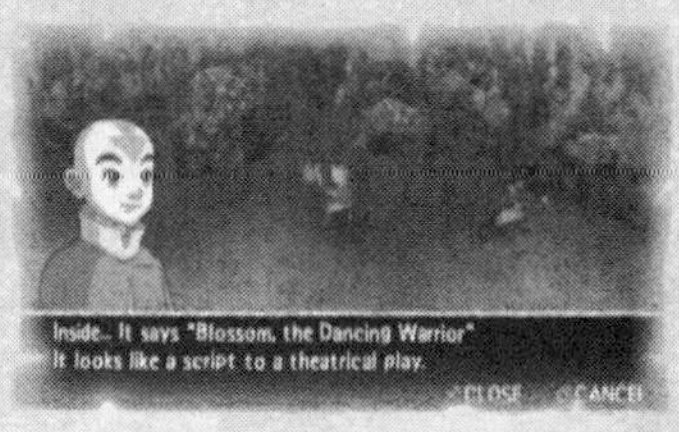

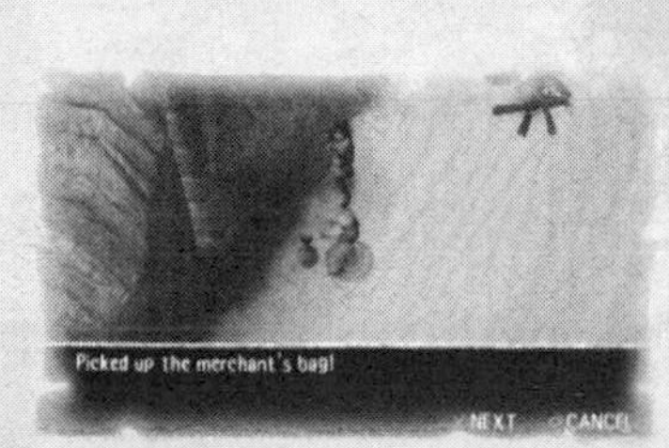

Another bag is located on the far east side of the island along the beach.

The last is found in the southwest corner of the island along the beach.

Gather all three of the bags and return them to the merchant to get the reward.

Chapter 6:

The Air Temple

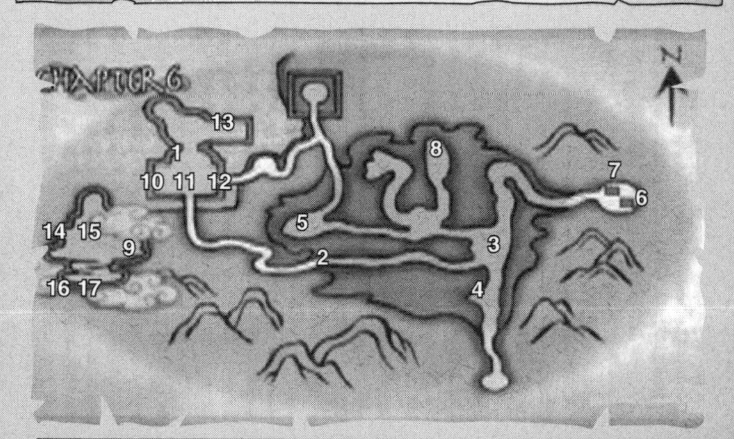

1. Strong Rope
2. Silk Rope
3. Flash Bomb
4. Health Remedy Full
5. Jade
6. Recovery Potion
7. Bison Whistle
8. Chi Remedy 100
9. Hermit's Ring
10. Herbalist
11. Merchant
12. Artisan
13. Silk Cloth
14. Tiger's Eye
15. Flax Cloth
16. Beast Fangs
17. Chi Remedy Full

Herbalist

Item	Cost
Health Remedy 30	78
Health Remedy 100	229
Health Remedy Full	712
Chi Remedy 30	57
Chi Remedy 100	186
Chi Remedy Full	594
Revival Potion	450

Merchant

Item	Cost
Exploding Bomb	54
Freeze Bomb	54
Flash Bomb	54
Bison Whistle	150
Fire Amulet	354
Rock Amulet	354
Water Amulet	354
Wind Amulet	354
Fire Ring	375
Rock Ring	375
Water Ring	375
Wind Ring	375

Artisan

Item	Cost
Bear Vest	1500
Sun Vest	1500
Dragon Vest	1500
Panda Vest	1500
Moon Vest	1500
Tortoise Vest	1500
Bear Belt	558
Sun Belt	558
Dragon Belt	558
Panda Belt	558
Moon Belt	558
Tortoise Belt	558

Defend the Statues

1. Ride Appa to the Air Temple
2. Examine the temple's doors
3. Use the twirling air at the base of the hill to climb the cliffs and reach the back entrance
4. Enter the temple and defeat the firebending machines as they assault the statues
5. Unlock the temple's front door and step outside

REWARD: 4,500 Skill Points

This quest is available at the start of *Chapter 6*.

Aang travels alone in this quest. The temple doors are locked tight when Aang reaches them and there's no way to open them. Check the chest behind the statue at the temple doors to collect a unique **Hermit's Ring**.

Go back down the hill to the base of the stairs and look for a swirling wind to the right. Stand in the wind and use a Bending Move to fly to the cliff above.

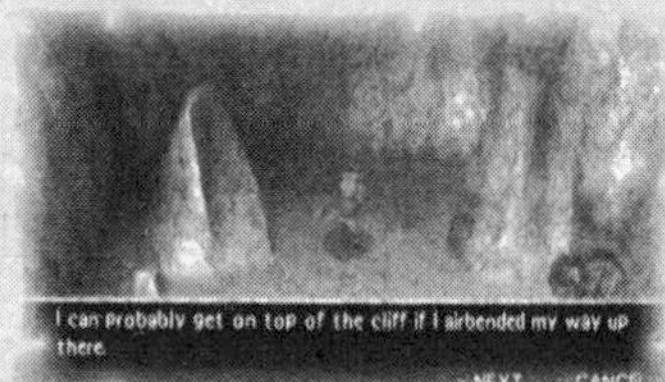

The road ahead consists of a series of cliffs. Use the winds to climb higher and higher. Each cliff is protected by airbending machines, so equip air resistance items. Don't miss the alternate route on the east side of the second cliff. This short hop leads to a chest containing a **Tiger's Eye**. Then there's a similar drop on the west side of the third cliff that leads to a **Flax Cloth**.

Climb the stairs at the top and enter the temple. Follow the center hall to find the statues being assaulted by firebending machines. You must defeat sixteen firebending machines before the statues can be destroyed. The energy bar at the top of the screen represents the health of the four statues. Pay close attention to the actions of each machine. Focus on those that are attacking the statues first, and then destroy the machines that are focusing on Aang. The basic Bending Combo works very well, but don't pass up opportunities to hit multiple enemies with Gale.

Use the west hallway to reach the front door. Don't miss the two chests (**Beast Fangs** & **Chi Remedy Full**) against the right wall before the exit. Defeat the earthbending machines at the front door and leave the temple to return to the others. This initiates the 'Investigation' quest.

Investigation

1. Speak to the villager about the machine at the building site
2. Travel to the building site in the east
3. Direct Aang to the building site also
4. Defeat the earthshaker

REWARD: 7,500 Skill Points

This quest is triggered at the end of the *Defend the Statues* quest.

Enter the village and seek a man in the northeast corner. He mentions a strange machine attacking the building site. The party might as well investigate while waiting for Aang to return.

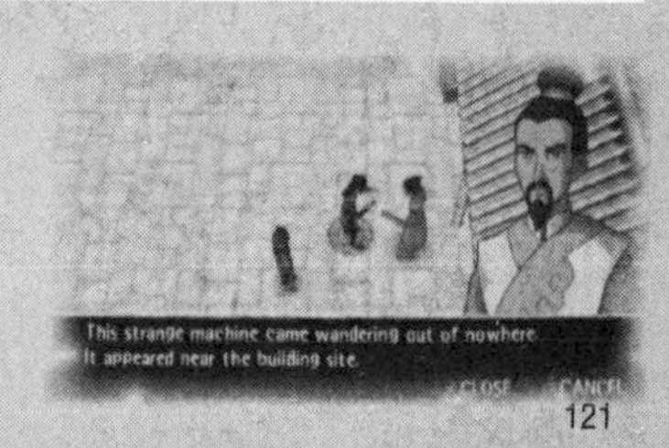

Run to the building site in the northeast corner of the map. The focus switches back to Aang upon the party's arrival. Aang must follow the others to the building site. Save outside the building site and take some time to finish any lingering quests before proceeding.

Earthshaker

Stay to the machine's side throughout the battle and attack its treads. Its attacks are always directed to the front or back, so the side is the only safe zone. Aang's Air Wave also works very well by allowing him to bombard the boss from a safe distance.

Beware of its short drilling action that stuns Aang. Prepare to run as soon as the stun effect wears off. You can often get away and avoid damage in the nick of time. Also look out for its tunneling attack, which causes the boss to disappear temporarily. Scan the ground for signs of the boss's location and get away fast, or Aang suffers a hit when the boss pops out of the ground.

Reopen the Road

1. Talk to the villager near the savepoint about the earthquakes
2. Travel the main road from the village to the building site in the east and clear the path
3. Report back to the man in the village

REWARD: 1,330 Skill Points & 580 gold

This quest is available at the start of *Chapter 6*.

Speak to the man next to the savepoint in the main village. Earthquakes have littered the road with rocks and branches blocking access to the new residential area to the east. Help clear the road.

There are three obstructions between the main village and the residential area. Follow the east road from the village and head south at the intersection. Then continue east through the large clearing with a statue to a second large clearing with four exits. Go north from here and follow the path to the residential area. The blockages are easily destroyed with any attack. Return to the village and report back to the man to earn the reward when the path is clear (and the journal updates).

The Broken Windmill

1. Talk to the man at the base of the windmill inside of the village
2. Collect a piece of Quality Bamboo from the woods
3. Mine for Crystal in the south
4. Have the artisan craft a new Air String
5. Repair the broken windmill

REWARD: 2480 Skill Points & 310 gold

This quest is available from the beginning of *Chapter 6*.

Look for a broken windmill at the northwest end of the main village. A man standing at its base mentions that only an Airbender can fix the windmil!. The repairs require Quality Bamboo, Crystal, and Air String.

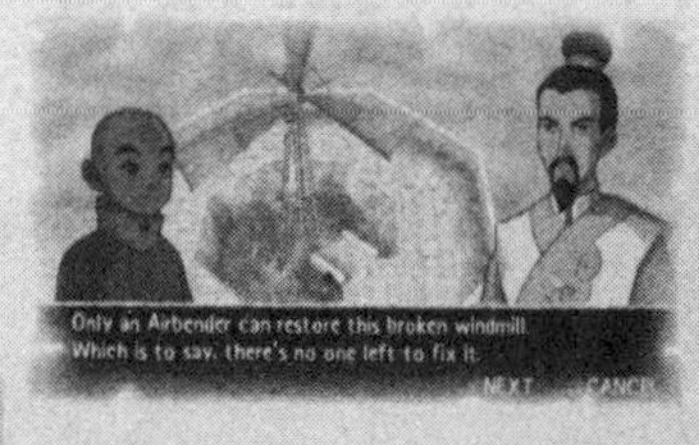

Bamboo can be found just about anywhere near the village, but only one spot delivers **Quality Bamboo**. There are two clearings on the north side of the map. Search the west clearing to find a lone bamboo tree. Cut it down with Aang's airbending to find the rare piece of Quality Bamboo.

The **Crystal** is found in the wild. Explore the clearing in the southeast section of the map. There's a huge boulder in the center and a bunch of smaller rocks against the northeast wall. Ignore the boulder and smash the smaller rocks to reveal a Crystal set into the wall.

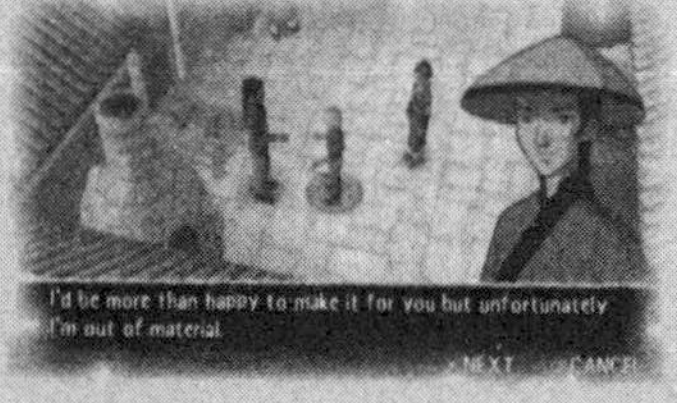

Select "Converse" and speak to the local artisan about the **Air String**. The artisan can create it, but only if you bring him three **Silk Ropes** and a piece of **Jade**. Fight creatures in the wild to find the necessary items then return them to the artisan to get the Air String.

Gather all of the parts then return to the broken windmill. Inspect the windmill's base to place the parts and then use a Bending Move to get it moving again.

Air String Revisited

1. Speak to the lady wandering around the north end of the village
2. Give her three Silk Ropes and a Jade

REWARD: 290 Skill Points & 180 gold

This quest becomes available once you complete *The Broken Windmill* quest.

Look for a lady wandering back and forth just south of the now functional windmill. She asks for three **Silk Ropes** and a **Jade** so she can have an **Air String** made. Give her the items to gain a small reward. This quest is repeatable.

Gathering Iron Sheets

1. Talk to the woman in the gazebo
2. Present the woman with two Iron Sheets

REWARD: 120 Skill Points & 250 gold

This quest is available from the beginning of *Chapter 6*.

Speak to the woman at the gazebo in the north half of the main village. Her husband needs building materials for the new residential section. Bring her two **Iron Sheets**, dropped by local creatures, to get a reward. This quest can be repeated until Chapter 6 ends.

The Spirit in the Garden

1. Speak to the old man in the village
2. Venture into the garden to the north of the village

REWARD: 1,110 Skill Points & Gyatso's Amulet

This quest becomes available upon Aang's return from the Air Temple during the 'Investigation' quest if 'The Broken Windmill' has also been completed.

Talk to the old man east of the village savepoint. He mentions a spirit has appeared in the garden. The garden is northeast of the village. Travel to the garden and speak to the tiger spirit. Aang is rewarded with a unique Gyatso's Amulet.

CHAPTER 7: THE FORTRESS

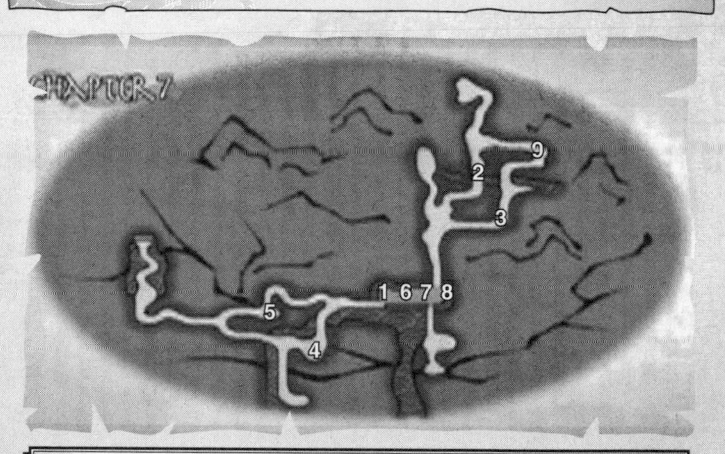

1. Exploding Bomb
2. Bison Whistle
3. Revival Potion
4. Beast Fangs
5. Beast Fur
6. Herbalist
7. Merchant
8. Artisan
9. Quest Item: Dictionary

ITEMS INSIDE EARTH TEMPLE

Moon Dogi (*Needs an exploding bomb or earthbending)
Jaeger Ring
Recovery Potion

ITEMS INSIDE HIDDEN TEMPLE

Super Crystal
Master's Dogi
Recovery Potion
Omniscient Ring (*Needs an exploding bomb or earthbending)

Herbalist

Item	Cost
Health Remedy 30	83
Health Remedy 100	244
Health Remedy Full	760
Chi Remedy 30	60
Chi Remedy 100	198
Chi Remedy Full	633
Recovery Potion*	1952
Revival Potion	480

*Only available after completing 'The Herbalist's Dictionary' quest

Merchant

Item	Cost
Exploding Bomb	57
Freeze Bomb	57
Flash Bomb	57
Bison Whistle	160
Fire Amulet	354
Rock Amulet	354
Water Amulet	354
Wind Amulet	354
Fire Ring	375
Rock Ring	375
Water Ring	375
Wind Ring	375

Artisan

Item	Cost
Dogi Armor	3000
Bear Vest	1500
Sun Vest	1500
Dragon Vest	1500
Panda Vest	1500
Moon Vest	1500
Tortoise Vest	1500
Bear Belt	558
Sun Belt	558
Dragon Belt	558
Panda Belt	558
Moon Belt	558
Tortoise Belt	558

The Dogi become available only after completing the Super Crystal quest.

Rescuing Friends

1. Speak to the villager wandering around the east side of town
2. Hike to the distant earth temple
3. Liberate Sokka
4. Rescue Katara
6. Set Haru free

REWARD: 10,000 Skill Points

Aang must find his missing friends, but first he needs some clues. Talk to the villager wandering around on the east side of town. He mentions a girl that left the village some time ago and headed west. That might be the culprit!

Enter the earth temple at the west edge of the map. There are four paths from the entrance. One is blocked by huge boulders and another by a large door. Follow the west path first. It leads to a room with four machines and a locked door at the back. Destroy the machines to open the door. The room beyond is where Sokka is being held captive. Destroy the pillar under his cage to free him.

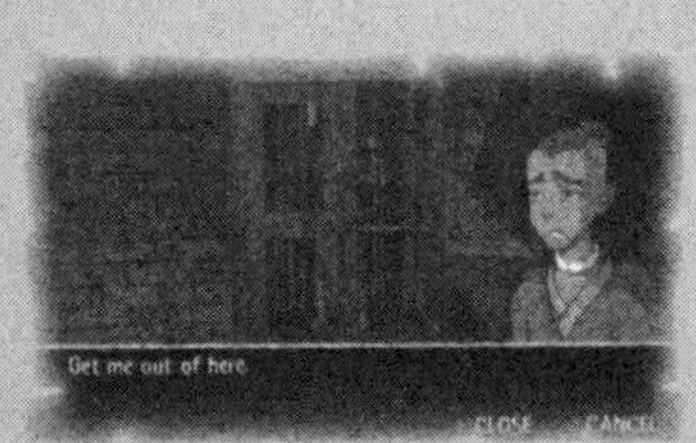

Return to the entrance and use Sokka's Exploding Bomb to clear the huge boulders blocking the second hallway. Check the chest behind the boulder to find a **Moon Dogi** then follow the hall north.

Backtrack to the entrance again. Take the far east path this time. Defeat the machines on the bridge to open the east door then enter the hall to find Haru. Use Haru's Cell Key to set him free. Check the chest in Haru's cell to find a unique **Jaeger Ring**.

Destroy the machines protecting the door that follows. Katara is in the room behind the door. She presents Aang with **Haru's Cell Key**.

The World of Machines

1. Open the southwest door in the earth temple using Haru's earthbending
2. Defeat the waterbending machine
3. Conquer the Avatar machine

REWARD: None (End Game Cinema & Credits)

This quest begins when 'Rescuing Friends' is completed.

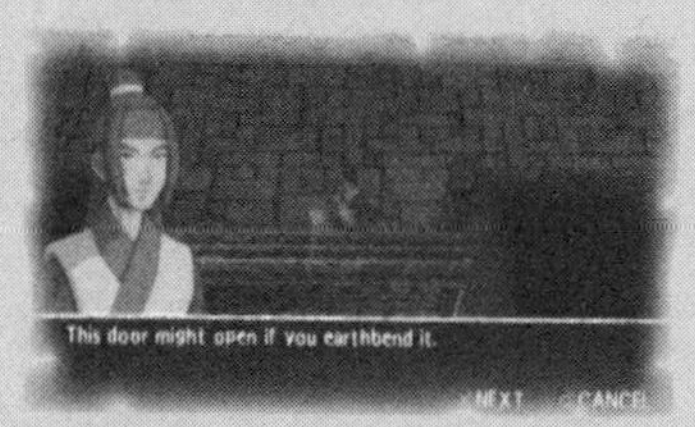

Use Haru's Bending Move to open the southeast door in the earth temple then proceed down the hall. Defeat the enemies ahead to open the door to the south. Don't miss the chest south of the door at the lava's edge that contains a **Recovery Potion**. Go around the lava and use the save point before the next room.

Waterbending Machine II

This battle is exactly the same as the fight with the first waterbending machine. Immediately set your ally to "don't attack" mode and run away from the boss moving clockwise around the oval. Keep running until the party is directly behind the boss. They can stay behind the enemy and remain safe for the duration of the battle.

Switch the ally back to "attack mode" and begin attacking the boss whenever it stops around a corner. Ranged attacks are fairly effective, but Bending Combos can also be very effective if used at the right moments. Continue chasing the boss around the oval and attacking until it collapses.

This is a good time to go back to the save point and save once more. Take a moment to return to town and complete any outstanding quests. The end of the game is nearing. Proceed down the stairs at the east end of the oval when ready to face the final boss.

Avatar Machine

There are two parts to this battle. The first part involves two characters and the boss. The enemy uses a simple pattern of a physical attack followed by an earthbending or firebending move.

Physical attacks can be dodged by giving the machine plenty of room. Get to the outside of the arena and its blades should miss when it spins around. You can then charge in and punch it a couple of times or use a quick bending move before the machine initiates a bending move of its own.

The large light on the front of the machine glows yellow or red depending on the move it's about to use. Red indicates the boss is about to use a firebending move, which is a huge jet of flame that chases the party around the room. Run in large loops while staying to the outside to avoid the attack

The yellow light indicates the boss is about to use an earthbending move. It slams the ground creating four large boulders that attempt to converge on their target. This move can actually damage the boss with a little trickery. When you see the yellow signal quickly run to a spot where the boss's left or right side is against the nearest wall. Wait for the boss to track your character and pause. Quickly dodge the slam that creates the boulders and run behind the machine. When the boulders appear they try to crush your character and instead ram into the boss causing around 200 points of damage.

When the boss's is defeated the second half of the battle begins. This time it's just Aang and the boss going one-on-one. The boss uses the same pattern as before, but it gains a waterbending move and an airbending move. Aang also becomes invincible for two minutes. You must defeat the boss within the time limit, or Aang is sent back the save point and the battle starts over from the mid point.

The airbending and firebending moves are the unchanged and can be dodged in the same manner. The waterbending move is preceded by a blue light. The boss spins around and creates a wall of water to its front then charges across the room. Run a circle around the boss to trigger the attack and quickly duck behind it as it charges. Aang can usually strike it a couple of times as it passes.

A green light signals an airbending attack is on the way. This is a simple cone of air shot in front of the boss. Run past its front to trigger the attack and keep moving to the boss's side. Aang can easily hit the boss several times before the attack finishes and the enemy recovers.

Remember to dodge the physical attacks between bending moves and take advantage of the boss's weak points during the airbending, waterbending, and earthbending attacks. Aang is super powered and quick as lightning, so two minutes is plenty of time. Don't forget his super move too. It can make all the difference when time is running short.

Take Back the Forest

1. Talk to the villager concerned about the machines to the north
2. Defeat the huge firebending machine in the northern clearing
3. Report back to the villager

REWARD: 2,810 Skill Points & Multi-color Braid

This quest is available from the beginning of *Chapter 7*.

Speak to the man in the west end of the village about the machines ruining the forest to the north. Someone must eliminate them before the forest is completely ruined.

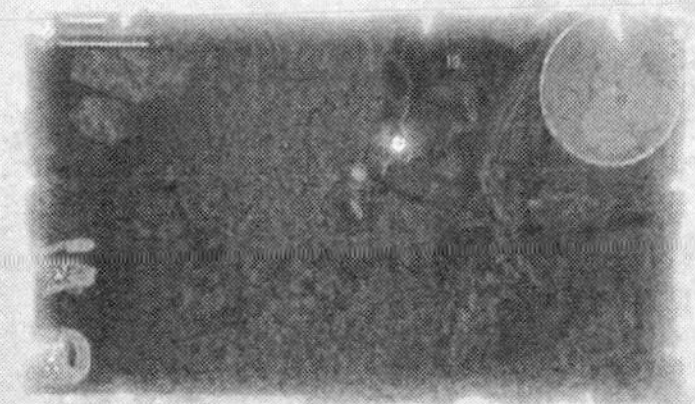

Enter the forest north of the village and make a beeline for the northern clearing. Aang discovers an enormous firebending machine upon arriving. Deal with it as you would other firebending machines. Aang's Bending Combo works very well and so does Gale. The machines abandon this section of the forest once the huge machine is eliminated. Return to the village and notify the man of your success.

Super Crystal

1. Speak to the artisan after finishing 'Take Back the Forest'
2. Enter the earth temple and defeat the waterbending boss
3. Check the bookshelves on the south side of the loop
4. Enter the cavern southwest of the village
5. Proceed to the second section of the cavern and go right, up, up, left, left, up, right
6. Collect the Super Crystal
7. Return the crystal to the artisan

REWARD: 3,550 Skill Points (1,500 Skill Points & 500 gold on later completions)

This quest becomes available once 'Take Back the Forest' has been completed.

The local artisan's business is booming now that the machines are gone. He's so happy he wants to create something special, but he needs a special ore to do so.

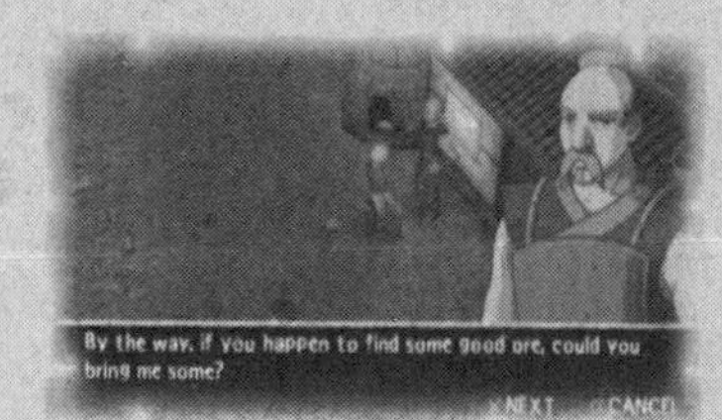

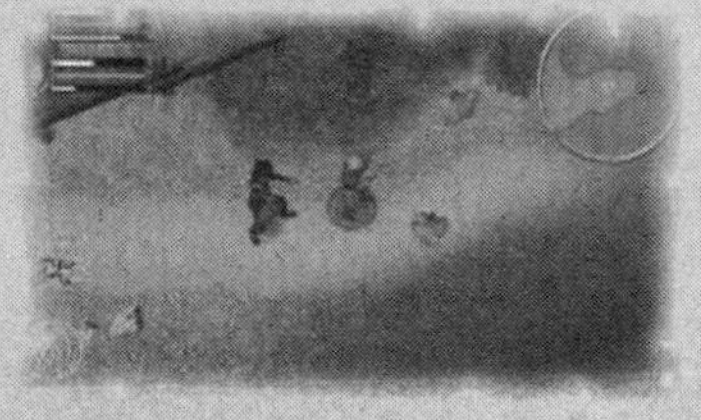

The ore is located in the sealed cave on the south end of the map. It only opens when the 'Sealed Up' quest is initiated during 'The World of Machines'. Proceed to the second section of the sealed cave, which is a maze where every section looks exactly the same. Go right, up, up, left, left, up and right. Normally you'd go up instead or right at the end, since a gazelle enters from the top, but look closely for some chickens on the right side of the screen. This marks the secret area where the ore is located.

The path leads to a dead end with the **Super Crystal** and a **Master's Dogi**.

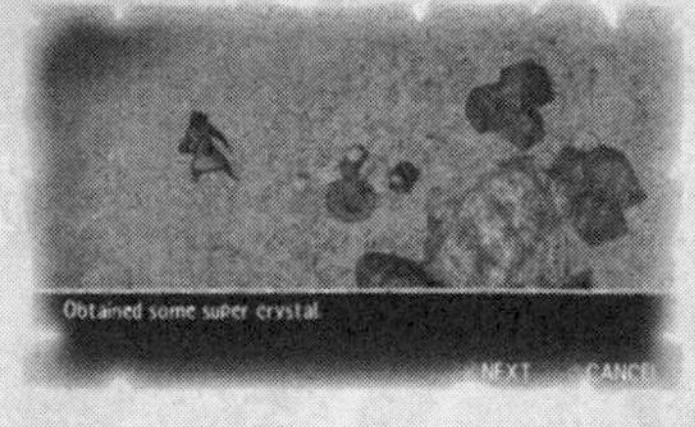

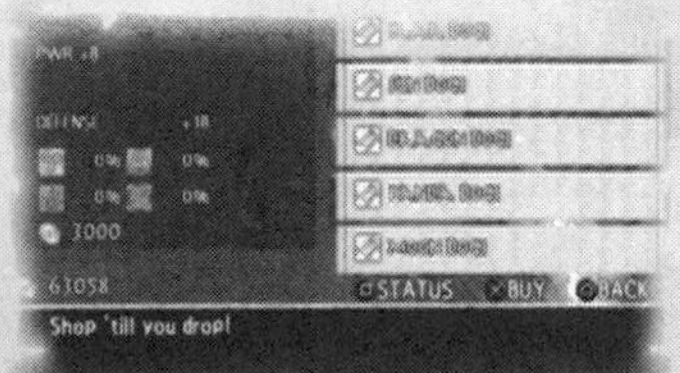

Return the Super Crystal to the artisan. He's thrilled and as a reward makes the extremely powerful Dogi armor available for purchase. This quest can be repeated until the end of Chapter 7.

The Herbalist's Dictionary

1. Talk to the herbalist in the village
2. Find and gather her lost dictionary
3. Return the book to the herbalist

REWARD: 2,200 Skill Points

This quest is available at the beginning of *Chapter 7*.

Speak with the village herbalist. She was picking herbs in the forest to the north when some machines began to chase her. She dropped a precious dictionary while fleeing. Retrieve the lost book for her.

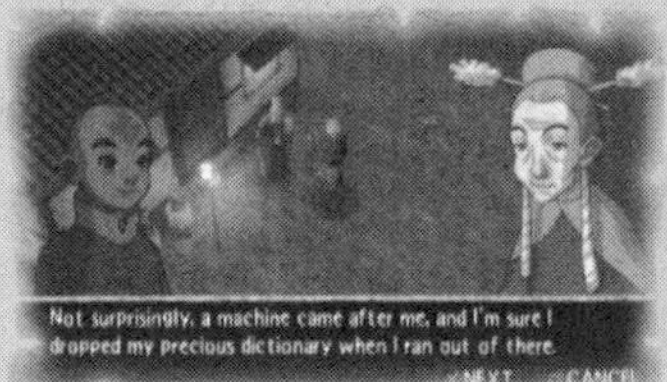

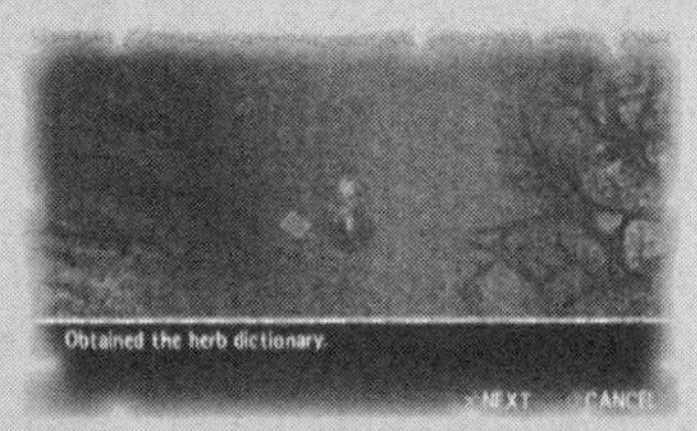

Enter the forest to the north and start searching. The **Herb Dictionary** is located on the ground in the far northeast corner of the map. It's a small grayish book, so it's fairly easy to walk past without noticing.

Bring the book back to the herbalist. She's so pleased that she offers to sell Aang a new item: **Recovery Potion**.

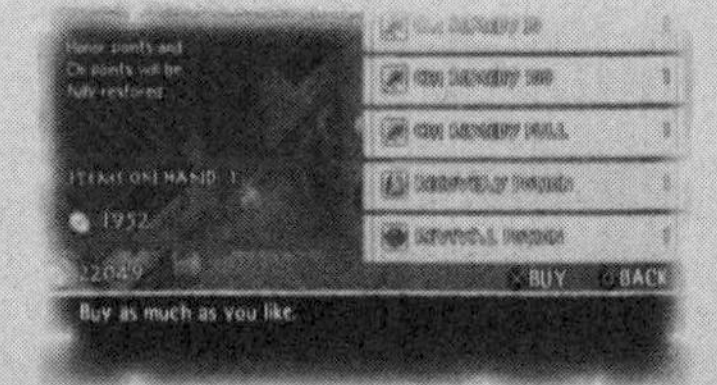

Health Food

1. Talk to the starving woman on the west side of the village
2. Get a Health Remedy 30 and bring it back to her

REWARD: 360 Skill Points

This quest is available from the start of *Chapter 7*

Look for a woman near the savepoint on the west end of the village. She's starving and asks for a Health Remedy 30. Give one to her to receive a small reward. The woman then hints about the cavern to the southwest, which is part of the 'Sealed Up' quest. This quest can be repeated.

Sealed Up

1. Defeat the waterbending boss in the earth temple during 'The World of Machines'
2. Search the bookshelves on the south side of the room
3. Find the sealed cavern entrance southwest of the village
4. Defeat the four giant machines to the west to clear the boulders blocking the path to the north
5. Get through the maze by going right, up, up, left, left, up and up
6. Defeat all of the enemies in five rooms within five minutes
7. Defeat the super earthshaker

REWARD: 4,000 Skill Points, 2,000 gold & White Dogi

This quest is available after defeating the waterbending boss during 'The World of Machines' quest.

Search the bookshelves on the south side of the room where you fight the waterbending boss during 'The World of Machines' quest. A book tells of a failed experiment locked in a southern cave. Return to the village and go to the clearing southwest of town to find a cavern blocked by stone doors.

Take Sokka or Haru along for this quest and plenty of healing items. It may be tempting to take Katara along for free healing, but you'll miss out on a valuable treasure near the end if you do so. She can always come along if you choose to run this quest again later.

The first section of the cavern consists of four paths to the west and one to the north. The northern path is blocked by two solid boulders that can't be destroyed with earthbending or bombs.

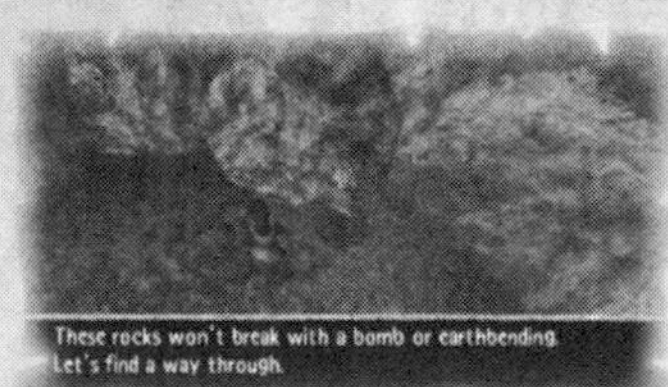

Each of the paths to the west leads to a huge machine (one fire bending, one water bending, and two earth bending). Defeat the four machines and the boulders vanish allowing you to explore deeper into the cavern. The machines sometimes drop '4 Element' gear when they're defeated. These are some of the best armor and accessories in the game. Replay this quest several times to try and collect all four pieces.

The northern path leads to a maze. Each section looks exactly like the last, but there's one specific way to get from the start to the third section of the cavern. Finding the correct route is fairly simple when you know what to do. Each section has four enemies in it. Defeat the enemies and a gazelle runs onto the screen. Pay attention. The direction from which the gazelle enters the screen is the way you should go next. Any wrong turn leads to a group of four machines and you'll need to reset the maze by going down and returning to the start The correct path is right, up, up, left, left, up and up.

There's a secret at the end of the maze. When the last enemy is defeated in the final part a gazelle runs in from the top of the screen, but some chickens enter from the right. The chickens are an indication of a dead end path that leads to the **Super Crystal** for the 'Super Crystal' quest and a unique **Master's Dogi**.

The third section consists of one long hallway made up of several rooms. There are four enemies in each of the five rooms past the start. You must clear each room of enemies and make it to the end in five minutes. Use a super move in the first room and the fifth room and it shouldn't prove to be too difficult.

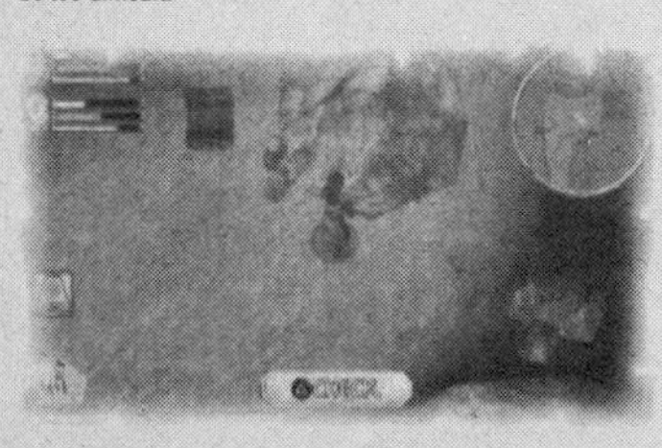

The final section is simpler. There's a path up and a path to the right. The path up leads to a chest containing a **Recovery Potion**. There's also a huge boulder in the room. Destroy it with Haru's earthbending or Sokka's Exploding Bomb to uncover a second chest containing a rare **Omniscient Ring**. The path to the right leads through some rocks and to the boss.

Earthshaker II

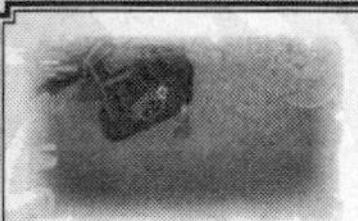

This battle is exactly like the previous battle except that the boss is stronger and you have the assistance of a second character. Stay to the machine's side again and attack its treads. The boss's attacks are always aimed forward or backward, so the side is the only safe area.

It can still stun the party with its drill. When that occurs, tap ⊗ rapidly and get ready to run. You can usually escape before being hit by another attack. Watch out for its underground drilling move again. Look for a dust cloud and avoid that area until the machine reappears.

NICKELODEON AVATAR: THE LAST AIRBENDER

Game Boy® Advance & Nintendo DS™ Versions

Game Boy Advance

North Pole Village

Once Aang is done meditating, head for the village. Be sure to use the **Save Stone** here, then head right. Katara says the Elder of the village wants to talk, so keep going right. He wants you to find Hiryu, the missing Waterbender. Head up from the village to enter the mountain area.

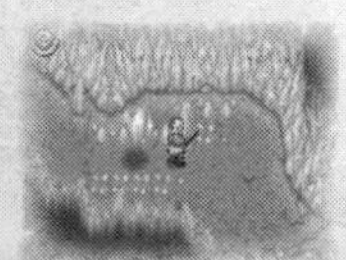

Push or pull the crate in the small area to open the path ahead. Inside the cave, watch the shadows for falling ice! Wait for a chance to sneak past.

There's a crate blocking the stairs. Move to the small swirl symbol on the ground and press against the wall until Aang floats up. Now you can pull the crate out of the way!

You can use Aang's Staff to smash the small pots lying around, but save them for now. Some hold **Herbs** that restore your characters' health if you pick them up and you'll need those after you clear out the enemy armadillo-wolves. Hit one, avoid its lunge, then hit it again to clear them all out. Hiryu's **Water Pouch** is just below! Grab it and take it to the Elder.

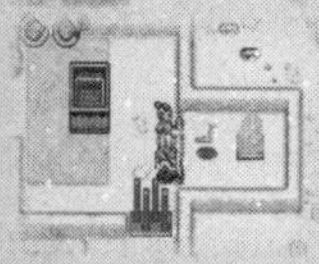

Sokka is in the training area behind the Elder. Use Aang's High Jump to reach the crystal and hit it with his Staff to open the gate. Once Sokka joins you, not only can you push the water-filled crates, but you can switch to him with Right Button. Use Sokka's Boomerang to hit the switches Aang can't reach.

Fire Nation soldiers have taken Katara! Their boat gets away, but Aang won't give up! Begin the trek to Appa. The path is blocked by a giant machine!

Boss: Fire Nation Climber Machine

This boss hurls fireballs from its main body. The attack is simple to avoid, but stay on your toes. The only way to hurt the boss is to first use Sokka's Boomerang to strike each of its arms, knocking it loose from the wall. Once the boss is on the floor and stunned, use Aang to hit its main body repeatedly. Once it gets back up, repeat the process until it's done for!

Sokka picks up his **Club** after the fight, giving him a strong attack that heavily damages enemies, but is very slow to swing. Climb up Appa's back to chase Prince Zuko's thugs!

Fire Nation Prison Island

Right away, Sokka's Club is useful, since it can clear out the large bushes that block your path. Use teamwork to push the water-filled crates, and Sokka's Club to remove the bushes that block their paths.

When you see the Fire Nation ship, some Fire Nation Swordsmen close in. It only takes a few swings of Aang's Staff to beat them. Plus, each blow stuns them for a second! The Yu Yan Archers are a little stronger and can hit you from a distance. Sokka's Boomerang attack can stun the soldiers for a few seconds, leaving them vulnerable.

The next area has a series of pressure switches to open the gates. Push the empty crates onto wood switches, and the water crates onto stone switches. You can't move the spiky box yet, so go up into the village.

Explore the village, then head right into the woods. Sokka needs to pull the lever so Aang can advance and push the crate onto the switch. Move on, taking out some more Fire Nation troops, and use Aang's High Jump to hit both crystal switches.

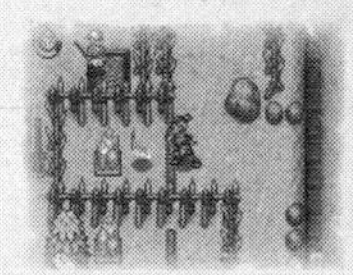

After this, Aang and Sokka need to split up once Sokka pulls the lever above. Press the Select Button to switch back and forth between the two, using their abilities to open the paths for each other. Sokka needs to take out an Archer by himself along the way. Once the Archer is down, get Aang to the wooden switch below where Sokka faced the Archer and reunite the two. The path loops back to the entrance, but there's also a chest with the **Air Blast Scroll** in it! Press the A Button with Aang to hurl a gust of air that moves objects and stuns enemies.

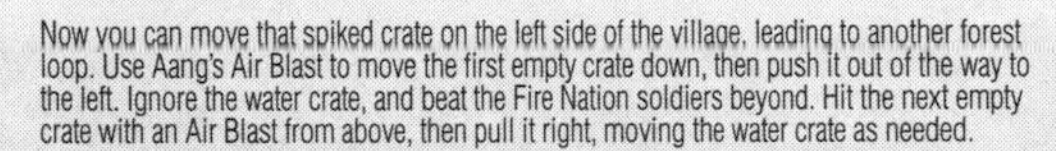

Now you can move that spiked crate on the left side of the village, leading to another forest loop. Use Aang's Air Blast to move the first empty crate down, then push it out of the way to the left. Ignore the water crate, and beat the Fire Nation soldiers beyond. Hit the next empty crate with an Air Blast from above, then pull it right, moving the water crate as needed.

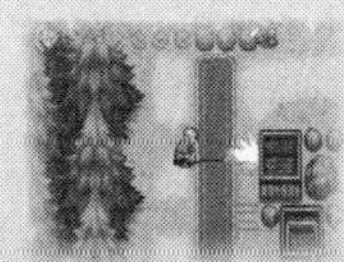

Use Aang's High Jump when you reach the swirl marks, and hit the empty crates with Air Blasts from the other side of the creek to open the path. The Spear Soldiers ahead are the strongest soldiers you've faced yet, but keep at them. Use Sokka's Club to clear a bush to the left and pick up the **Health Potion** you saw earlier; it increases Aang's health bar.

Fight your way right through a bunch of Fire Nation soldiers, and you reach a chest with some **Soldier Uniforms**. Now you can sneak into the prison and rescue Katara! Head up from the village and use the uniforms to enter the Prison. Use the Save Stone in the courtyard before you enter the main building, though!

The inside is crawling with guards. Be very careful, since there's little chance to heal inside! The area looks more complicated than it is, since most side-paths are blocked off, forcing you to go one way. ***Remember that gold door on the right for later!*** On the second floor, you have to clear out a room full of guard to open the gate to a crystal switch. There are several **Herbs** in pots on the other side of the gate, but only use what you need.

You come back to this large flame in a bit, but for now go left and enter the door. Have Sokka pull the lever, then send Aang to stand on the wood panel. Switch back to Sokka and use his Boomerang on the crystal switch. Send Aang up and move the empty crate there up with an Air Blast from below. Then return Aang to Sokka and move on through the now-open gate to the lower level.

Take the path under the grate to an area with three crystal switches. Once you hit one with Sokka's Boomerang, you only have three seconds to hit the other two! If all three are lit, the gate ahead opens. If you didn't Air Blast the crate earlier, you have to go back and do it to move forward. There are several guards, so move slowly and take them on one at a time. Take the **Silver Key** in the chest once the guards are down and go back to the previous area.

Open the silver door to the right of the flame to rescue Katara, who joins you on your new mission to free the Maker! Use her Water Whip to clear out the flames and face a Sub-Boss! The Firebender here can create a large explosion around him after a short hop-kick, or shoot fireballs in three directions. Stay back and wait for him to use a move, sidestep it, rush in and attack once or twice with Aang, then retreat and repeat. Remember that if anyone in your party runs out of life energy, it's game over! When the Firebender falls, he gives up the **Gold Key**. Run back and get the Herbs in the area to heal up, and open the gold door to the right of Katara's cell. There's another **Health Potion** there, and this time Sokka gets the boost! Go forward and use the Save Stone before taking on the Boss.

Boss: Fire Nation Bomber

Like the Machine previously, you cannot hurt this boss until he is stunned. Move very carefully to avoid his small bombs, lure them to one corner then as soon as he throws one, run to the other. Stay away from the wall so Sokka and Katara stick close to Aang, or they'll get left behind and caught in the blast!

He eventually throws a large bomb to the center of the room. It takes a while to explode and has a wide blast, so don't let it! Use Aang's Air Blast to push it into the Bomber to stun him. Then leap in and attack until he gets up! Just remember to stay back when you first Air Blast the bomb, or you'll be caught in the blast too!

As soon as he gets up, run away! He starts spinning and moving to the other side of the room. Like the bombs, try to lure him to one corner, since he can't move up or down as fast. He throws more bombs the weaker he gets. However, you can avoid them easily if you're careful. It should only take three large bombs to bring him down.

Once the Bomber is down, go right and hit the crystal to open the cell door. Enter the Maker's cell and open the chest to get the **Heal Scroll**, which lets Katara heal the entire party when they all have full Chi—very handy! Head down then left, and use all three to push the full water crate onto the metal plate switch.

Use Katara's Water Shift ability to move the water out of the spiked crate and into one of the empty ones to the side. Then use Aang's Air Blast to move the crate. Below, use Water Shift again to move the water from one crate to the other, then push them into the pressure plates to open the gate.

Once you're through the gate, go right all the way and open the gold door there to get another **Health Potion** to improve Katara's health bar! Head back left and go up the steps to each a room full of small pots, each with an **Herb** in it. Head out the door and jump down the ledges, heading left into the woods.

Use Katara's Water Shift on the river to put some more water into the water crate above, then push it onto the pressure plate. The gate opens and reveals a chest with the **Ice Bridge Scroll**. Use this new ability to continue heading left by crossing the streams. Remember that you can't form an Ice Bridge over whirlpools!

There's another Firebender as you move left, but he's no different from the previous one. Clear him out, and you're one Ice Bridge away from Appa and your next destination, Omashu!

Earth Kingdom City Omashu

Follow the path to the palace and the throne room of King Bumi, who lets you into the Royal Library. Leave the palace and go right. However, you find that you need an Earthbender - like Haru - to enter. A guard moves, giving you access to a ladder to the underground passages.

In the passage, you eventually come across a half-full ditch of water. Push the water-filled crate close to the ditch, then use Water Shift to pull water from the crate and fill the ditch, letting Katara use Ice Bridge. The next ditch needs two crates' worth of water to fill, so pull the lower one close! There's a Save Stone in the next area, be sure to use it. Push as far up and left as possible and use Ice Bridge to enter the door just above.

The next section is tricky. Use Water Shift to empty the right crate, dumping the water into the creek. Then use Air Blast to push the now-empty crate right, then up onto the pressure plate. Don't hit the left crystal switch yet! Use Water Shift again to empty one of the spiked crates to the left, then use Air Blast to open the path. Now use Boomerang to hit the crystal from as far as possible and run for it as soon as the crystal lights up! You only have 12 seconds to get up and through the gate before it closes!

Back up on the surface, you need to run along the paths while avoiding the mail crates. Slip in immediately behind them and leap off as soon as possible. The crates do a little damage, but it can build up! Thankfully, the conveyors don't affect your movement.

Back underground, use Ice Bridge and cross the open gate to the left. Head up and use Ice Bridge again near the crystal switch, then use Boomerang to activate it. Air Blast pushes the spiked crate out of your way so you can get back down. Head up and open the chest for an **Ice Bridge Upgrade**, which lets you make Bridges three squares long! Use it to head down.

You're returned to the Save Stone, so head left from there, skip the ladder up, and keep going left, then down. Push the crate onto the wooden plate to advance. Head along until you reach an area with a crystal switch. Use Boomerang to hit the switch, then head down and left to find another switch. Boomerang it, then use Water Shift to empty the water crate to the right. Air Blast it from the left, then send Aang up the now-open path to claim the **Air Vent Scroll**.

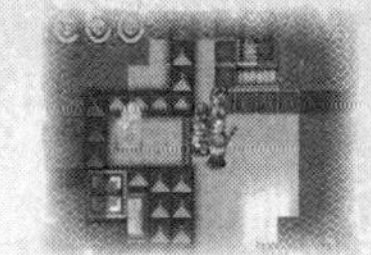

Go back to the right where the water crate blocks your path. Push the closed crate onto a vent, then use Air Vent on the other one to flip the crate over! Now pull it close to the water crate, use Water Shift, then move the newly-filled crate as far down and to the left as possible. Water Shift the water from that crate to the empty one that is now partially on the stone pressure switch to the left to open a gate in the far upper-left! Continue using Ice Bridge to make your way through the gate to pick up a **Health Potion**!

Drop off the upper ledge where you picked up the Potion and head down. Push the crate there onto a vent and flip it with Air Vent, then push it onto the pressure plate to the right. Water Shift some water into it to open the gate down-right.

Use Ice Bridge to go as far up and to the right as possible, then do it again so that Sokka can hit the crystal with his

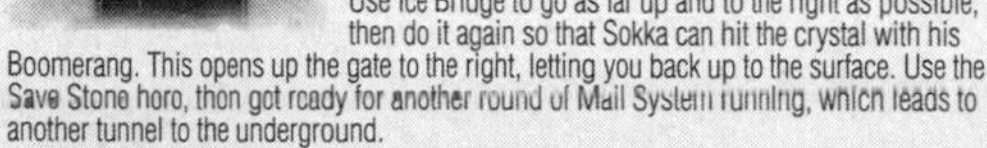

Boomerang. This opens up the gate to the right, letting you back up to the surface. Use the Save Stone here, then get ready for another round of Mail System running, which leads to another tunnel to the underground.

Underground, Katara reveals the ability to walk through water fountains using the A Button. Have her trip the pressure plate, then use the Select Button to switch to Aang and Sokka. Have them move up and use Air Blast to push the spiked crate as far down and left as possible, then to the right with a single shot so it's lined up with the wooden plate. Air Blast it up onto the plate, then have them move up and stand on the plate above. Switch back to Katara, and Ice Bridge your way up and open the chest for another **Ice Bridge Upgrade**, giving you a Bridge four squares long! Form an Ice Bridge to the right so Aang and Sokka can rejoin Katara, then go left.

Have the entire party stand on the pressure plate, and Boomerang the crystal to open the left gate. This puts you back in the room with the Save Stone, but now you can cross the water directly above it and enter the door there, which eventually leads to a ladder to the surface.

Keep going left, and use Air Blast to move the spiked crate left. Move around and use Water Shift to move the water from the upper crate to the spiked crate, then Air Blast the empty crate to the left. Pull the empty crate back to the right as far as you can, and Water Shift the water *back* from the spiked crate. Push the water crate left, then Air Blast the spiked crate to the right. This gives Aang access to the High Jump spot so he can claim the **Health Potion** giving Sokka a health boost!

Go talk to Haru to the left, then hit the crystal and Air Blast the spiked crate upwards. Haru has cleared out an earth block, which gives you a shortcut to the Library door. Talk to Haru to enter!

Guards are blocking your progress inside the Library, so go right and down the ladder. When you find a crate, Water Shift its contents into the ditch. Then make a two-by-two-square Ice Bridge so you can push the now-empty crate onto the pressure switch. This takes you to a ladder leading to the area behind the right guard. Use Sokka's Club from below to destroy a brush, then Boomerang from the left to hit the crystal switch. Return to the underground now.

Back underground, re-make the Ice Bridge and push the crate onto the left pressure plate. Water Shift water from the creek into the crate until it trips the switch and opens the stone gate up. Return to the center area and enter! There's a **Weird Item Map** inside, take it and continue on to the exit to the left, not the way you came in!

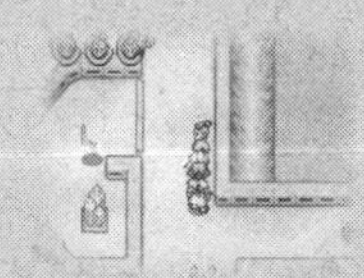

There's a chest there that has the **Circle Boomerang Throw Scroll**, which gives Sokka's boomerang some new skills! Use it to hit the crystal switches and move left. The last crystal switch takes some tricky positioning to hit. Head down, and Haru warns of the invading Fire Nation troops! Talk to Bumi, who points you to Four Paws Island. Sadly, you have to find your own way out of the Palace!

Use the Save Stone, then Water Shift the crate-water into the ditch. Make a large Ice Bridge so you can push the crate halfway onto the switch, then go back to the left side of it. Water Shift water back into the crate to open the gate. Use the Circle Boomerang Throw on the crystal to the right, then stand on the pressure switch and use the Circle again to the left, which permanently opens the gate.

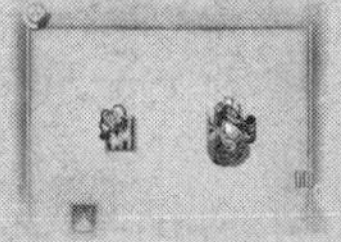

Above, Air Blast the spiked crate from the left, then send Aang up the passage. There's a Fire Tank there waiting for him! You can't damage it, but Aang's Air Vent can flip it over! You just need to lure it over one of the vents. Head for the left vent *immediately*, and it should drive right over it and you can flip it over right away! Head right and hit the crystal switch it guards.

Move on, and have Sokka pull the switch ahead. Aang and Katara need to step on the pressure switch, which lets Sokka move up, and deal with a Rock Thrower Machine! Thankfully, it stays still for long stretches and takes its time between attacks, giving Sokka time to stun it with the Boomerang, then rush in and hit it with the Club. Keep at it until it falls. This opens the gates so Aang and Katara can reunite with him and enter the next level down.

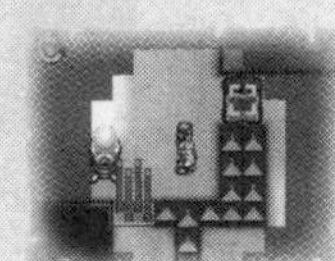

Now Katara has her own Machine to deal with past a water fountain. The Typhoon Machine spins and charges after Katara. Use Water Shift from the right side of the area to dump its water into the ditch when it spins. It only takes one Shift to stop it and let Katara pass, and trip the plate to open the gate ahead.

There are several Fire Nation soldiers above ground, including a Firebender. Bash your way through them! After the Fire Troops, Aang must High Jump up and dash up a mail system gauntlet to reach a crystal switch, letting the party go up.

There are even more Fire Nation troops in the next area, including yet another Firebender. If you go up through the gate above that opens when he's down, you face another Firebender, and can use the Circle Boomerang Throw to reach the next area. Go right, however, and you have quite a few more Firebenders to go through… first one, then two at once, then *three* at once! Try to tackle them one at a time, and keep your health up by using Katara's Heal at each opportunity! If you clear out the three Firebenders, you can claim a **Health Potion** for Katara. The gate to the left leads to the same exit to the next area as the left route.

There's more mail system carts up ahead, just take your time and watch the patterns before moving on. Be sure to use the Save Stone before you move on.

Boss: King's Aide

Looks like you have to take out the king's aide! Just keep running, avoiding his fairly simple attacks until he moves the giant stone he's standing on. Run onto a grate and get off before he smashes you under it! Quickly run to another grate and use Air Vent to knock him off it, leaving him stunned and vulnerable to Aang's staff attacks.

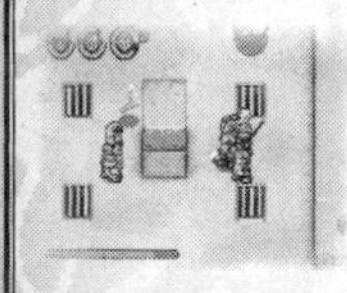

Once he's knocked off, he tries to stay on the opposite side of the rock tower. Dodge the rock discs and charge up the Circle Boomerang Throw. It's a bit tricky to get the right position to hit him with it but the move stuns him long enough for you to get some more hits in and destroys any stone discs it hits. Afterwards, he returns to the tower and repeats the pattern, so you should too! The attacks come a little faster each time, but you shouldn't have any troubles.

Once he's down, you can move on to Appa, and Four Paws Island!

Four Paws Island

Luckily there's a village on Four Paws Island. Use the Save Stone there and explore around, checking out the ruins. You can't do much in the ruins, so head right into the forest.

Hordes of Hog Monkeys are running around, and you can't attack them, so simply rush through the gaps in their charges. There are also Armadillo Wolves here, but they're no stronger than when you faced them at the North Pole.

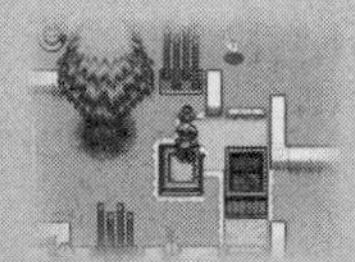

Sokka needs to pull the lever above so Aang and Katara can trip a switch, letting Sokka move up. Open the chest, giving Sokka **Bombs** he can use to destroy the big rocks in the area. Move everyone up and left, and use the Circle Boomerang Throw to hit the uppermost crystal, letting the party reunite. Bomb the left rock and bring the water crate right, and pull the empty crate onto the plate, and Water Shift between the two crates to trip the switch. Move up and collect the **Health Potion**! Now head left, bombing the rocks to enter the village again.

Continue down into the next section of ruins. Bomb the rock blocking the gray statue, then pull it right to reveal steps underground. The second crate you need to move there needs a rock destroyed first that's outside of Sokka's Bomb throw range, so toss one then hit it with Air Blast to push it to the rock. This allows access to the chest containing the **Sacred Caverns Key**. Go up and to the left from the village to the big doors!

You have to deal with a Rock Thrower Machine immediately! Just like before, use Sokka's Boomerang to stun it, then smash it with his Club. A Fire Tank comes next, but this one is trickier to get over a vent. Flip it with Air Vent, then move it onto the stone plate to open the gate to the left.

Once you're back outside, clear out the Armadillo Wolves, and dodge the charging Hog Monkeys as you go right. When you reach the area with the water crate, Water Shift its contents into the right pond, then pull it down. Create an Ice Bridge on the edge of the left pond so you can push the crate onto the plate and advance.

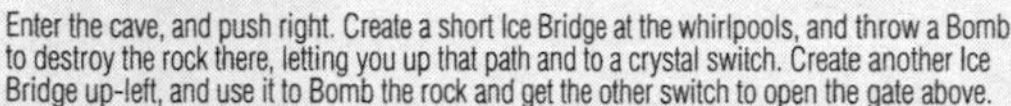

Enter the cave, and push right. Create a short Ice Bridge at the whirlpools, and throw a Bomb to destroy the rock there, letting you up that path and to a crystal switch. Create another Ice Bridge up-left, and use it to Bomb the rock and get the other switch to open the gate above.

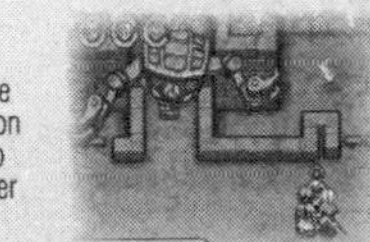

The next puzzle is tricky. Water Shift the crate's contents into the pool, then make a two-by-two bridge to the small island. Air Blast the empty crate onto it. Make your way to the larger island, then make an Ice Bridge big enough to pull the crate onto it. Go up, then make another bridge to pull the crate onto the pressure plate above.

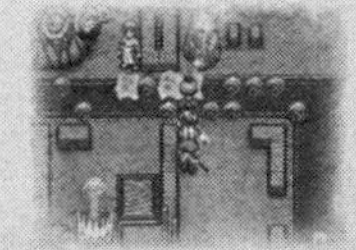

After the Maker retreats behind the iron door, use the Save Stone and head straight down and through the passage, which leads to another Fire Nation Rock Climber Machine. Take it out the same way you did the first one, except you need to use the Circle Boomerang Throw to hit the arm on the right! This one recovers much faster than the first, but it's still an easy battle. The road it blocks eventually leads to a crystal switch above the iron door.

From the Save Stone, go down and to the right toward a water-filled area. Create an Ice Bridge at the top of the lower pond so you can move the water crate onto it. Water Shift its contents into the pond so you can Air Blast the crate to the right, then Water Shift to fill it again and activate the pressure switch.

Now, Katara needs to go through the fountain, letting Aang and Sokka go right. Send Katara up, and make an Ice Bridge long enough to put one block by the rock above. Throw a Bomb onto the Bridge so the rock is blown away.

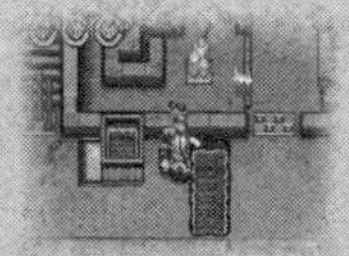

Get Katara as far down and left over the large lake with the small islands, so she ends up on solid ground just below where Aang and Sokka are. Have her make an Ice Bridge through the whirlpools so the two guys can cross, then have her make an Ice Bridge across the water from left to right, connecting at the rock. Throw a Bomb over the fence and Air Blast it into the rock. This lets Katara down so she can stand on the plate that lets the party reunite.

You end up outside, with another batch of Hog Monkeys to avoid. Send Aang up with the High Jump, and run right while dodging Hog Monkeys on the long road. Run up and follow the path until it leads to a crystal switch. Hit it, then ***go back the way you came***! Do ***not*** move the spiked crate! Go left through the long Hog Monkey gauntlet to get a **Health Potion**, then return Aang to the others, and go right.

Keep going, and there's another Hog Monkey run to deal with. Use Katara's Ice Bridge to give yourself some more room to stay safe, and closer to the next safe spot as you zigzag up the Hog Monkey run.

Back underground, Water Shift the crate water into the ditch, and make an Ice Bridge to push it onto the plate. Water Shift water out of the ditch into the crate to trip the plate, opening the gate to the right. Use Circle Boomerang Throw to hit the switch from a distance, and loop-the loop up and around. Go through the gate you threw the Boomerang through into the next area.

Send Katara through the water fountain, and push left over the lake, heading up at the first opportunity. Water Shift the crate water into the ditch to reach a crystal switch, and Water Whip it. Move the empty crate as far left and down as possible, and Water Shift water back into it. Go left and Water Shift from the crate to fill the ditch so you can cross it. Head down and Ice Bridge your way over the lake; continue down to where the rock is. Make an L-shaped Ice Bridge for Sokka's Bomb to land on, then Air Blast it and smash the rock, letting Katara move down and hit the plate to reunite the party.

In the next section, make another Ice Bridge, toss a Bomb, then wait. You need to carefully time your Air Blast so the Bomb explodes next to the rock, or else it will fall into the water. Hit the A Button at the first white flash for proper timing, and the rock should be destroyed. Move on, Water Shift the water from the spiked crate, and create an S-shaped Ice Bridge using the plank across the creek. Use Air Blast to maneuver the crate across the bridge and onto the plate, then Water Shift water into it to activate the plate. This reveals a crystal switch that opens the gate to ***another*** switch, the second of three that opens the iron door.

Now go up-left from the iron door (after saving, of course). You need to do a lot of Water Shifting here! From below the gate, Water Shift water from the left ditch into the crate, then from the right ditch into the left ditch until that's full! Use the Ice Bridge to cross, then push the full crate onto the plate.

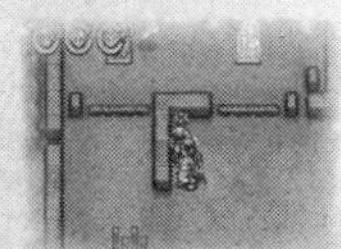

Above that, use Sokka's Boomerang to hit the rightmost crystal, then dash left, charging up his Circle Boomerang Throw. You only have 6.5 seconds to use it to hit the other two crystals to the left, which opens the gate. Hug the left wall and throw from just above the little symbol to nail both in one shot. This lets you hit the spiked crate with an Air Blast and push it right, so you can move to the next section.

Use a combination of Ice Bridge and the Boomerang to hit the next crystal. Go left past the gate, and use Ice Bridge and Circle Boomerang Throw to hit the crystal there, opening the next gate.

There's an inactive Typhoon Machine just below, but you need to activate it! Water Shift some water into it, then let it chase you downwards. Once it's in range, Water Shift the water from it into the ditch ahead so you can Ice Bridge across it.

Head up the steps and make a long Ice Bridge into the pond in the very center. Use Circle Boomerang Throw to hit all three crystal switches with one attack, opening the lower gate. Now, go back to the ditch you crossed, and Water Shift twice, putting the ditch water into the Typhoon Machine. Lure it down and to the left, then do two quick Water Shifts into the crate. Push the full crate onto the pressure plate.

In the next area, have Sokka pull the lever and send Aang and Katara on ahead. Bypass the spiked crate and head around, where a Fire Tank waits. Run down, lure it onto the center vent, and quickly rush up and Air Vent from the left to flip it over. Create a two-by-two Ice Bridge across the left creek, and push the tank to the other side. Air Blast upwards, pushing the spiked crate onto the plate. Now, when Sokka releases the lever, the gate in front of him stays open!

Send Sokka up, Bombing through the rock. Use his Club to clear out the bush, then push the upside-down crate onto the vent it exposes. Send Aang and Katara back right, and Air Vent from the right to flip the crate, then have Sokka move it so only a corner of it is on the pressure plate. Get Aang and Katara back on the other side, and Water Shift some water from the ditch into the crate, activating the pressure switch. Send Sokka down, then have Aang and Katara move the Fire Tank onto the lowest pressure plate, so they can reunite with Sokka. From this point, a simple pressure plate and Boomerang move grant access to the next section.

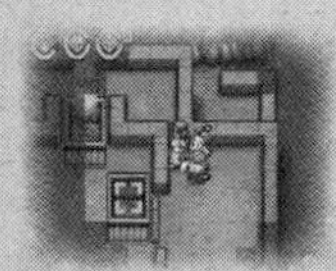

Head up at the first opportunity, and Air Blast the crate twice so it goes as far right as possible. Go down and skip the High Jump spot and move up the stairs. Toss a Bomb over the low wall, and use an Air Blast so it destroys the rock to the left. Then Air Blast the crate to the spot the rock was at before. Move up a little more and Water Shift the water from the high crate into the one you first Air Blasted. Now, send Aang up, move the crate, and hit the crystal switch behind it so the party can move on. You're back at the main hall, and the crystal just ahead open the gate to the final crystal you need to open the iron gate!

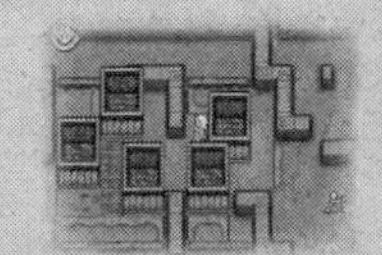

Head up through the iron gate. Aang needs to High Jump up and work his way through a maze of crates. Air Blast the leftmost crate from below, then go up and Air Blast the second crate from the right so it goes down. Go between the crates and pull the last crate right so you can get through and hit the crystal switch.

It's a trap! Rush back and through the open gate, dropping down into the area to the right.

Boss: Giant Drill Machine

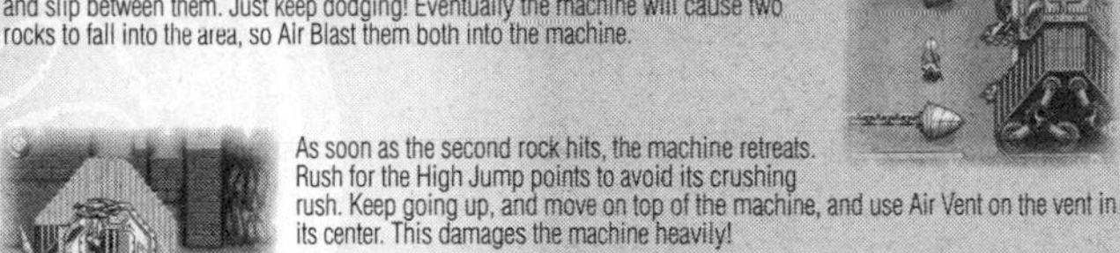

You have to do a lot of dodging here! Watch for the twin drills to poke from the walls, and slip between them. Just keep dodging! Eventually the machine will cause two rocks to fall into the area, so Air Blast them both into the machine.

As soon as the second rock hits, the machine retreats. Rush for the High Jump points to avoid its crushing rush. Keep going up, and move on top of the machine, and use Air Vent on the vent in its center. This damages the machine heavily!

The next round of drilling is a simple back-and-forth pattern from above. Simply get in one spot and dodge the drill as it comes down at you. Eventually it will create two more rocks, so repeat the High Jump and Air Vent combo.

Finally, it will do the twin drill attack, but one from the wall above, and one from the side. Again, just keep dodging until it produces two rocks, Air Blast, High Jump, and Air Vent, and the machine is destroyed.

Go right, and prepare to find a new area. Time to hunt down the Maker and get Aang's friends back!

The Maker's Fortress

This mysterious new land has some nasty machines waiting for you right out of the gate! First of all, head right as soon as possible, and High Jump to reach a crystal switch.

Drop back down and go left, High Jump up, and take on a Fire Tank. Head left as soon as possible to lure it onto the upper vent, and Air Vent to flip it over, letting you at the other crystal switch. Now all you can do is avoid the attacks of the Rock Thrower and Typhoon Machines and rush into the now-open giant door!

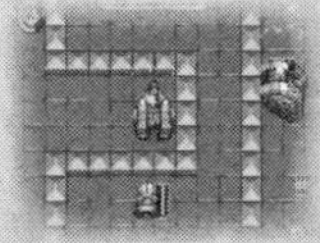

Two Fire Tanks are inside! Dodging their attacks is tricky, but if you're willing to take a hit or two, sticking near the grate in your passage lures them both onto the grates in theirs. Air Vent at the right time to flip them both over and advance. Keep advancing until you reach a crystal switch, freeing Katara!

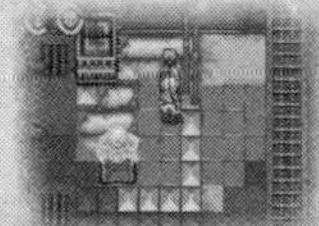

Now that you have control of Katara, have her step on the wooden plate and bring Aang down. Drop down and another gigantic drill machine advances from the left! Hitting the drills is game over, so run right immediately, and hit the crystal switch to open the gate so you can keep running. The drill won't stop, so don't wait! Air Blast the spiked crate ahead up into the upper vent, then Air Blast it onto the stone plate. Cross the water ditch, and Water Shift some water into the crate to open the gate.

Keep Katara in front, using Ice Bridge to cross the water. Make a bridge so you can Air Blast the spiked crate onto the wood plate, and Ice Bridge your way to the gate. Thankfully, time stops when you're preparing the Ice Bridges. Follow the path, using the top of the Machine as a bridge back to the start of the area.

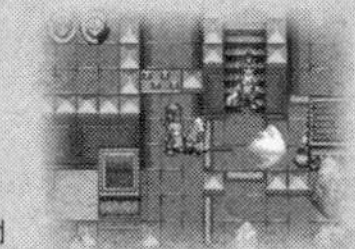

Now Katara can Ice Bridge across the water to the right, following the path. Use Water Whip to hit the crystal switch at the end, freeing Sokka. Have him Boomerang the crystal below, then get out of the way. Make an Ice Bridge at the left side of the pool, then move Aang and Katara so he can Air Blast the spiked crate right. Put a Bomb in the corner next to the rock, and Air Blast it to make sure it's far enough to blow up the rock. Now Air Blast the crate from above, make an Ice Bridge so Sokka can go right, and Bomb the rock to reunite the team. They can now push the full water crate away, but before you drop, switch to Sokka and charge up the Circle Boomerang Throw.

There's another giant drill machine here, of course! Keep Sokka in the lead and release the Circle Boomerang Throw so it hits the crystal and opens the gate. Switch to Katara and run right.

Make an Ice Bridge using the platforms so the spiked crate has a clear path to the plate. Be sure to do this from the upper section to save a few valuable seconds! Air Blast it from the top, then back up so it's even with the bridge. Air Blast it four times to get it onto the stone plate and run right, then Water Shift some pond-water into the crate to open the gate. You need expert timing for this, and can't make a mistake!

Push the next water crate out of the way and keep going. Use Sokka's Club to destroy the bush (ignore the rock!), then Air Blast the flipped crate onto the right vent. Air Vent to flip it over, then Water Shift the contents of the spiked crate into the empty one. Now you can Air Blast the spiked crate away.

Quickly switch to Katara and create an L-shaped Ice Bridge from the bottom of the pool. Grab and pull the full crate across the bridge, and as soon as it trips the plate, run for it! The drill machine can't go any further, leaving you free to use the Save Stone ahead.

Now you have to split up the party again. Send Katara through the fountain and keep going up until she drops a level, which opens a gate. Cross it and have Sokka pull the lever, letting Aang take the center path and trip a plate. Send Sokka up all the way until the gate blocking Aang opens. Time to take on the Maker and her nastiest machine yet!

Boss: Maker's Element Bending Machine

The Bending Machine's first attack is a simple forward fireball, like the Rock Climber you first faced. Stand back, directly in front of the nozzle and Air Blast once the fireball appears, and it's knocked back into the Machine for heavy damage! When the side nozzles start moving, rush up in front of the nozzle. First the left one spits a tongue of fire that sweeps from left to right, so move right a bit and hit the nozzle from the side with the Air Blast. Then the right nozzle spits scalding steam from right to left, followed by fire from the left again. Finally, the two shoot together, so move up in front of the main cannon to avoid it, and hit it with the Air Blast a few more times! Keep it up and soon the action shifts to Katara.

When Katara is active, the Machine pushes her back with gusts of wind wile spitting rocks at her. Dodge the rock while pressing forward, and create a wide Ice Bridge across the water that gets you as far right as possible, plus lets you dodge any rocks. Once there, hit the vent with a Water Whip to do massive damage! The action shifts to Sokka if you connect with the Water Whip, or automatically after a set amount of time.

When it shifts to Sokka, rocks drop from the ceiling in a predictable pattern in a three-by-three grid. Use Boomerang to repeatedly hit the cover to the left, moving up and down to avoid the rocks as they fall.

Once the action goes back to Aang, the pattern remains the same, only a little quicker, and the side nozzles' blasts reach farther, forcing you to move more. Katara's second round is pretty much the same. Sokka's second round has a different rock pattern, hitting only the outer edges of his area. The center is safe, but too far for his Boomerang to hit the vent.

Aang's next round mixes up the double-nozzle-blast, forcing you to move from side to side! Because they keep moving, you don't really have time to Air Blast it during this attack. Hit the center nozzle *once* then run to the back of the room, because the nozzles are about to shoot an X-shaped blast! If you're quick, you can destroy this part of the machine this round!

Now, Katara must deal with two rocks at once each time it tosses them out. But the goal is the same, push right, Ice Bridge, and Water Whip. The third Whip destroys her side of the Machine! Back to Sokka, the rock pattern changes again, but you should have no problems dodging them and using the Boomerang to finish it off.

With the Maker's machine down, the threat is over! Congratulations!

Nintendo DS

Long ago, the four nations of Water, Earth, Fire and Air, lived together in perfect harmony. When the nation of Fire launched an attack which upset this balance, only the Avatar - master of all four elements - could stop them. Unfortunately, it was when the world needed him most that he vanished. A hundred years have since passed and my brother and I have discovered the new Avatar—an Airbender named Aang. Although his airbending skills are great, he has much to learn. But I do believe, with time, Aang has the potential to save the world and restore balance.

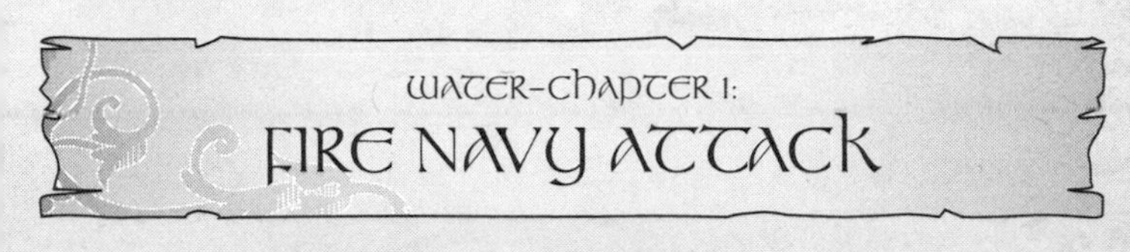

WATER-CHAPTER 1: FIRE NAVY ATTACK

As you are talking to your trusty flying bison Appa about penguin sledding, Katara runs up to inform you that Master Wei needs to speak with you right away.

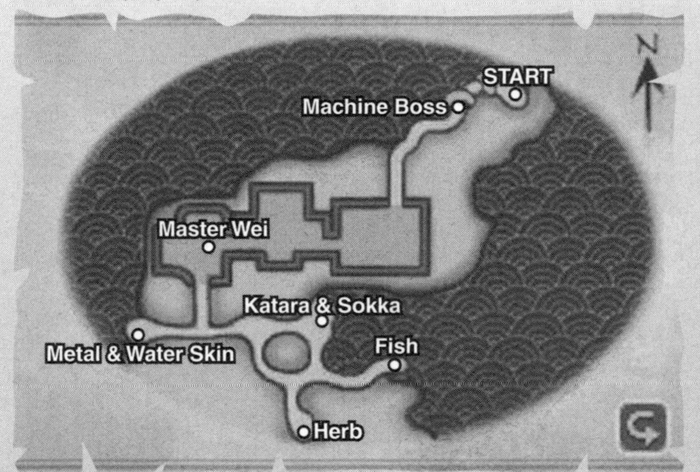

On your journey to speak with Master Wei, be sure to stop and talk to the villagers milling about town. A young girl tells you of her ailing mother and the healing herbs she needs to become well. Offer to find the precious healing herbs for her and bring them back.

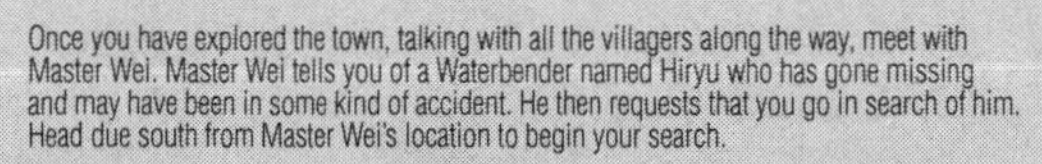

Once you have explored the town, talking with all the villagers along the way, meet with Master Wei. Master Wei tells you of a Waterbender named Hiryu who has gone missing and may have been in some kind of accident. He then requests that you go in search of him. Head due south from Master Wei's location to begin your search.

Before heading west to investigate Hiryu's disappearance, walk east and explore the area. You come across fish swimming in the ocean near the south east edge of the map. Maybe you should bring Katara here later and see if she can catch one. Walk as far south as you can and pick the herb growing there. Now head west to continue investigating the Waterbender's disappearance.

There appears to have been some type of struggle in the area as indicated by numerous sets of foot prints and general disarray. You find something "shiny" and a water skin just like the one Katara has. Head back to Master Wei and report what you have found.

Master Wei examines what you have brought him and knows something is not right. He informs you that Katara went looking for her brother, Sokka, and he's worried about her as well. When he sends you out to find her, take the Healing Herb B to the girl in town; she rewards you with a STR source. Head back out the south gate to search for Katara.

You find Katara and Sokka arguing about chores to the east of the south gate. As soon as you can get a word in edgewise, you tell them Master Wei is worried and escort them back to town.

Before going back to Master Wei, lead Katara to the spot you saw the fish. You enter a mini-game in which you use your stylus to follow the shadow of the fish and help Katara use her waterbending skills to catch it.

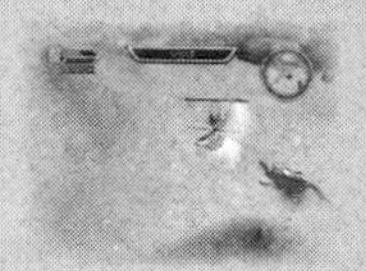

On the way back to town, the ground begins to shake and there is a large crashing sound. The Fire Nation is attacking! Katara stays with Master Wei and fights while you and Sokka run around town fighting off the Fire Nation soldiers raiding the village. Aang sends Sokka to the eastern part of town while he heads north. Battle the four soldiers you come across, picking up any items they drop after you've defeated them. Zuko bends a giant fireball at Master Wei, knocking him down. He then uses Wei's weakened state to get Katara to leave on his ship with him.

When Aang and Sokka return to Master Wei they learn of Katara's fate. Determined to rescue her, they run to Appa's location in the north east so they may ride him and follow Zuko's ship, but encounter an enemy blocking the way.

Machine Boss

The Machine boss has three types of moves within its attack pattern. The first is three fire balls shot in a row. You can avoid the fire balls by running to the bottom left of the screen where they won't be able to reach you. The second is a sweeping fan of fire that moves from side to side. Use your chi defense move to hover above the fan. The third attack occurs if you get within close range of the machine; it swipes at you with one of its arms.

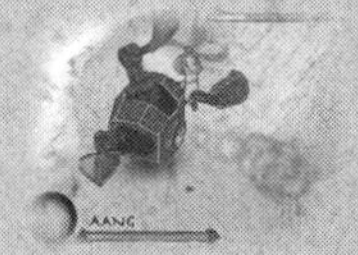

To defeat this maniacal machine:

1) Hover above its fan of fire when the fan is sweeping back up the area
2) Release your hover and use your normal attack to wear it down.

You'll have to repeat this process several times, but it works like a charm.

More Tips: Using your defense move, move in close to the Automata. Aim for its weak point which is the Fire Nation symbol in the middle. If the Automata attacks with his flame thrower, use your bending defense move (fly up) or run into the safety zone which is located on the left side. You will be safe there.

EARTH-CHAPTER 2: AMONG THE ENEMY

Aang and Sokka are clearly troubled by this unknown entity they've encountered. As they cross the ocean upon the back of Appa they find Zuko's ship anchored at an island. The island seems to be a Fire Nation stronghold and they notice a military type building. Is Katara all right?

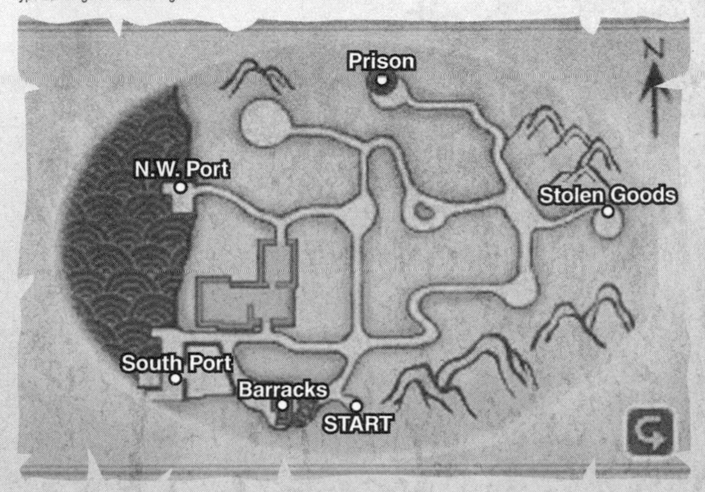

Begin this chapter by first running to the port located to the south west. You find Zuko's ship, but Zuko and Katara are nowhere to be found. Go to town and ask around, maybe someone saw something.

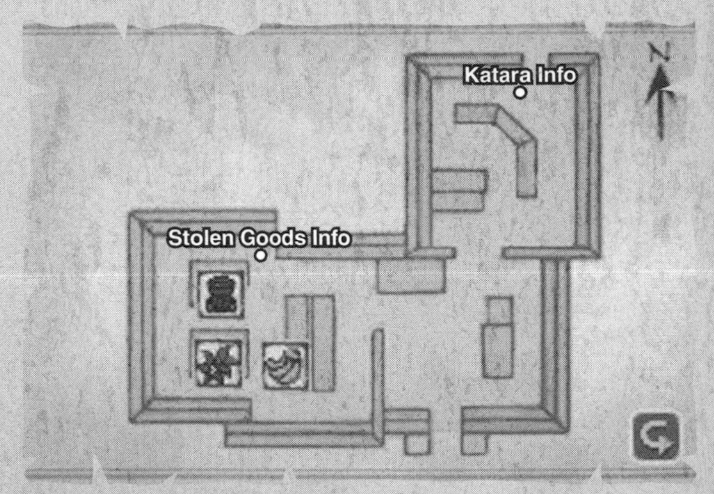

Someone said that they saw a boy and a girl being taken to the prison in the north. The girl was wearing the same clothes as Sokka, that girl must be Katara! You also learn that the building to the south is a barracks for the Fire Nation. There are two captains in charge of the Fire Nation soldiers—one good, one bad and that shipments of goods have been short for some reason.

Stock up on any health items you can afford and head north. Before you investigate the prison, go to the north west port and talk to the shipper. He will tell you that goods have been disappearing from ships and that someone in town may know something.

Go back to town and inquire about the missing goods. You find out that someone saw some men stealing goods from the ship yard and taking them to the east. Go to the far east of the field map to investigate.

When you get to the far east, you discover piles of goods out in the open. When you move in to get a closer look you are jumped by Fire Nation soldiers and the "bad" captain. Defeat them and as a reward the shipper gives you 200 gold.

Go back to town, stock up on supplies, and head to the prison. When you reach the prison you realize that there are too many soldiers to easily pass and decide to head back to town and re-think your plan.

Aang decides the best idea is to sneak into the barracks and "borrow" soldiers uniforms so that he and Sokka will be able to walk through the front door at the prison. When you arrive at the front of the barracks it is heavily guarded, run around to the back of the building and go in that way.

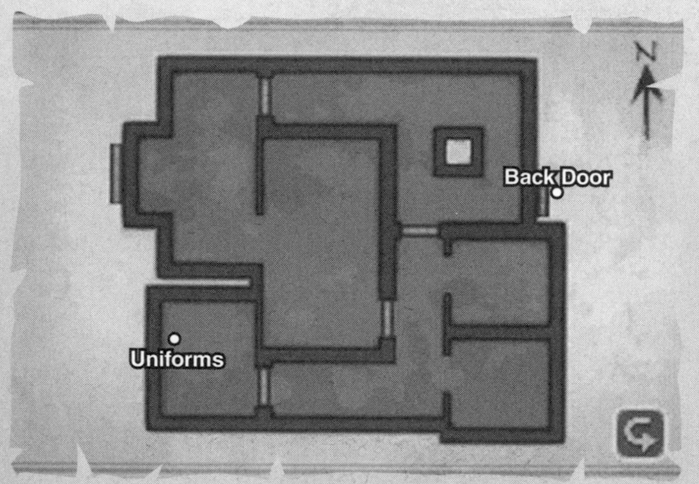

Once inside you overhear the captain telling the soldiers that they stink. He not so delicately tells them they need to bathe. Once the conversation has finished, head to the baths and grab the two soldier uniforms sitting on the shelves. Before you exit the barracks, talk to the soldiers on duty and get any extra information you can.

Now that you have the soldier uniforms, head to the prison. The rooms the soldiers occupy are located on the second floor. In the last room you will find the prison key. Run down to the basement floor where the prison cells are and free the man in the last cell before you get to Katara. Be sure to enter his cell after you release him and grab the items inside. Free Katara and grab the items in her cell then open the door to the next chamber.

Talk to Lian and open the door to her cell. The warden appears and wants to show you his weapon; he's extremely proud of it.

Warden Boss

The Warden wields a staff with fire on both ends. He attacks by shooting fire balls at you and making long semi-circular swings with his staff. Attack him at close range on the opposite side from which your other team members are attacking.

More Tips: Don't get too close or he will unleash an attack that cannot be blocked. Use Katara or Aang and use a bending move from afar to defeat this enemy. Run around and keep away from being directly in front of him.

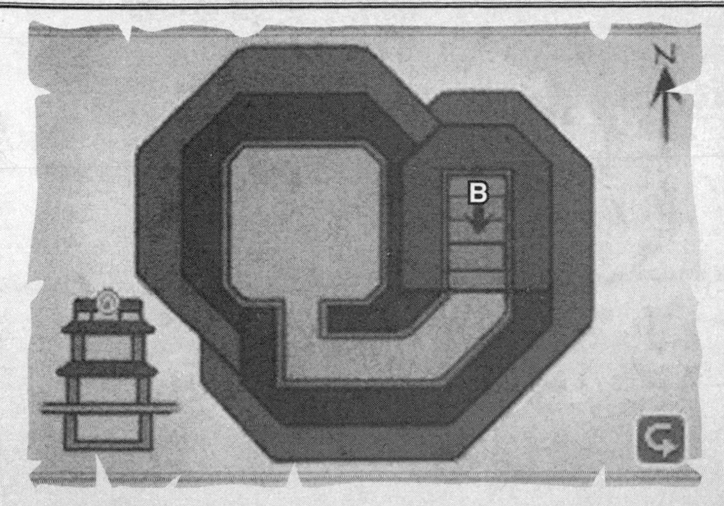

N
B

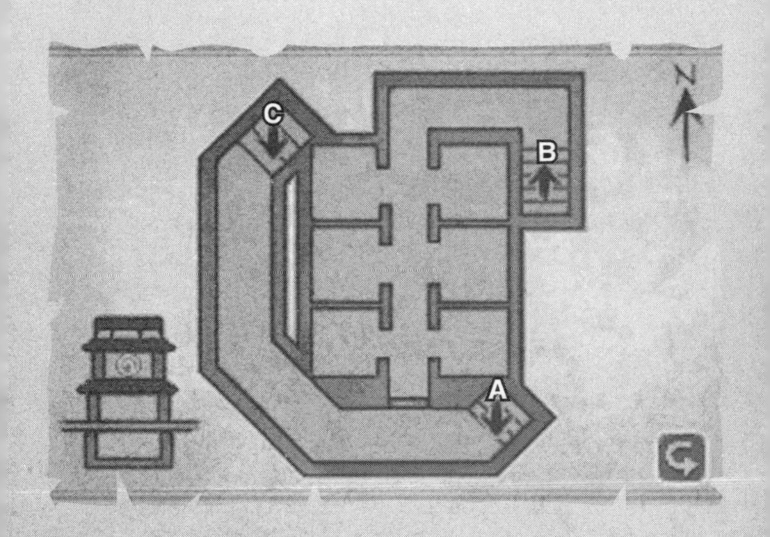

N
C
B
A

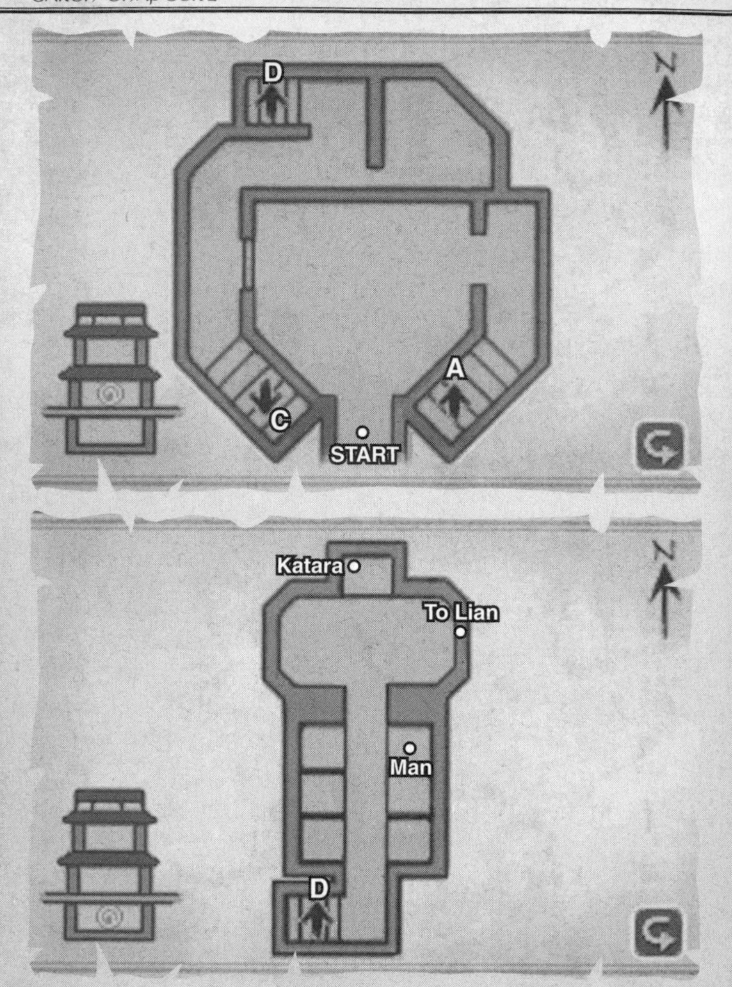

EARTH-CHAPTER 3:
THE FOREST

The Fire Nation is up to something. The team has managed to rescue Katara safely and are now headed for a village in the heart of the Earth Kingdom that was pointed out by a note discovered in Lian's cell. There is a vast forest there with a mysterious air about it.

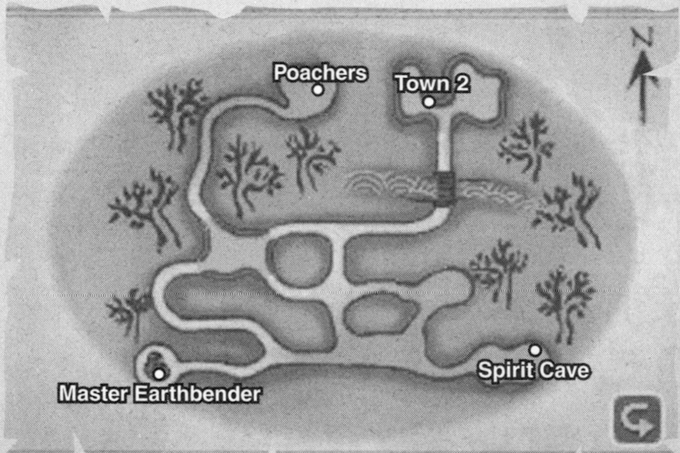

When you start this chapter someone from a nearby village comes and asks for help. With his village under attack, the village elder asks your team to go and help. Stock up on supplies and then head to the neighboring village. On your way you realize that the bridge is out. Katara uses her waterbending skills to build an ice bridge.

When you arrive in the neighboring village, you see Haru battling machines to no avail as he is outnumbered. Swoop in and help defeat the enemies. After you finish of the mechanical attackers, Haru tells you that his father hasn't returned and asks that you help him. Walk around the side of the village you are on and collect the items in two chests then run over to the other side of the village and fight the machines attacking Haru's dad and the other villagers.

When the battle is finished, Haru's father tells Haru that he should join your team on your quest to find out where the machines are coming from and why they are attacking. Haru's father also informs you that an Earthbender, Yuan was taken. He requests you go back to the other village and let the elder know that the machines have been defeated.

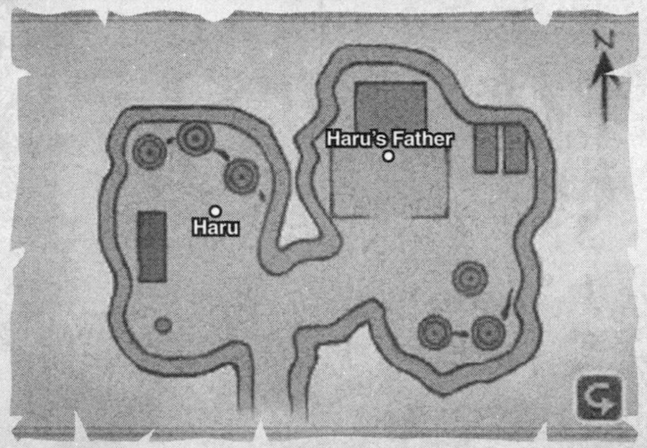

The elder will give Haru a letter to present to an Earthbender that is training in the south. Stock up on supplies and converse with the herbalist. This will trigger a Momo mini-game.

Rubyfruit Guard

In this "mini-game" Momo must protect ten rubyfruits from sneaky rats while the little girl goes home to retrieve a basket. Move Momo around the fruit, chasing away any rats that approach. If you are successful, the little girl will give Momo two rubyfruits, which when used, add to the user's power rating.

After Momo returns from his adventure, give the two rubyfruit to the team members with the lowest power rating. Before you head out of town, talk to all the villagers again. One of them will tell you about poachers to the north that are trapping Hog Monkeys.

Exit the town from the northwest exit and continue north. When you reach the poachers, fight them and release the Hog Monkeys. When the monkeys leave, collect the many herbs left in their place. Head out to find the Earthbender training in the woods.

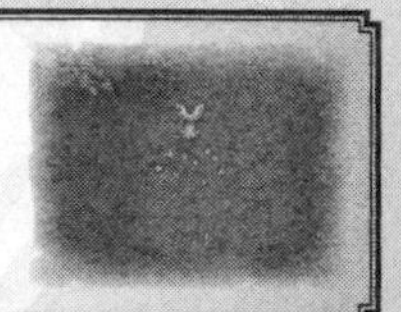

Find the master Earthbender in the southwest area of the map marked by boulders. Show the elder's letter to him and he will train Haru. Once Haru has completed the training he will be rewarded with more power and strength.

Return to Haru's father where he tells you to search for the earth spirit. He is not clear on the exact location, just that it is in the forest. Head to the southeast corner of the map and enter the cave you find there.

There you find the spirit in the east part of the cave. Be sure to explore the caves first in order to find some helpful health items. When you're ready, go to the east side of the cave and fight the spirits first form.

Earth Spirit Boss

The earth spirit tests your worthiness by battling you in the form of a great bison. His only vulnerable spot is his head so concentrate your attacks there. Watch out for his paws which he will swipe at you.

Once you have defeated the earth spirits first form, he transforms to his second and tells you that you already know where you are supposed to go, but only Aang seems to understand this.

More Tips: His only vulnerable area his is head. Using Sokka or Haru is recommended here. The Boss' attacks cannot be defended against so watch for his attack moves so you can avoid them and then launch your attack in between.

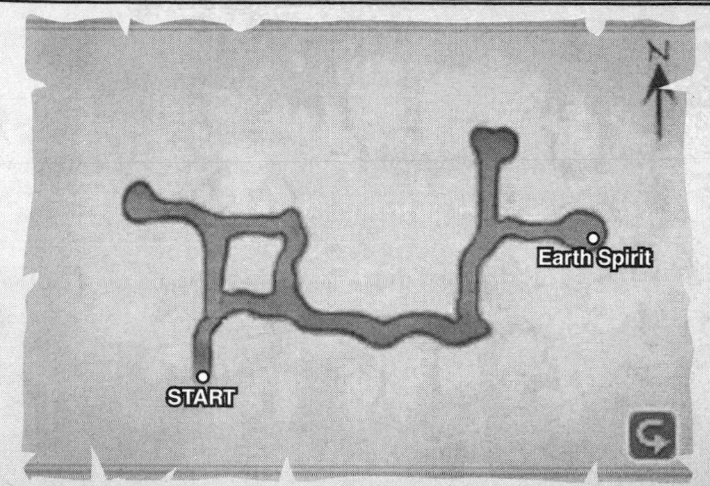

EARTH-CHAPTER 4:
OMASHU

Haru joins the team and makes it a lively bunch, but the mystery of the machines deepens further. Aang says they're off to see a King. However, the mystery behind the statement by the Spirit, "plant it at the core of the earth and there you'll find your answer," has yet to be solved. "The center of the Earth..." Earth = Earth Kingdom. The center of the Earth is Omashu! And a king there could only mean one person!

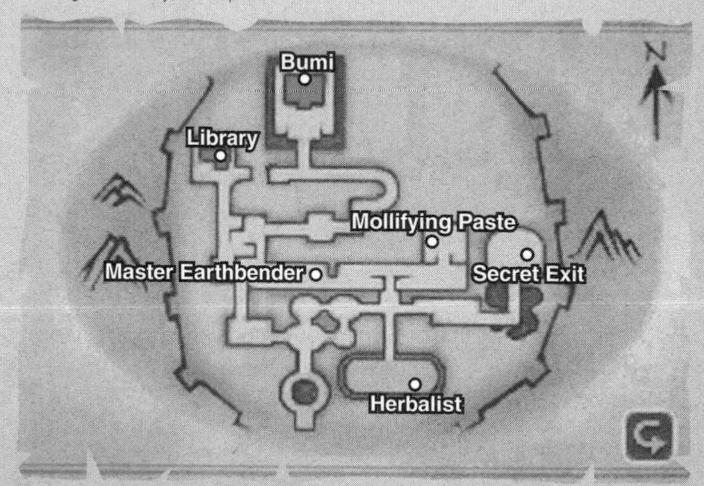

When you go and talk to King Bumi and tell him what you are looking for, he says the answer may be found in the library. As you are about to head to the Library, the Consul pipes in and says only Master Earthbenders are allowed in the Library and anyone else is breaking Earth Kingdom tradition. Bumi points out however, that Aang is not bound by Earth Kingdom law as he is not an Earthbender.

The guards at the library refuse to let you in. Go around to the back of the building; there is a small vent that Momo can fit through. (Use the B button to sneak through.)

Button Pusher

In this "mini-game," Momo must press colored buttons in order to unlock the back door to the library. All of the buttons must be green. Set it up so that the buttons are green, red, red, green, green, red. Then press the center green button and they all change to green.

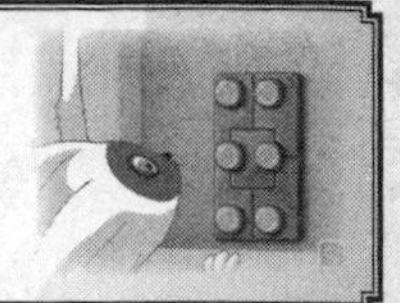

Once Momo has unlocked the door, head inside. Haru stays outside; he does not want to break any Earth Kingdom traditions. You need to sneak past guards to get to the other side of the library. The first room you must sneak in, walk forward to the bookshelf (holding the B button) and wait for the guard to walk to the right to slip past him. Walk north through the room and when you reach a spot where you can go right, in between two bookshelves, do so. Walk to the middle of the book shelf and wait for the guard to turn to the left and walk past him.

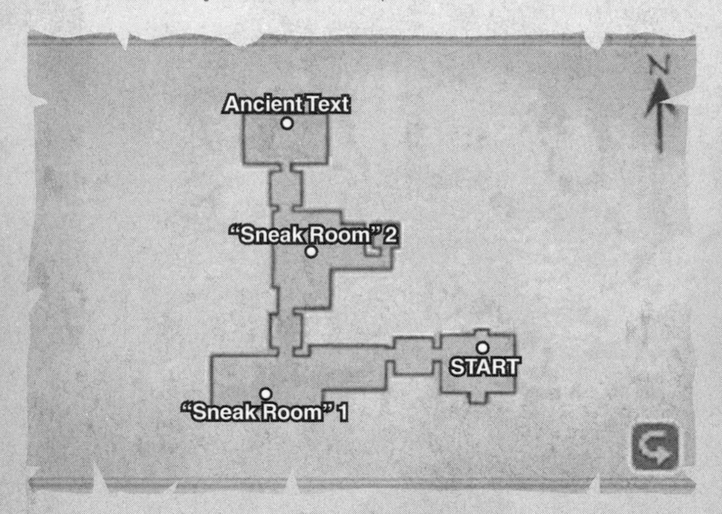

The second room to sneak through has three guards. Walk to the mid-point of the first bookshelf and wait. A guard that is patrolling the library walks right next to you. As long as you stand at the mid-point of the shelf, you remain out of sight. When he heads back to the north, go all the way to the left of the room and slowly walk up the hall. Stopping when you see the guard posted between the bookshelves ahead. When he turns to the left, go right. Be sure the guard patrolling the hallway is still heading north before you do so.

After you cross the hallway, pass one bookshelf and then start to pass another. There's another guard. Wait for him to turn to the north then walk behind him. Enter the room in front of you. Inside you find three chests containing stat boosting items. Exit the room and wait for the guard to turn again and stop at the end of the bookshelf. Confirm that the coast is clear and then head north to the door at the top of the room.

When you get inside, you find a map of an island with strange writing, a picture of a stone statue and the depiction of Benders fighting machines. Aang doesn't know of this island so you need to go ask Bumi about it.

Bumi says he can help you but that he first needs Mollifying Paste. Your team agrees to retrieve it for him by heading to the spot Bumi marked on your map. On your way to the merchant you come across an Earthbender who asks Haru if he'd like to test his skills. Say, "Yes" and begin. Haru must break 30 boulders to be deemed worthy and receive his stat building rewards. After he has completed this test, head to the merchant.

The merchant says he can make you some mollifying paste but he needs three ingredients: a platypus-egg, nuts and powdered medicinal herb. He gives you an herb to take to the herbalist and the other two ingredients you must find. Their locations are marked on your in game map.

Hidden Rooms

Before you deliver all of the ingredients for the mollifying paste to the merchant, search the walls of the kingdom. If you find a section of wall that is lighter than the others, try opening the section, there are hidden rooms behind these light spots that contain items.

Once you've gathered all the ingredients required for the mollifying paste, take them to the merchant. After he gives you the paste, the Fire Nation attacks. Haru stays behind and fights while the rest of the team makes their way to the king.

Give Bumi the paste, he slathers it on his lips—it is lip balm after all. He tells you the island is Four Paws Island and it is so ancient it isn't on any map. He shows you where to go and then sends you to the east side of the kingdom where a guard is waiting to usher the team to safety.

Exit the castle and head east. When you get to the spot marked on your map, the guard opens a secret passage and the Consul will promptly shut it. Haru has to battle him so the team can escape.

Consul Boss

The Consul warps around the battlefield, popping up and shooting boulders at you. When he teleports down, run around until he comes back up, making it harder for him to target you. Use Haru's chi attack Shoot Rocks to deal damage to the Consul. If the Consul pauses, Haru can run in for a few close range regular attacks, but the Consul is fast with his defense so close attack opportunities are few.

More Tips: Use Haru in this battle. When the Consul disappears below ground, watch for the location where he will reemerge and attack the area repeatedly. When the Consul unleashes his 4-boulder attack, do not hesitate and either use your blocking move or run around to evade his attacks.

Earth-Chapter 5:
The Sacred Caverns

Haru defeats the Consul but something seems to be moving behind him. What is this "plan" the Consul was talking about? Will Aang and the team find out? Thanks to a clue they found in the library, the team learns about an island called Four Paws which is not depicted in the map from King Bumi. The team heads there with anticipation.

When you start out on Four Paws Island you only have one clue to follow—find the stone statue. Follow the southern shore around the island to the northeast tip. On your way to this location, you come across a man having trouble catching fish. Katara gives him the fish she caught at the north pole. When you reach the northeast tip of the island, you see the statue you saw in the library. Head down the stairs nearby.

As you descend into the chamber, your team is ambushed by machines. Battle them and once they are defeated, press on. You discover a relief of the entire island. Walk around to the back of the sculpture and remove the blue ball. When you do so, a light shines down on part of the island. The ball has ancient writing on it that none of you are able to read. Head out of the chamber and over to the town to see if you can find anyone who can read it.

When you arrive in town look for an elderly gentlemen and ask his opinion of the blue ball. He tells you it describes in detail the origins of the people of Four Paws Island. He also tells you it is a key to the Sacred Caverns.

Stock up on supplies and talk to everyone in town. A young boy will take a particular interest in Sokka's boomerang. He likes it so much he begs Sokka until he gives in. The boy promptly walks off with it and Sokka must chase after him. When the boy gets into trouble, Sokka rescues him and the boy gives him a strength stat booster.

Before you head to the sacred caverns which are just north of the village, go through the center pathway through the mountains in the middle of the island. When you reach the circular area you will encounter a large angry beast that does not wish to let you pass. Aang tries to reason with it, but the beast only seems to understand battle. The beast will run around the area in circles and if you get too close it will clap its hands together and smash you. Use Aang's Air Blast attack to strike from a distance. Once the creature is defeated, run up and get three bunches of bananas and a Water Scroll.

Have Katara learn the scroll right away as it allows her to heal fallen team members. Head to the sacred caverns and insert the keystone into the wall and enter the opening. There are two passageways that need to be opened up; they are marked in red and blue on your in-game map. You need to get the red wall down before you can lower the blue wall.

The key for the red wall is located in the northeast corner of the caverns. The key for the blue wall is behind the red wall. Once the blue wall is down, enter the passageway and at the end you find Lian.

Lian

Lian has created a big bad machine and beating it shall prove to be quite the challenge. You must strike it from the front while avoiding its water blasts. When it charges forward run to the safety of one of the several nook's in the cavern wall. Haru's Shoot Rocks attack is especially effective and almost never misses. If anyone on your team is defeated, use Katara's newly learned Heal move and bring them back.

More Tips: A ranged attack works best here. When the enemy closes in, it will enter its charging motion. When it charges, run into the safety zone along the cavern walls. Katara's bending attacks work well against this Boss.

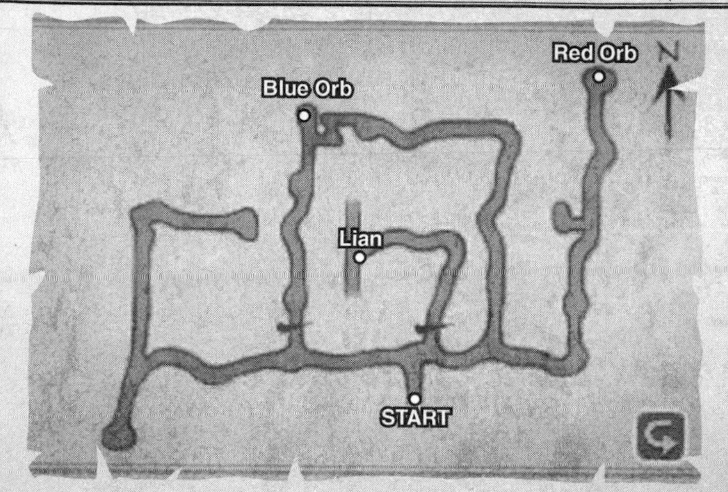

Air-Chapter 6:
The Air Temple

The machines are a product of Lian's grand plan and she plans on harnessing their power to claim her stake in the world. When Lian said she "could sever his ties to the spirit world, leaving him powerless", Aang intuitively knows that she is headed for his home, the Air Temple. Keeping his feelings of fear and danger in check, he heads for the Air Temple.

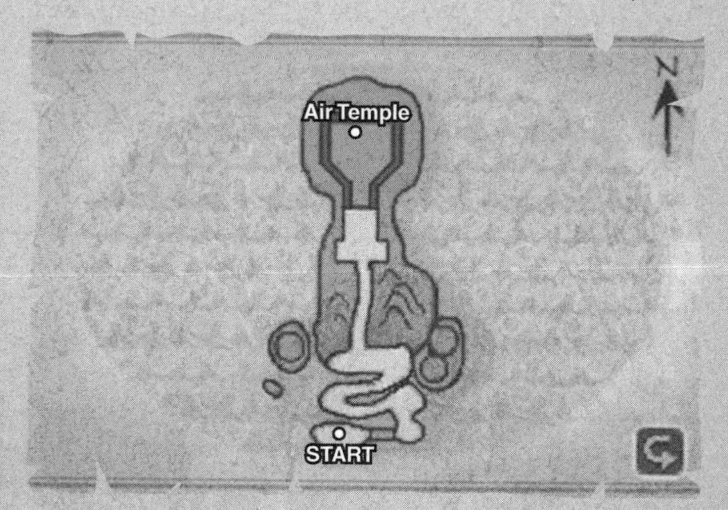

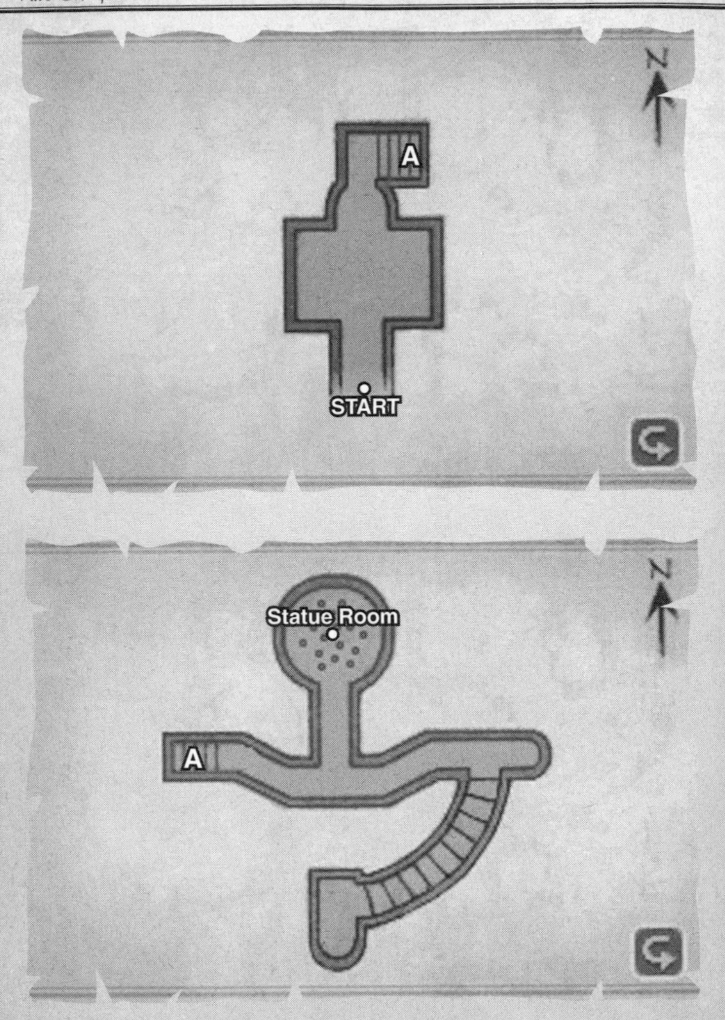

Aang heads for the Air Temple alone. Run up the path to the temple, fighting any machines you come across. Before you enter the room marked on the in game map, run to the top of the temple and grab the items placed there. Head into the marked room and defeat the machines that await.

When Aang defeats the enemies, you will switch back to the rest of the team, who are growing antsy for Aangs return. They decide to walk around town to gather information. The team finds out that: the air temple people are building a new home deeper in the woods but it is infested with machines and there is a cliff to the north that has a warm feeling.

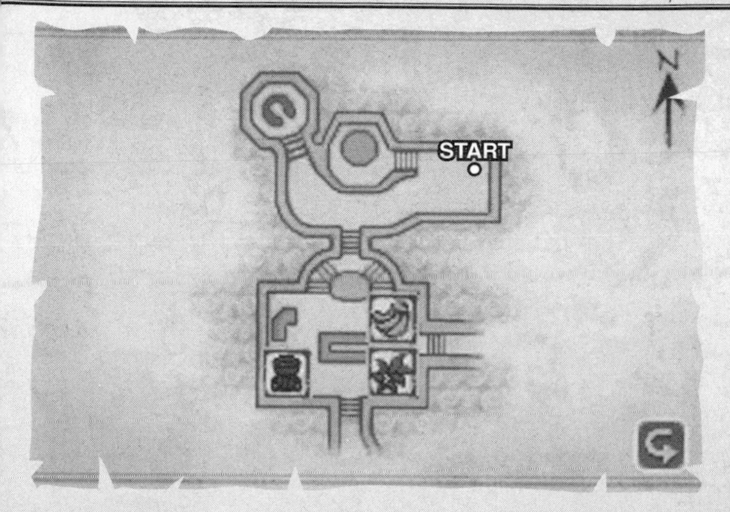

Stock up on supplies and head out to explore the area. To the south east you will come across an Earthbender training who will offer to test Haru's ability. When Haru passes the test, he will receive a scroll from which he can learn Shoot Rocks 2. Learn Shoot Rocks 2 right away and then head north east to the building site.

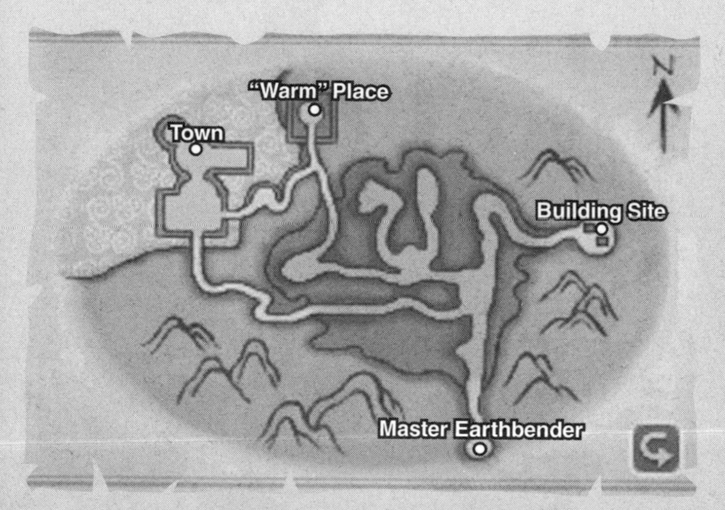

When the team reaches the building site they find that there are three groups of machines roaming the area they must defeat. When the battles are done you will switch back to Aang, who realizes the rest of the team may need him. Run back down the hill and ride Appa to town.

The rest of the team is nowhere to be found and you must now figure out where they have gone. Walk around town gathering information. You learn that they may have gone to the building site. Go to the spot with the unique atmosphere in the northwest and play Four Nations with Gyatso. After you play your game, Gyasto will disappear and leave behind an air scroll.

Read the scroll and learn Tornado Attack then head to the building site. When you arrive you will find a large hole preceded by a big drilling machine that you must now battle.

Drill Boss

The Drill Boss digs down into the soil and then back out again all the while poking its drill bit out at you. Avoid the drill attacks while your chi meter refills and then perform your Tornado attack. Repeat this process until the drill is defeated.

More Tips: When the Drill machine disappears into the ground, it is difficult to gauge where it will reappear. Take care not to get caught when it reemerges from the ground. The machine's attack covers a wide area so do not bother a half-hearted attempt at running away; as soon as you see its attack motion, use your defensive move or quickly run away.

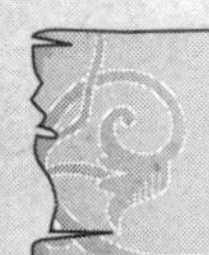

EARTH-CHAPTER 7: THE FORTRESS

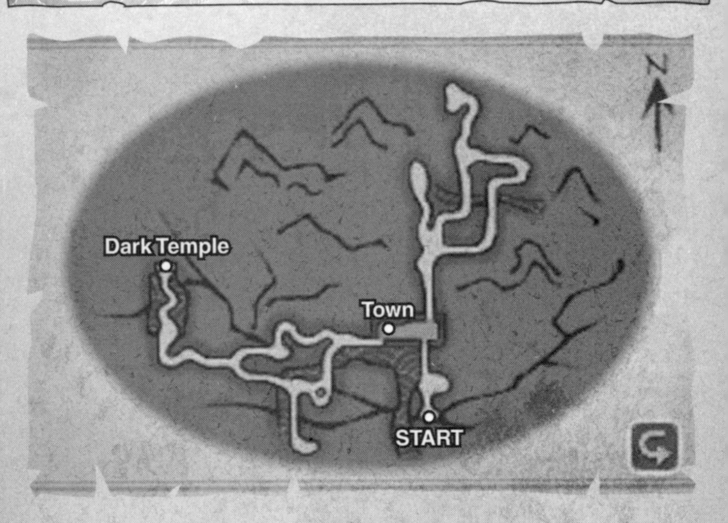

Aang sees the sad expressions Momo and Appa have and tries to encourage them so that they can enter the dark and foreboding hole. Inside is a very long tunnel and the group proceeds with Aang and Momo on Appa's back. After a little while, the team comes to a desolate area where row upon row of dead trees stand. All Aang hopes for now is the safety of Haru, Sokka and Katara.

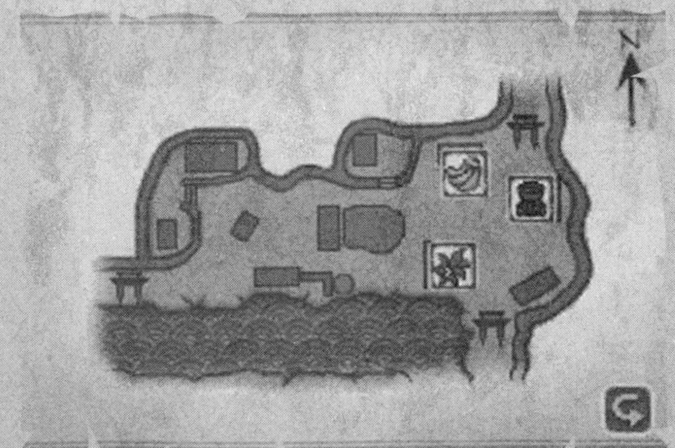

Head forward and enter town. Talk to everyone you come across in order to gather information. You learn that the machines have polluted the area so much that nothing grows and the water is contaminated. You also learn that there's a dark temple to the west. Stock up on supplies and head towards it.

When you enter the temple go to the room in the north west and free Sokka. Sokka has a wrench that Lian dropped and he gives it to you. Go to the next hall and free Katara then return to the "main" hallway. Walk east all the way to the end of he hall and enter the room at the end. Free Haru and enter his cell to pick up a DEF source.

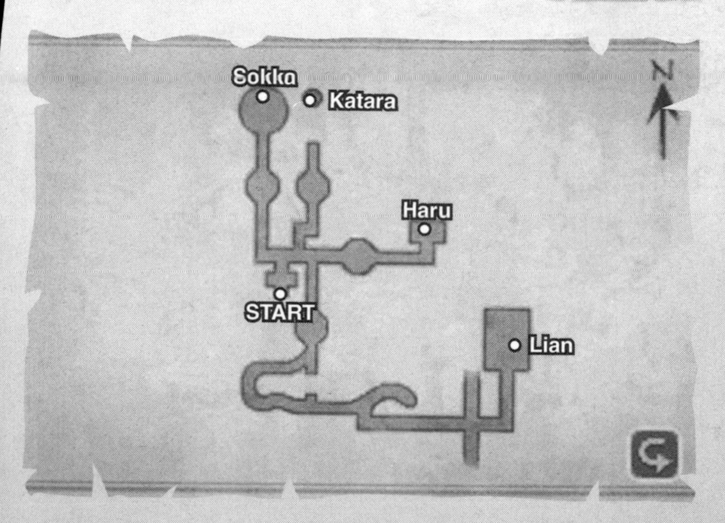

Now head west back down the main hallway. When you get to the hall to the south turn down it and make your way westward. You come to a spot where you must battle a machine that is like the machine you fought in your first battle with Lian. Fight it the same way, using the strongest chi attacks each member now knows.

After you finish off the machine, head to the end of the hallway. When you get there you find Lian and the missing Benders working on a massive machine. The Benders have become sympathetic to Lian's fight and do not wish to be "rescued".

Lian 2

This battle has two parts, the first of which goes by fairly quickly. Switching to Haru and using his Shoot Rocks 2 attack makes it go even faster. The machine only moves back and forth, the weapons mounted on top rotate around however.

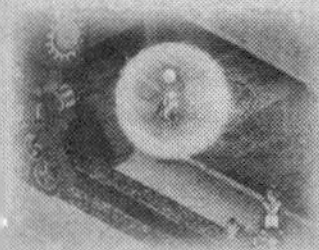

When the team has beat the machine, Lian takes a cheap shot at Aang, but Katara pushes him out of the way. The shot hits her and knocks her out. When this happens, Aang transforms into the Avatar form, making him faster than normal.

In this new form, Aang battles Lian's machine alone. Run around the outer edges of the room while your chi meter refills and attack with the Staff Strike move. Continue battling using this method to destroy Lian's precious machine.

More Tips: The first Boss is basically the same as the one in chapter 5. Use the same echnique to defeat it.

or the Ultimaton, evade its attacks and then attack yourself. Repeat this procedure until the Ultimaton is ultimately defeated. s attacks have a wide range so make sure to take care when doing this.

NICKELODEON AVATAR: THE LAST AIRBENDER
Official Strategy Guide

Written by Mark Androvich, David Cassady, Jason Rosmir, & Greg Sepelak

BradyGames Publishing
An Imprint of DK Publishing, Inc.
800 East 96th Street, 3rd Floor
Indianapolis, Indiana 46240

BradyGAMES Staff

Publisher
David Waybright

Editor-In-Chief
H. Leigh Davis

Director of Marketing
Steve Escalante

Creative Director
Robin Lasek

Licensing Manager
Mike Degler

Credits

Senior Development Editor
Christian Sumner

Screenshot Editor
Michael Owen

Book Designer
Colin King

Production Designer
Bob Klunder

ISBN: 0-7440-0880-8

Printing Code: The rightmost double-digit number is the year of the book's printing; the rightmost single-digit number is the number of the book's printing. For example, 06-1 shows that the first printing of the book occurred in 2006.

09 08 07 06 4 3 2 1

Manufactured in the United States of America.